William R Keech

PAPER
STONES

PAPER STONES

A History of Electoral Socialism

Adam Przeworski and John Sprague

The University of Chicago Press
Chicago and London

ADAM PRZEWORSKI is Martin A. Ryerson Distinguished Service Professor of
Political Science, University of Chicago, and the author of *Capitalism and Social
Democracy.* JOHN SPRAGUE is professor of political science, Washington
University in St. Louis. He is the author of *Voting Patterns of the U.S. Supreme
Court* and is co-author with Adam Przeworski of *Systems Analysis for Social
Scientists.*

The University of Chicago Press, Chicago 60637
The University of Chicago Press, Ltd., London
© 1986 by The University of Chicago
All rights reserved. Published 1986
Printed in the United States of America

95 94 93 92 91 90 89 88 87 86 5 4 3 2 1

This project was supported in part by grants from the National Science
Foundation, SOC75-17906 to the University of Chicago and SOC75-17456
to Washington University.

LIBRARY OF CONGRESS CATALOGING-IN-PUBLICATION DATA

Przeworski, Adam.
    Paper stones.

    Bibliography: p.
    Includes index.
    1. Elections—History. 2. Voting—History.
3. Socialist parties—History. I. Sprague, John.
II. Title. III. Title: Electoral socialism.
JF1027.P79   1986   324.9   86–6984
ISBN 0–226–68497–0

Contents

Prologue

One should stress the importance and significance which, in the modern world, political parties have in the elaboration and diffusion of a conception of the world, because essentially what they do is to work out the ethics and the politics corresponding to these conceptions and act, as it were, as their historical 'laboratory'.

Antonio Gramsci

No political party ever won an electoral majority on a program offering a socialist transformation of society. At the end of the nineteenth century, as socialist parties entered into the competition for votes, they saw in universal suffrage an institution that would allow the working class to proceed from "political to social emancipation," as Marx had put it fifty years earlier. Elections were to open the "parliamentary road" to socialism; they were to bring about a "peaceful revolution" from a society based on the exploitation of workers to one that would provide conditions for universal liberation. Barricades were no longer needed when workers could cast ballots: votes were "paper stones."

The syllogism was simple and persuasive. Since most people suffer from poverty and oppression inherent in the capitalist organization of society, and since elections are decided by numbers, socialism would become the electoral expression of an immense majority. Great masses would provide the mandate for legislating society into socialism. Socialism was the telos, universal suffrage was to be the instrument, and yet it has never happened, at least not thus far.

Involvement in electoral politics was inevitable if socialist parties were to establish roots among workers. Nor could it be merely symbolic. As long as participation in electoral competition is instrumental for improving the conditions of workers in the short run, any political party that seeks a mass following must avail itself of this opportunity. In spite of the distrust which the plunge into electoral politics often evoked among socialists, abstention was never a feasible option. Workers did not become organized as a political party everywhere; but wherever they can, working-class parties do participate in electoral competition.

Observers often saw dilemmas in the involvement of workers in any of the institutions of capitalist society, including elections. "Whatever seeks to extend itself under domination runs the risk of reproducing it"—this would be the fate of working-class organizations under capitalism (Horkheimer 1973:5). In order to realize the revolutionary goal of bringing about socialism, working-class parties must avail themselves of the opportunities that exist in capitalist society. But to the extent to which electoral participation is instrumental in improving the condition of workers within the confines of capitalism, socialism is no longer urgently necessary. Socialism cannot be achieved without participation in democratic institutions, but participation erodes the will for socialism: this is the frequently bemoaned dilemma of democratic socialism. Yet the protagonists—socialist leaders who marched their parties onto electoral battlefields—never saw their choice as a dilemma. They entered electoral politics with the goal of winning an overwhelming popular mandate for socialism, even if they were compelled to enter by the need to improve the immediate conditions of workers. They entered with ultimate goals and they knew they would win.

This divergence between cause and purpose is perhaps a sign of rationalization. Yet the crucial question is not about the motivations of party leaders but about the effect of electoral participation on the movement for socialism. It is a question about conditions which are independent of anyone's will, about the structure of the situation in which a socialist movement finds itself in a democratic capitalist society.

The decision to participate is but a prologue to the history of socialism, but prologues delimit the entire play. Once leaders of socialist parties decided to enter into electoral competition, the electoral system structured their future choices. To be effective in elections—for whatever goals—a party must win votes, and votes are measured in numbers. Hence the perpetual issue facing the parties that organize workers is whether or not to seek electoral suoport elsewhere in the society. Leaders of socialist parties must repeatedly decide whether or not to seek electoral success at the cost, or at least the risk, of diluting class lines and consequently diminishing the salience of class as a motive for the political behavior of workers themselves.

Contrary to the enthusiastic expectations with which socialist leaders initially joined the game of elections, workers—the proletarians who "had nothing to sell but their labor power" and "nothing to lose but their chains"—never became a numerical majority in any society. Hence the electoral mandate for socialism could not be obtained from workers alone. Democratic institutions played a perverse trick with socialist intentions—the emancipation of the working classes could not be the task of workers themselves if this emancipation was to be accomplished through elections.

Given the minority status of workers, leaders of class-based parties must choose between a party homogeneous in its class appeal but sentenced to perpetual electoral defeats or a party that struggles for electoral success at the cost of diluting its class orientation. This is the alternative presented to socialist, social democratic, labor, communist, and other parties by the particular combination of class structure and political institutions found in democratic capitalist societies.

This choice is not between revolution and reform. There is no a priori reason—pace Lukacs (1971:60)—and no historical evidence to suppose that a minority, class-pure, electoral party of workers would be any more revolutionary than a majority party heterogeneous in its class basis. Indeed, class-pure, electoral parties of workers, of which the Social Democratic Party of Germany (SPD) during the Weimar period is perhaps the prime example, can be committed exclusively to the defense of corporate interests of workers within the confines of capitalism. A pure party of workers constituting a majority of the electorate could have perhaps maintained its commitments without compromise, as socialists said they would when they saw the working class as majoritarian. But to continue as a minority party dedicated exclusively to ultimate goals in a system which requires a majority—more, an overwhelming mandate—to attempt to realize these goals would have been absurd. Keeping a party class pure produces at best a sect of guardians of the eternal flame (Schumpeter 1942). To gain electoral influence for whatever aims, from the ultimate to the most immediate, working class parties had to seek support from other people, to enter into alliances, and to make compromises. The decision to participate in elections ineluctably altered the logic of revolutionary transformations. A majority composed of workers could not provide the mandate for socialism because workers never became a majority. The only question was whether a majority for socialism, and indeed for any more proximate goals, could be obtained by seeking electoral support among people other than workers.

With the support of workers alone or of the people in general, electoral majorities turned out to be an elusive goal. No party won an electoral majority on a program offering a socialist transformation of society, but very few won majorities with any program. Elections rarely result in majorities: about one election in fifteen yields the majority of votes cast to a single party. And there is no reason to stop at the magic number of 50 percent. Why has no party ever obtained an overwhelming mandate in a free election, for anything? How does it happen that no party has ever obtained the support of one-half of those entitled to vote? When, at the beginning of the century, socialist leaders witnessed the spectacular growth of their electoral strength, winning an overwhelming majority seemed just a matter of time, indeed of a few elections. And yet all extrapolations remained frustrated—socialist parties settled down to some share of the vote typically inferior to 50 percent. All growth was arrested as it approached 50 percent, almost as if electoral institutions were designed in a way that would prevent any political force from obtaining overwhelming support for any social transformation.

What kind of system is it that socialists got themselves into? Can parties that appeal to workers win an overwhelming majority of votes given the class structure of industrialized capitalist societies? Is there an inherent dilemma that makes an electoral mandate for socialism impossible to obtain? Is this a dilemma that makes an overwhelming victory of any party, behind any program, impossible? What is the range of choice available to socialist parties? Have they exploited the opportunities historically available to them?

To answer these questions we need to know why people vote the way they do. We do know much about voting; few social phenomena have been studied as extensively as the voting behavior of individuals. With the aid of surveys, social scientists have accumulated detailed information about the voting patterns of persons located variously in the social structure and characterized by differing opinions, attitudes, and preferences. While in southern France small farmers are more likely to vote Left, in Italy landless agricultural laborers are more prone to do so. A Swedish manual worker is almost certain to vote for the Social Democrats if he graduated from high school, if his father was also a manual worker, if he works in a large factory, and is a union member. But we would be surprised to find anywhere but in Austria an elderly Catholic widow voting socialist. And yet, in spite of this rich empirical knowledge, the reasons why these people vote the way they do remain unclear.

The first surveys of voting were conducted with the hope that a few factors would turn out to have a dominant impact on the direction of voting, that their list would be short, and the explanation almost complete. Yet it is sufficient to look at Appendix A to *Voting* (Berelson et al. 1954) to see what happened to this hope— over two hundred factors had some bearing on the vote. It seems as if everything had some relation to the way people vote and with nothing being truly decisive.

Most hopes were pinned on class. Class is indeed one factor for which there are good reasons to expect that it should shape patterns of voting. ''A relation between class position and voting behavior,'' a typical argument ran, ''is a natural and expected association in the Western democracies for a number of reasons: the existence of class interests, the representation of these interests by political parties, and the regular association of certain parties with certain interests. Given the character of the stratification order and the way political parties act as representatives of different class interests, it would be remarkable if such a relation were not found'' (Alford 1967:68–69; also Alford 1963). And it was often found, for example by Lipset: ''The simplest explanation of this widespread pattern is simple economic self-interest. The leftist parties represent themselves as instruments of social change in the direction of equality; the lower-income groups support them in order to become economically better off, while the higher-income groups oppose them in order to maintain their economic advantages. The statistical fact can then be taken as evidence of the importance of class in political behavior'' (1963:29). If societies are differentiated in terms of class, if persons similarly located in the class structure share interests, and if parties differ in representing these interests, then indeed people can be expected to vote on the basis of their class position.

Many people do. Survey studies indicate that between 60 and 80 percent of the voters in Western Europe and the Anglo-Saxon countries cast their ballots in a manner consistent with their location in the class structure. But these patterns are far from overwhelming. A large part of British workers choose the Conservatives, supposedly out of deference for their inherited skills in handling the complex matters of governance. Women generally tend to vote for conservative parties more frequently than men of the same class. Religious persons often express their confessional identification at the polls. Ethnic, linguistic, racial, or regional identification leads to voting that cuts across class divisions. Indeed, some observers have concluded that religion rather than class is the most important determinant of voting (Rose and Urwin 1969). Several students of voting behavior maintain that it is identification with parties rather than with any social groups that motivates voting decisions, arguing that there are good psychological reasons why class should not matter (Converse 1958). Still others see voting not as a matter of expressing identifies or prior commitments but as calculated decisions made independently by individuals for each election.

Most of these explanations—in terms of class, age, sex, education, religion, ethnicity, party identification, or region—have the same logic. They cite individual attributes to explain individual acts. In this logic some social distinctions are first objectified as cleavages. Places in these cleavages are attributed to individuals, and after this reduction the locations in the structure of society appear as individual traits, such as worker, Catholic, or woman. These traits are thought to determine acts because they are viewed as representing interests, internalized norms, psychological attachments, and the like.

Through this reduction the locus of causality is placed within each individual. Social relations are reduced to statistical distributions of individual traits. A successful explanation of voting behavior in this mode of analysis consists of finding a statistical covariation between individual traits and acts. If one trait is not sufficient, more are brought to bear the weight of explanation. If class is not sufficient, it must be because religion also matters: "Part of the explanation of these deviations has already been pointed out: other characteristics and group affiliations such as religious belief are more salient in particular situations than high or low social and economic position" (Lipset 1963:240).

But why is class important in molding individual voting behavior in some societies but not in others, during some periods but not during others? Why do individuals sometimes vote on the basis of class, sometimes on the basis of confessional attachments, sometimes because of loyalties to parties, and at times because of the overwhelming charm of someone's grin? Why are Norwegians more likely to vote on the basis of class than the French? Why are Swedish workers more prone to vote for the Social Democratic Party today than they were sixty years ago?

These are not questions about individuals. For even if individual acts tend to coincide with individual traits, why do particular traits become causes of individual acts? In nature, causes are causes and no one can do anything to alter them. The causal structure of the natural world is given, but the causal structure of society is not. The causes of individual behavior are produced by people in interaction with one another.

Reduction does not suffice as an explanation because the causal path from individual traits to individual acts passes through the totality of social relations. "The counting of 'votes'," as Gramsci put it, "is the final ceremony of a long process. . . ." (1971:193). This is a process of creating images of society, of forging collective identities, of mobilizing commitments to particular projects for the future. Class, religion, ethnicity, race, or nation do not happen spontaneously as reflections of objective conditions in the psyches of individuals. Collective identity, group solidarity, and political commitment are continually transformed—shaped, destroyed, and molded anew—as a result of conflicts in the course of which political parties, schools, unions, churches, newspapers, armies, and corporations strive to impose a particular form of organization upon the life of society. The relation between places occupied by individuals in society and their acts is a contingent historical outcome of struggles that confront interests and images, that involve preferences and strategies, that bring victories and defeats. The political behavior of individuals can be understood only in concrete historical articulation with these conflicts—particular traits become causes of individual acts when they are embedded within a definite structure that has been imposed upon political relations at a given moment in history.

The organization of politics in terms of class is not inevitable. There is nothing inherent in capitalism and nothing in the logic of history that would make the emergence of classes as collective subjects inexorable. Class position structures daily experience, generates a certain kind of knowledge, endows people with interests, and may even evoke an understanding of a shared lot, a feeling of solidarity. But this experience need not become collectivized as one of class. As Marx said and Gramsci was fond of repeating, individuals become conscious of social relations in the realm of ideology, people become aware of conflicts of interests at the level of ideology. "It is not the simple *existence* of oppressive conditions," Michels points out, "but it is the *recognition of these conditions by the oppressed,* which in the course of history constituted the prime factor of class struggle" (1962:228). Class relations are not transparent at the level of the "immediate" (Gramsci), the "lived" (Althusser 1971) experience—the experience which is simply a reflection on everyday life. This experience may be one of poverty, of compulsion, of inequality, of oppression. It may be one of similarity. But it is not an experience of class.

Even similarity need not breed solidarity, as Olson (1971) has shown. Indeed, Marx and Engels noted in the *Communist Manifesto* that "the organization of proletariat into a class, and consequently into a political party, is continually being upset by the competition among workers themselves" (1967:144). People who are in a similar situation and who have identical interests often find themselves in competition with one another.

Thus the division of society into classes does not necessarily result in the organization of politics in terms of class. The "system of interests" need not become the "system of solidarities" (Pizzorno 1966). "The simple objective conditions of producers," Sartre emphasized, "defines the concrete man—his needs, his vital problems, the orientation of his thought, the nature of his relationships with others: it does not determine his belonging to a class" (1958:96). Nor is this experience as simple as Sartre supposed, since it is not the only objective experience. If "objective" means experience that is inherited by individuals and independent of their will, then being a Catholic in Italy is an objective experience, as is being a black in the United States, or a woman in Switzerland. The people who perpetuate their existence by selling their capacity to work are also men or women, Catholics or Protestants, Northerners or Southerners. They are consumers, taxpayers, parents, and city dwellers. They may be mobilized into politics as workers, but they may also become Catholic workers, Catholics, or Bavarian Catholics. Hence, in spite of the wealth of information we have today about patterns of individual voting, the explanatory question remains open: why do people vote the way they do?

Our central thesis is that the voting behavior of individuals is an effect of the activities of political parties. More precisely, the relative salience of class as a determinant of individual voting behavior is a cumulative consequence of the strategies pursued by political parties of the Left. Hence, this is a study of voting, but not of voters, that is predicated on a theory of the system of economic and political organization under which political parties develop their strategies and individuals cast their votes.

The organization of politics in terms of class is always a contingent result of conflicts in the course of which multiple political forces strive to maintain or to alter existing social relations. Along with other organizations, political parties forge collective identities, instill commitments, define the interests on behalf of which collective actions become possible, offer choices to individuals and deny them. Is society composed of classes or individuals with harmonious interests? Are class relations the fundamental line of social conflicts or are they subordinate to some other divisions? What are the classes? Are class interests antagonistic or do they encourage cooperation? Which classes represent interests more general than their own? Which are capable of leading the entire society? These are the issues in which political parties can play a crucial role.

Different parties, however, play different roles. Conflicts over the political salience of class are characterized in any capitalist society by a basic structural asymmetry. The organization of politics in terms of class can be attempted at most by one specific class, workers.[1] In any conflict between workers and capitalists the principal visions of society are one of class and one of universalism, and both of these ideologies rationalize class interests. The claims of workers are particularistic, and when workers organize as a class they seek to impose upon the entire society the image of classes, each endowed with particularistic interests. Specifically, to legitimize their claims workers must show that capitalists are also a class, whose interests are particularistic and opposed to other classes. Capitalists, in turn, only in moments of folly represent themselves as a class under democratic conditions. The response to the particularistic claims of the working class is not a particularism of the bourgeoisie but ideologies which deny altogether the salience of class interests, either by posing a universalistic model of society composed of individuals-citizens whose interests are in harmony or by evoking alternative particularisms of religion, language, ethnicity, etc. Hence, ideological conflicts rarely, if ever, concern the legitimacy or justice of the claims made by various classes. Instead, they juxtapose the class ideology put forth by the spokesmen for workers to nonclass alternatives. Consequently, the relation between parties and classes is not the same for different classes.

This argument does not imply that workers' organizations never make universalistic claims, portraying their interests as those of the entire society, not only for the future but also at the present. Indeed, this kind of a universalistic stance is to be expected of any party seriously engaged in competition for votes. Our argument is rather that class is salient in any society, if, when, and only to the extent to which it is important to political parties which mobilize

---

1. Farmers organized their own parties in several countries, particularly in Scandinavia. The goal of these parties was to defend the particular interests of farmers in an increasingly industrial society, not to impose upon politics an organization of conflict in terms of class.

workers. Workers are the only potential proponent of the class organization of politics—when no political forces seek to mobilize workers as a class, separately from and in opposition to all other classes, class is absent altogether as a principle of political organization. Hence, historical variations concerning the salience of class as a determinant of political behavior can be attributed to the strategies pursued by political parties, especially parties of the Left.

I

Electoral Participation and Its Consequences

Republicans before everything, we do not indulge the crazy idea of appealing to a pretender's sham prestige or a dictator's sword to secure the triumph of our doctrine. We appeal only to universal suffrage. It is the voter whom we want to set economically and politically free.

Alexandre Millerand, in 1902

THE DECISION TO PARTICIPATE

The crucial choice was whether or not to participate. Earlier events resulted in establishing the principle of democracy in the political realm. Yet political rights were merely formal when accompanied by the compulsion and inequality that reigned in the social realm. As it emerged around 1850, socialism was thus a movement that would complete the revolution started by the bourgeoisie by wresting from it social power just as the bourgeoisie had conquered political power. The recurrent theme of the socialist movement ever since has been this notion of extending the democratic principle from the political to the social, in effect primarily economic, realm.

Yet precisely because the principle of democracy was already present in the political institutions, the means by which socialism could be achieved appeared as a choice. The project of the early, communitarian socialists was to build a society within the society, a community of immediate producers associated in workshops and manufactures, cooperating as consumers and administering their own affairs. This society of associated producers was to be

Portions of this chapter first appeared in the *New Left Review*, no. 122 (July 1980) in a somewhat different form.

built in complete independence from the bourgeois world; it was simply to bypass the emerging capitalist, and to a great extent industrial, order. Yet as soon as the new bourgeois society developed its specific political institutions—the popularly elected parliament—the posture of aloof independence could not be sustained. One could no longer maintain, as Proudhon had, that social reform cannot result from political change. Even if political action was indeed ineffective in bringing about social reform, once established, the new political institutions had to be treated either as an enemy or a potential instrument. The choice had become one between direct and political action—a direct confrontation between the world of workers and the world of capital or a struggle through bourgeois political institutions. Building a society within the society was not enough. The conquest of political power was necessary. As Marx argued in his Inaugural Address to the First International in 1864, "To be able to emancipate the working class, the cooperative system must be developed at the national level, which implies that it must dispose of national means. . . . Under these conditions, the great duty of the working class is to conquer political power" (1974:80). Hence Marx claimed that workers must organize as a political party and this party must conquer power on the road to establishing the socialist society. But the tormenting question was whether this party should avail itself of the already existing institutions in its quest for political power. Political democracy, specifically suffrage, was a ready-made weapon for the working class. Was this weapon to be discarded or was it to be wielded on the road from political to social emancipation?

The anarchist response was resoundingly negative. What anarchists feared and claimed was not only that political action is unnecessary and ineffective but that any involvement in bourgeois institutions, whatever its purpose and whatever its form, would destroy the movement for socialism. The Anarchist Congress at Chaud-de-Fonds warned in 1870 that "all workers' participation in bourgeois governmental politics cannot have other results than the consolidation of the existing state of affairs, and thus would paralyze socialist revolutionary action of the proletariat" (Droz 1966:33). The consideration of an improvement in the workers' situation within capitalist society—a discussion of international codes for the protection of labor at the founding meeting of the

Second International in 1889—brought Anarchists to exclaim immediately that whoever accepts reforms is not a true socialist (Joll 1966:45). Alex Danielsson, one of the founders of the Swedish Social Democracy, maintained in 1888 that electoral participation would change socialism "from a new theory of society and the world into a paltry program for a purely parliamentary party, and at that instant the enthusiasm in the workers' core will be extinguished and the ideal of social revolution degenerate into a pursuit of 'reforms' that will consume all the workers' interests" (Tingsten 1973:352). As Errico Malatesta observed in retrospect, "Anarchists have always kept themselves pure, and remain the revolutionary party par excellence, the party of the future, because they have been able to resist the siren song of elections" (Guerin 1970:19).

Those who became socialists were the ones who decided to utilize the political rights of workers in those societies where workers had them and to struggle for these rights where they were still to be won. The abstentionist current lost its support within the First International after 1873 and the newly formed socialist parties, most founded between 1884 and 1892, embraced the principles of political action and of workers' autonomy (Haupt 1980).

Yet the attitude of socialist parties toward electoral participation was ambivalent at best and this ambivalence was not theoretical. Little is to be gained by interpreting and reinterpreting every word Marx wrote about bourgeois democracy for the simple reason that Marx himself and the men and women who led the newly founded parties into electoral battles were not quite certain what to expect of electoral competition. The main question—one which history never resolved because it cannot be resolved once and for all—was whether the bourgeoisie would respect its own legal order in case of an electoral triumph by socialism. If socialists were to use the institution of suffrage—established by the bourgeoisie in its struggle against absolutism—to win elections and to legislate a society toward socialism, would the bourgeoisie revert to illegal means to defend its interests? This is what had happened in France in 1851, and it seemed likely that it would happen again. But on several occasions Marx entertained the possibility that in England or in Holland a counterrevolution would not occur if workers won the majority in the parliament. Marx's general appraisal of the democratic eventuality was a conditional one. He wrote in 1879 that "a historical development can only remain 'peaceful' so long as it is not opposed by the violence of those who wield power in society at that time" (McLellan 1971:201).

Thus, the essential question facing socialist parties was whether, as Hjalmar Branting posed it in 1886, "the upper class [would] respect popular will *even when it demanded the abolition of its privileges*" (Tingsten 1973:361). Sterky, the leader of the left wing of the Swedish Social Democrats, was among those who took a clearly negative view. "Suppose that . . . the working class could send a majority to the legislature; not even by doing this would it obtain power. One can be sure that the capitalist class would then take care not to continue along a parliamentary course but instead resort to bayonets" (Tingsten 1973:361). No one could be completely certain. Austrian Socialists, for example, promised in their Linz program of 1926 to "govern in strict accordance with the rules of the democratic state," but they felt compelled to warn that "should the bourgeoisie by boycotting revolutionary forces attempt to obstruct the social change which the labour movement in assuming power is pledged to carry out, then social democracy will be forced to employ dictatorial means to break such resistance" (Leser 1976:145). The main doubt about electoral participation was whether revolution would not be necessary anyway, as August Bebel put it in 1905, "as a purely defensive measure, designed to safeguard the exercise of power legitimately acquired through the ballot" (Schorske 1972:43).

Under these conditions the attitude toward electoral participation was understandably cautious. Socialists entered electoral politics gingerly, "only to utilize them for propaganda purposes," and vowed "not to enter any alliances with other parties or to accept any compromises" (Resolution of the Eisenach Congress of the SPD in 1870). At best, many thought, universal suffrage was one instrument among others, albeit one that had "the incomparably higher merit of unchaining the class struggle," as Marx put it in 1850 (1952:47). Elections were to be used only as a ready-made forum for organization, agitation, and propaganda. The typical posture is well illustrated by this motion offered in 1889: "Since Sweden's Social Democratic Workers' Party is a propaganda party, i.e., it considers its main objective to be the dissemination of information about Social Democracy, and since participation in elections is a good vehicle for agitation, the Congress recommends participation" (Tingsten 1973:357). Elections were also useful in providing party leadership with a reading of the revolutionary fervor of the masses. But this is all they seemed to promise at the moment when socialists decided to participate. The last edition of *The Origins of Private Property, Family, and the State* which appeared during Engels' lifetime still contained in 1891 the assertion that universal suffrage is merely "the gauge of the maturity of the working class. It cannot and never will be anything more in the present-day state" (1942:158) and continued somewhat ambivalently, "but that is sufficient."

Each step toward full participation rekindled controversies. The German Social Democratic Party argued whether to allow one of its members to become the Deputy Speaker of the Reichstag, whether to vote on the budget, even whether to trade votes in the second round of elections (Schorske 1972). The Norwegian Labor Party refused in 1906 to trade votes in the second round even though absolutely no compromise was implied (Lafferty 1971:127). In 1898, a survey of the opinions of prominent leaders of the Second International showed that while interventions into bourgeois politics were thought to be at times advisable, six of the respondents voted "*jamais*" with regard to participating in a government, eleven admitted it was possible only "*très exceptionnellement,*" and a minority of twelve thought that such participation is either always desirable or at least it was in the case of Millerand (Fiechtier 1965:69–75). Of the sixty-nine Swedish Social Democrats polled by telegram whether the party should join the Liberal government in 1911, sixty-three responded against participating (Tingsten 1973:418). While some parties "suspended" class struggle and entered into coalition governments before the end of World War I, even in Great Britain the decision to form the first Labour government in 1924 was a subject of intense polemics and was rationalized as an opportunity to acquire experience necessary for the socialist era (Lyman 1957).

Opponents of participation seem to hold a permanent place in the political spectrum. As established parties take each step toward full participation, new voices emerge to continue the tradition according to which the belief in the parliamentary battles "between frogs and mice" (Luxemburg 1967:37) is simply a manifestation of what Marx called under very special circumstances "parliamentary cretinism" (1952:77). "Integration is the price," Horkheimer repeated in 1940 in the anarchist *memento*, "which individuals and groups must pay in order to flourish under capitalism" (1973:5). "Elections, a trap for fools," was the title of an article by Sartre on the eve of the 1973 French parliamentary elections. "*Voter, c'est abdiquer*" shouted the walls of Paris in 1968.

ELECTORAL PARTICIPATION AND CLASS ORGANIZATION

The reason why involvement in representative politics of bourgeois society has never ceased to evoke controversy is that the very act of taking part in this particular system shapes the movement for socialism and its relation to workers as a class. The recurrent question is whether involvement in electoral politics can result in socialism or must strengthen the existing, that is, capitalist, social order. Is it possible for the socialist movement to find a passage between the two reefs charted by Rosa Luxemburg: "abandonment of the mass character or abandonment of the final goals?" (Howard 1973–74:93). Participation in electoral politics is necessary if the movement for socialism is to find mass support among workers, yet this participation appears to obstruct the attainment of final goals. Working for today and working toward tomorrow appear as horns of a dilemma to many observers who argue, as E. H. Tawney did about Labour, that the "Party can be either a political agent, pressing in the Parliament the claims of particular groups of wage earners or it can be an instrument for the establishment of a socialist commonwealth. What it cannot be is both at the same time and in the same measure" (1923).

Participation imprints a particular structure on the organization of workers as a class. These effects of participation upon internal class relations have been best analyzed by Luxemburg: "the division between political struggle and economic struggle and their separation is but an artificial product, even if historically understandable, of the parliamentary period. On the one hand, in the peaceful development, 'normal' for the bourgeois society, the economic struggle is fractionalized, disaggregated into a multitude of partial struggles limited to each firm, to each branch of production. On the other hand, the political struggle is conducted not by the masses through direct action, but in conformity with the structure of the bourgeois state, in the representative fashion, by the pressure exercised upon the legislative body'' (1970:202).

The first effect of the structure of the bourgeois state is thus that wage earners are formed as a class in a number of independent and often competitive organizations, most frequently as trade unions and political parties, but also as cooperatives, neighborhood associations, clubs, etc. One characteristic feature of capitalist democracy is the individualization of class relations in the realms of politics and ideology (Lukacs 1971:65–66; Poulantzas 1973). People who are capitalists or wage earners within the system of production all appear in politics as undifferentiated individuals-citizens. Hence, even if a political party succeeds in organizing a class on the terrain of political institutions, economic and political organization need not coincide. Multiple unions and parties often represent different interests and compete with each other. Moreover, while the class base of unions is confined to certain groups of people more or less permanently employed as wage earners, political parties which organize workers can also mobilize people who cannot be members of unions. Hence there is a permanent tension between the narrower interests of unions and the broader interests represented by parties. Class organized as a participant does not appear as a single actor in concrete historical conflicts (Miliband 1977:129).

The second effect is that relations within the class become structured as relations of representation. The parliament is a representative institution—seating individuals, not masses. A relation of representation is thus imposed upon the class by the nature of political institutions. Masses do not act directly on behalf of their interests, they delegate this activity. This is true of unions as much as of parties, and the process of collective bargaining is as distant from the daily experience of the masses as are elections. Leaders become representatives. Masses are represented by leaders. This becomes the mode of organization of the working class.

The organizational dilemma extends even further. The struggle for socialism inevitably results in the *embourgeoisement* of the socialist movement. This is the gist of Roberto Michels' classical analysis. The struggle requires organization; it demands a permanent apparatus, a salaried bureaucracy; it calls for the movement to engage in economic activities of its own. Hence socialist militants become bureaucrats, newspaper editors, managers of insurance companies, directors of funeral parlors, and even barkeepers. All of these are petty bourgeois occupations. "They impress," Michels concluded, "a markedly petty bourgeois stamp" (1962:270). As a French Communist dissident wrote recently, "The working class is lost in administering its imaginary bastions. Comrades disguised as notables occupy themselves with municipal garbage dumps and school cafeterias. Or are these notables disguised as comrades? I no longer know" (Konopnicki 1979).

A party that participates in elections must foresake some alternative tactics: this is the frequently diagnosed tactical dilemma. As long as workers did not have political rights, no choice between insurrectionary and parliamentary tactics was necessary. Indeed, political rights could be conquered by those who did not have them only through extraparliamentary activities. César de Paepe, the founder of the *Parti Socialiste Brabançon* wrote in 1887 that "in using our constitutional right and legal means at our disposal we do not renounce the right to revolution" (Landauer 1959, I:457). This statement was echoed several times, notably by Engels in 1895. Danielsson maintained, in a more pragmatic vein, perhaps thinking that revolution is a matter of opportunity rather than right, that Social Democrats should not commit themselves to "a dogma regarding tactics that would bind the party to act according to the same routine under all circumstances" (Tingsten 1973:362). That a mass strike should be used to achieve universal suffrage was not questioned, and both the Belgian Parti Ouvrier and the Swedish Social Democrats led successful mass strikes that resulted in extensions of the suffrage.

Yet as soon as universal male suffrage was obtained, the choice between legal and extraparliamentary tactics had to be made. John McGurk, the chairman of the Labour Party, put it sharply in 1919: "We are either constitutionalists or we are not constitutionalists. If we are constitutionalists, if we believe in the efficacy of the political weapon (and we do, or why do we have a Labour Party?) then it is both unwise and undemocratic because we fail to get a majority at the polls to turn around and demand that we should substitute industrial action" (Miliband 1972:69). To win votes of people other than workers, particularly the petite bourgeoisie, to form alliances and coalitions, to administer the government in the short-run interest of workers, a party cannot appear irresponsible or give any indication of being less than wholehearted about its commitment to the rules and the limits of parliamentarism. At times the party must even restrain its own followers from actions that would jeopardize electoral progress. Moreover, a party oriented toward partial improvements, a party in which leaders-representatives lead a petty bourgeois life-style, a party that for years shies away from the streets cannot "pour through the hole in the trenches," as Gramsci put it, even when this opening is forged by a crisis. "The trouble about the revolutionary left in stable industrial societies," observed Eric Hobsbawm (1973:14–15), "is not that its opportunities never came, but that the normal conditions in which it must operate prevent it from developing the movements likely to seize the rare moments when they are called upon to behave as revolutionaries. . . . Being a revolutionary in countries such as ours just happens to be difficult."

This dilemma became even more acute when representative democracy ceased to be merely a tactical instrument and became accepted as the basic tenet of the future socialist society. Socialist parties eventually recognized in political democracy a value that transcends different forms of organization of production. Jean Jaurès claimed that "the triumph of socialism will not be a break with the French Revolution but the fulfillment of the French Revolution in new economic conditions" (1971:71). Eduard Bernstein (1961) saw in socialism simply "democracy brought to its logical conclusion," and this statement has been ritually repeated by social democrats ever since. Representative democracy became simultaneously the means and the goal, simultaneously the strategy and the program, instrumental and prefigurative. But this commitment made even more critical the question whether, as Harold Laski (1935:77) put it, capitalist democracy would "allow its electorate to stumble into socialism by the accident of the verdict at the polls." "Is democratic socialism, then, impossible?"—Peter Gay's biography of Bernstein dramatized this dilemma. "Or can it be achieved only if the party is willing to abandon the democratic method temporarily to attain power by violence in the hope that it may return to parliamentarism as soon as it is secure. Surely this second alternative contains tragic possibilities: a democratic movement that resorts to authoritarian methods to gain its objective may not remain a democratic movement for long. Still, the first alternative—to cling to democratic procedures under all circumstances—may doom the party to continual political impotence'' (1970:7).

SOCIALISM AND ELECTORALISM

Finding dilemmas, or inventing them, is an occupation for spectators, not activists. People who are out to change the world do not dwell upon the inexorable logics of futility: they lead masses to the final victory. Socialists entered into elections to obtain an overwhelming mandate for revolutionary transformation of society, to legislate the society into socialism. This was their aim and their expectation.

Socialists entered into elections with ultimate goals. The Hague Congress of the First International proclaimed that the ''organization of the proletariat into a political party is necessary to insure the victory of social revolution and its ultimate goal— the abolition of classes'' (Chodak 1962:39). The first Swedish program specified that ''Social Democracy differs from other parties in that it aspires to completely transform the economic organization of bourgeois society and bring about the social liberation of the working class'' (Tingsten 1973:118–19). Even the most reformist among revisionists, Alexandre Millerand admonished that ''whoever does not admit the necessary progressive replacement of capitalist property by social property is not a socialist'' (Ensor 1908:51).

These were the goals that were to be reached through legislation, on a mandate of an electorally expressed majority, as the will of the universal suffrage. Socialists were to abolish exploitation, to destroy the division of society into classes, to remove all economic and political inequalities, to finish the wastefulness and anarchy of capitalist production, to eradicate all sources of injustice and prejudice. They were going to emancipate not only workers but humanity, to build a society based on cooperation, to rationally orient resources and energies toward satisfaction of human needs, to create social conditions for an unlimited development of personality. Rationality, freedom, and justice were the guiding goals of the movement.

These were ultimate goals. They could not be realized immediately for economic as well as political reasons. But socialists were unwilling to wait for the day when these aims could be finally accomplished. They claimed to represent the interests of workers and of other groups not only in the future but in the present as well, that is, in capitalist society (Kautsky 1971). The *Parti Socialiste Française,* led by Jaurès, proclaimed at its Tours Congress of 1902 that the party, "rejecting the policy of all or nothing, has a programme of reforms whose realization it pursues forthwith," and listed fifty-four specific demands concerning democratization, secularization, organization of justice, family, education, taxation, protection of labor, social insurance, nationalization of industries, and foreign policy (Ensor 1908:345ff). Swedish Social Democrats in 1897 demanded direct taxation, development of state and municipal productive activities, public credit including direct state control of credit for farmers, legislation concerning working conditions, old age, sickness, and accident insurance, legal equality, and freedoms of organization, assembly, speech, and press (Tingsten 1973:119–20).

This orientation toward immediate improvements was never perceived by its architects as a departure from ultimate goals. Since socialism was inevitable, there would be no reason why immediate measures should not be advocated by socialist parties: there was no danger, not even a possibility, that such measures could prevent the advent of the inescapable. As Karl Kautsky maintained, "it would be a profound error to imagine that such reforms could delay the social revolution" (1971:93). "Precisely because it is a party of revolution," Jaurès argued against Jules Guesde, "the Socialist party is the party most actively reformist" (Fiechtier 1965:163). Ultimate goals were going to be realized because History was on the side of socialism; also, reforms would strengthen the working class. Revisionists within the movement were, if anything, even more deterministic than those who considered insurrectionary tactics. Millerand argued, for example, in the Saint-Mande speech that "Men do not and will not set up collectivism; it is setting itself daily; it is, if I may be allowed the phrase, being secreted by capitalist system" (Ensor 1908:50).

Even when socialists left the protection of history to rediscover a justification for socialism in ethical values, no dilemma appeared in the consciousness of socialist leaders. Bernstein's famous renunciation of final goals did not imply that they remain unfulfilled but rather that they would be best realized by concentrating on proximate aims. Jaurès, speaking about the conquest of political power by workers, provided the classical image: "I do not believe, either, that there will necessarily be an abrupt leap, the crossing of an abyss; perhaps we shall be aware of having entered the zone of the Socialistic State as navigators are aware of having crossed the line of a hemisphere—not that they have been able to see as they crossed a cord stretched over the ocean warning them of their passage, but that little by little they have been led into a new hemisphere by the progress of their ship" (Ensor 1908:171). Reforms constitute steps; they gradually accumulate toward a complete restructuring of society. Anticipating Bernstein, George von Vollmar, the leader of the Bavarian wing of the SPD, declared at the Erfurt Congress: "Beside the general or ultimate goal we see a nearer end: the advancement of the most immediate needs of the people. For me, the achievement of the most immediate demands is the main thing, not only because they are of great propagandist value and serve to enlist the masses, but also because, in my opinion, this gradual progress, this gradual socialization, is the method strongly advocated for a progressive transition" (Gay 1970:259). Forty years later, at a crucial moment of Swedish history, P. A. Hansson repeated: "What lies at the basis of confidence and secures our victory . . . is our attempt to put to the people practical proposals for the solution of issues that are of interest to them in their daily lives—a policy that is by no means new, a policy that does not exclude the idea that the duty to the future, and to the greater aims that may never be neglected by a social democratic party, is fulfilled" (Tingsten 1973:289). It was never apparent to those oriented toward concrete, immediate improvements that one could not traverse the road to a socialist future by taking practical steps.

Thus the electoral commitment became almost absolute, and questions of tactics were reduced to choices of electoral strategies while party leaders continued to maintain that electoralism involves no dilemma. Participation in elections was based on the belief that democracy is not only necessary but that it is sufficient for reaching socialism. "If one thing is certain," Engels wrote in an 1891 letter that was to meet with Lenin's acute displeasure, "it is that our Party and the working class can only come to power under the form of the democratic republic. This is even the specific form of the dictatorship of the proletariat" (1935:486). Jaurès saw in democracy "the largest and most solid terrain on which the working class can stand, . . . the bedrock that the reactionary bourgeoisie cannot dissolve without opening fissues in the earth and throwing itself into them" (Derfler 1973:59). Millerand was as always incisive: "To realize the immediate reforms capable of relieving the lot of the working class, and thus fitting it to win its own freedom, and to begin, as conditioned by the nature of things, the socialization of the means of production, it is necessary and sufficient for the socialist party to endeavor to capture the government through universal suffrage" (Ensor 1908:54).

There was no dilemma between electoralism and socialism because socialism would be reached simply by winning elections.

GREAT EXPECTATIONS

Socialists entered elections because they had to be concerned about immediate improvements of workers' conditions. Yet they entered in order to bring about socialism. Is this divergence between cause and purpose a symptom of rationalization? Was the pathos of final goals just a form of self-deception?

Such questions are best left for psychologists to resolve. But one thing is certain, socialists were deeply persuaded that they would win elections, that they would obtain for socialism the support of an overwhelming numerical majority. They put all of their hopes and efforts into electoral competition because they were certain that electoral victory was within reach. Their strength was in numbers, and elections are an expression of numerical strength. Hence, universal suffrage seemed to guarantee socialist victory, if not immediately then certainly within the near future. Revolution would be made at the ballot box. Among the many expressions of this conviction is the striking apologia delivered by Engels in 1895: "The German workers . . . showed the comrades in all countries how to make use of universal suffrage. . . . With the successful utilization of universal suffrage . . . an entirely new method of proletarian struggle came into operation, and this method quickly developed even further. It was found that state institutions, in which the rule of the bourgeoisie is organized, offer the working class still further opportunities to fight these very state institutions." And Engels offered a forecast: "If it [electoral progress] continues in this fashion, by the end of the century we

shall . . . grow into the decisive power in the land, before which
all other power will have to bow, whether they like it or not"
(1960:22).

The grounds for this conviction were both theoretical and practical. Already in the *Communist Manifesto,* Marx and Engels described socialism as the movement of the "immense majority"
(1967:147). In an 1850 article on "The Chartists" in the New
York *Daily Tribune* and then again in 1867 in the Polish émigré
newspaper *Głos Wolny,* Marx repeated that "universal suffrage is
the equivalent of political power for the working class of England,
where the proletariat forms the large majority of the population. . . ." But even if the first electoral battles would not end in
triumph, even if the proletariat was not yet a majority, electoral
victory seemed only a matter of time because capitalism was
swelling the ranks of the proletariat. The development of factory
production and its corollary concentration of capital and land were
to result rapidly in the proletarianization of craftsmen, artisans,
merchants, and small agricultural proprietors. Even "the physi-
cian, the lawyer, the priest, the poet, the man of science" were
being converted into wage laborers according to the *Communist
Manifesto.* This growth of the numbers of people who were forced
to sell their labor power for a wage in order to survive was not
accidental, temporary, or reversible—it was viewed as a necessary consequence of capitalist development. Hence, it was just a
question of time before almost everyone, "all but a handful of
exploiters," would become proletarian. Socialism would be in the
interest of almost everyone, and the overwhelming majority of the
people would electorally express their will for socialism. A young
Swedish theoretician formulated this syllogism as follows in
1898: "The struggle for the state is political. Its outcome is therefore to a very great extent contingent upon the possibility open to
society's members—whose proletarianism has been brought
about by the capitalist process—to exercise their proper influence
on political decision-making. If democracy is achieved, the
growth of capitalism means a corresponding mobilization of
voices *against* the capitalist system itself. Democracy therefore
contains an automatically operative device that heightens the opposition to capitalism in proportion to the development of capitalism" (Tingsten 1973:402). History spoke through the people.

People spoke in elections. And no one doubted that history would make people express their will for socialism.

This was a good theory by positivist and by practical criteria. The proportion of the proletariat—manual industrial workers—in the population was increasing, even if slowly, in most countries. In Germany, manual industrial workers constituted 19 percent of the adult population in 1882, 25 percent in 1907. In Sweden, the proportion of workers increased from 12 percent in 1900 to 18 percent in 1910. Belgium, along with Great Britain, was the most industrialized country in Europe at the turn of the century—workers increased from 27 percent of adult population in 1892 to 30 percent in 1910. In France the proportion of workers hovered around 28 percent of adults and in Denmark around 14 percent at the turn of the century. At the same time, small property was being destroyed. Bernstein may have been an effective strategist but he was not much of a data analyst. In Germany, the proportion of people who were self-employed and did not employ others fell from 27 percent in 1882 to 20 percent in 1907; in Denmark from 25 percent in 1901 to 22 percent in 1920; in France, after a temporary increase, it diminished from 13 percent in 1901 to 11 percent in 1921; and in Sweden the small proprietors decreased from 25 percent in 1900 to 23 percent in 1910.

More importantly, these expectations, based on a conviction about the future course of history, were almost immediately vindicated by the electoral successes of socialist parties. The German party grew, despite repression, from 125,000 votes in 1871 to 312,000 in 1881, to 1,427,300 in 1890, and finally to 4,250,000 on the eve of World War I. Indeed, as soon as the Anti-Socialist laws were allowed to lapse, the SPD in 1890 became the largest party in Germany with 19.7 percent of the vote. By 1912 their share of 34.8 percent was more than twice that of the next largest party. No wonder that in 1900 Bebel could make "explicit the widely held assumption of his fellow socialists that the working class would continue to grow and that the party would one day embrace a majority of the population" (Schorske 1972:43). Several parties entered even more spectacularly into the competition for votes. Finnish Social Democrats won the plurality, 37 percent, in the first election under universal suffrage, in 1907. The Austrian Social Democrats won 21 percent after male franchise was made universal in 1907, 25.4 percent in 1911, and the plurality of 40.8 percent under the new boundaries in 1919. The Belgian *Parti Ouvrier* won 13.2 percent when the *régime censitaire* was abolished in 1894 and kept growing in jumps to win in 1925 the plurality of 39.4 percent, a success which ''stimulated them to hope that continuing industrialization would produce an increasing socialist working-class electorate'' (Mabille and Lorwin 1977:392). Even in those countries where the first steps were not equally dramatic, electoral progress seemed inexorable. In the religiously politicized Netherlands, socialism marched in big steps, from 3 percent in 1896 to 9.5, 11.2, 13.9, and 18.5 in 1913. The Danish party obtained 4.9 percent in 1884, the first election it contested, only 3.5 percent in 1889, but henceforth the party never failed to increase its share of the vote until 1935, when it won 46.1 percent. Here again, ''there was a general expectation that as the sole party representing the labour movement, it would achieve power through an absolute majority of the electorate'' (Thomas 1977:240). The Swedish party began meekly, offering candidates on joint lists with Liberals; it won 3.5 percent in 1902, 9.5 in 1905, 14.6 in 1908; jumped to 28.5 percent in 1911, after the suffrage was extended; increased its share to 30.1 and 36.4 in the two successive elections of 1914, and with its left-wing offshoot won the plurality of the vote, 39.1 percent, in 1917. The Norwegian Labour Party grew about 5 percent in each election, from 1897 when it obtained 0.6 percent onward to 1915 when its share reached 32.1 percent.

Practice was confirming the theory. From election to election, the forces of socialism were growing in strength. Each round was a new success. A few thousand at best during the first difficult moments, socialists saw their electorate expand into millions. The progress seemed inexorable; the majority and the mandate for socialism embodied therein were just a matter of a few years, a couple of elections. One more effort and humanity would be ushered into a new era by the overwhelming expression of popular will. ''I am convinced,'' Bebel spoke at the Erfurt Congress, ''that the fulfillment of our aims is so close that there are few in this hall who will not live to see the day'' (Derfler 1973:58).

2

The Dilemma
of Electoral Socialism

*If any external element contributed to put Marx somewhat out
of date, it is the elections.*

Engels to Bernstein, 30 November 1881

THE MAGIC BARRIER

In some mysterious way the electoral progress of socialist parties
was arrested as soon as they approached the magic barrier of numerical majority. It seems as if the system of electoral competition contained a built-in spring that pushed the socialist vote down
each time it neared 50 percent. Between 1944 and 1978 four socialist parties obtained, on the average, between 40 and 50 percent of the vote: in Austria, Norway, the United Kingdom, and
Sweden. Four parties saw their vote stabilized between 30 and 40
percent. The Left as a whole—socialist parties, communist parties, and other left-wing groups combined—saw its average vote
slightly exceed 50 percent in Sweden and Norway. In most other
countries, the share of the total Left hovered between 40 and 50
percent (see table 2.1).

In country after country the same story was repeated. In
Belgium, the *Parti Ouvrier* won a plurality of 39.4 percent in
1925; this turned out to be their best performance ever. In Denmark the long climb reached its peak when Social Democrats won
46.1 percent in 1935, again a result that was never approximated
later. In Finland, a civil war interrupted social democratic progress; then the communist split developed, and now the two par-

Table 2.1 Average Shares of the Vote of Major Socialist Parties
and the Total Left, 1917–78

	Socialist Party		Total Left	
Country	1917–43	1944–78	1917–43	1944–78
Austria	40.0	44.9	40.5	48.2
Belgium	35.3	31.1	37.7	35.6
Denmark	37.4	37.1	38.1	45.4
Finland	33.1	24.8	38.8	42.7
France	19.7	18.3	30.8	43.3
Germany	24.5	37.0	36.4	38.1
Ireland	11.5	12.4	11.5	12.4
Iceland	16.4	14.5	23.0	33.3
Italy	28.5	13.6	31.5	42.7
Luxembourg	29.0	34.0	33.5	46.4
Netherlands	21.9	28.3	24.8	36.1
Norway	31.7	44.0	36.3	50.5
United Kingdom	31.4	44.5	31.8	44.7
Sweden	40.8	46.0	47.3	51.2
Switzerland	26.3	25.4	27.7	28.3

Source: Bartolini 1979.

ties combined hover a few percentage points under fifty. In
France the moment of triumph was in 1936 when the Popular
Front received 59 percent of the vote; in 1945 the Left as a whole
won 49.9 percent and had to wait until 1981 to match this performance. German Social Democrats never recuperated during the
Weimar period from the "great schism" and the subsequent communist split; after World War II the Communist Party was dele-
galized while Social Democrats began to climb into the 40 percent
range. The Norwegian Labour Party suffered a series of splits
after 1920, consolidated without communists by 1927, and has
been winning almost 50 percent of the vote since 1945. Finally, in
Sweden, Social Democrats experienced some great days at the
polls but kept their majority mostly because of alliances with
Agrarians or the tacit support of the Communists. In almost all
cases, electoral progress continued more or less until a party won
the plurality; then their vote stabilized and continued to oscillate
around some stable level.

This experience is not uniform. By relative standards the

Swedish Social Democratic Party has been quite successful electorally during most of its history while, say, the Dutch Party has been less so. But by invoking relative standards one forgets that absolute standards exist as well; one proceeds as if the common fate did not require an explanation. And yet, what different histories have in common illuminates the limits of our historically inherited possibilities. Before asking why this party has been more successful than that one, can we ignore the fact that no party has succeeded in terms of its own dreams and designs, that not one has brought to realization the very purpose of its foundation?

WORKERS AS A MINORITY

The first reason why socialists never won the victories they foresaw is that workers never were and never would become a numerical majority in their respective societies. The victories which socialists had expected to win in elections were to be furnished by workers. The proletariat—acting on its interest and conscious of its mission—was to be the social force carrying society into socialism. But who were these proletarians who were to provide the electoral mandate for socialism?

The proletariat appeared as a distinct class in the course of the industrial revolution. Bergier (1973:397) succinctly summarized this process: "The introduction of a new power source superseding that of man, wind, or running water soon wrought a clear distinction between the industrialist, who owned this comparatively expensive machine and the looms it drove, and the worker, who was paid to run it." As feudal restrictions were being abolished, first *les classes laborieuses*—all those who worked—became separated from *les classes inférieures*—all those who were not distinguished by birth or position within the old society. Then the newcomer appeared: *la classe ouvrière* (Furet 1963:473). Workers were distinct from artisans because they owned none of the tools they used and worked where the tools were. They were distinct from serfs and slaves because they were legally free to choose their employer. They were distinct from beggars because they worked. The very term "proletariat" acquired a standardized meaning, denoting those who sell their labor services to a capitalist for a wage. It was first introduced in France, and then in Germany by Lorenz von Stein in 1842 (Sombart 1909:6). By 1848, and perhaps earlier in 1830 in Lyon or in 1818 at Peterloo, the political reactions of the lower classes to the new conditions of industrialism ceased to assume the form of sporadic riots against prices or taxes. The proletariat broke away from *le peuple* and for the first time marked its political presence (Marx 1952; Hobsbawm 1964).

Workers were expected by socialists to become the moving force for socialism because of two aspects of the position which they occupied in capitalist society. Workers had both an interest in abolishing capitalism and the capacity to organize socialism. They were the ones who were exploited in the manner specific to the new form of the organization of production—they were forced to sell their capacity to work for a wage which only allowed them to sustain that capacity. Around 1848 proletarians were the poor and miserable people who were thrown off the land and forced to sell themselves, as a commodity, "like every other article of commerce," to a capitalist. They were "an appendage of the machine," of whom "only the most simple, most monotonous, and most easily acquired knock was required" (Marx and Engels 1967:141; cf. Engels 1958 and Marcus 1975). Proletarians were the people—men, women, and children—who toiled day and night, next to a machine, in noise and dirt, producing they knew not what and why just to survive until the following day so that they could sell themselves again. Workers were exploited, they were poor, they were oppressed, and they would revolt against the system of which they were the principal victims. They would "throw off their chains."

But poverty and oppression were not the only reasons workers were endowed by Marx and his fellow socialists with their historic mission. Proletarians were crucial because they utilized the modern means of production in the developing industrial society. Although farmers, artisans, and craftsmen still produced some things that people required, they would be replaced by modern industry. As Branting put it, "the working class alone belongs to the future" (Tingsten 1973:159). Moreover, although some other people—merchants, intermediaries, servants, officials—also worked, their labor was not indispensable to satisfying human needs. Indeed, the people who did not make things with their hands were "social parasites who, finding all avenues of productive work closed to them, try to eke out a miserable existence through a variety of occupations, most of which are wholly superfluous and not a few injurious to society . . ." (Kautsky 1971:85). Hence proletarians occupied a unique position, for they were the only ones who would be necessary in the future to make all that which society required, and they could make it on their own. As Mandel (1971:23) emphasized, Marx and Engels "assigned the proletariat the key role in the coming of socialism not so much because of the misery it suffers as because of the place it occupies in the production process."

In the middle of the nineteenth century, the concept of the proletariat was unambiguous. The theoretical denotation of proletariat defined in terms of wage labor coincided with the intuitive concept of workers as manual, principally industrial laborers. A Norwegian industrialist remarked: "If a working man doesn't smell of filth and sweat two miles off, he isn't much of a fellow" (Bull 1955:67). Not until 1888 did Engels find it necessary to introduce a definition of the proletariat as a footnote to the English edition of the *Communist Manifesto*. According to this definition, "by proletariat is meant the class of modern wage labourers who, having no means of production of their own, are reduced to selling their labour power in order to live." Kautsky echoed this definition in the influential commentary on the Erfurt Programme: "Proletarians, that is to say . . . workers who are divorced from their instruments of production so that they can produce nothing by their efforts and, therefore, are compelled to sell the only commodity they possess—their labour power" (1971:43).

Around 1890, exactly at the time socialist parties were entering into electoral battles, those who sold their labor power for a wage were almost exclusively the manual laborers in mining, manufacturing, construction, and in some countries agriculture and forestry. In industry (including mining and construction)—which was supposed to represent the future of society—wage earners other than manual workers were very few.[1] According to the 1882 German census, there were about 1.5 million employers, 3.5 million manual workers, and only 90 thousand clerical and technical personnel in this sector. In France in 1881 there were 1,169,000 employers, about 3 million manual workers, and 236 thousand

1. Unless noted otherwise, all the references to class structure are based on data reconstructed specifically for this project. For the description of sources and procedures see Appendix: Data.

office employees of any kind (Toutain 1963). The respective figures for Sweden in 1900 were 125 thousand employers, 442 thousand workers, and 22 thousand office and technical personnel. At
the same time in Denmark there were 27 thousand office and clerical staff, 62 thousand employers, and 160 thousand manual
workers. Proletarians were wage earners, and wage earners were
manual industrial workers. Proletarians were workers, not clerks
or officials.

This was the proletariat that was expected to carry socialism to
its electoral majority. It consisted of manual workers employed in
mining, manufacturing, construction, transport, and sometimes
agriculture.

This proletariat was not and would never become a numerical
majority of any society. The proportion of the population manually employed as wage earners in industrial activities at no time
surpassed 50 percent in any country.[2] Even if agricultural workers
are added to this group, the proportion of the workers in the adult
population never approached one-half in the four countries for
which detailed information on the class structure can be reconstructed—Sweden, France, Denmark, Belgium. And the numbers
presented in table 2.2 include among workers the inactive members of their households.[3] If adult dependents of workers, primarily wives not working outside the household, were not
included, only rarely would workers exceed one-quarter of the
adult population.

The relevant proportions from the electoral point of view,
however, are among persons who have the right to vote, the elec-

2. Our own data are taken from Belgium, Denmark, Finland, France, Germany, Norway, and Sweden. Hobsbawm (1978) refers to British data according to
which workers would have constituted 75 percent of the population around 1870
but neither his definition of workers nor of population is quite clear. Other studies
do not show workers to have been a majority in Great Britain. Workers were never
the majority in Italy (Sylos Labini 1972) or in Japan (Okasaki 1958).

3. We used household classification of the population, that is, we classified all
people who were not gainfully employed outside the household in the category of
the head of household. In most censuses, the head of household is the gainfully
employed person if there is only one such individual, and it is the male whenever
both husband and wife are employed. In other words, all the persons who are
gainfully employed outside the household were classified by their own occupation
but those not employed outside were typically put in the category of the senior
working male.

Table 2.2 Workers as a Proportion of Adult Population, Census Years

Year	Belgium	Denmark	Finland	France	Germany	Norway	Sweden
1882					27.0		
1890	26.7					26.6	
1895					31.6		
1900–1901	30.2	22.4		36.0	34.1	28.4	19.2
1906–7				33.5			
1910–11	29.9	21.8	22.2	34.2		26.9	27.6
1920–21	30.3	24.3	23.6	35.4		30.7	35.3
1925–26				36.1			
1930–31	28.7	22.9	20.8	34.2	34.3	28.9	35.0
1933					33.9		
1936				29.6			
1940		28.9	21.2				34.5
1946–47	22.5					29.7	
1950		29.4	23.9		32.2[b]	32.0	36.4
1954				27.7[a]			
1960–62	20.6	29.3	22.5	26.8	32.9	31.1	33.8
1968			20.3				
1970				24.7			

Note: Workers include manual wage earners in mining, manufacturing, construction, transport, and agriculture, as well as their inactive adult household members.

[a] The French series is not directly comparable from 1936 to 1954. The 1954 figure calculated in the same way as the 1936 one would be 25.1.
[b] Under new borders.

torate, rather than the population, and these proportions differ unless suffrage is truly universal.

The introduction of universal male suffrage preceded the birth of socialist parties in Denmark and Switzerland, the two countries where the legacy of 1848 proved to be lasting. In France universal suffrage experienced a more tumultuous history and was introduced for the third time in 1876, more or less at the same time as the first explicitly socialist parties were formed. Universal male suffrage also coincided with the establishment of the first socialist parties in the newly unified Germany in 1871. In other countries socialist parties had to struggle for the right to vote. The relationship between suffrage and socialist electoral participation is examined in table 2.3.

Table 2.3 Timing of Socialist Entry into Elections and of Suffrage Reforms

Country	(1)	(2)	(3)	(4)	(5)	(6)	(7)
Austria	1889	1897	1907		1919		
Belgium	1885[a]	1894	1894	45.7	1948	38.4	22.2
Denmark	1878[a]	1884	1849	28.1[b]	1915	24.6	23.9
Finland	1899	1907	1906	22.0	1906		22.0
France	1879	1893	1876	36.5[c]	1946	33.9	24.9
Germany	1867	1871	1871	25.5	1919	34.2[d]	34.0[d]
Italy	1892[a]		1913		1945		
Netherlands	1878	1888	1917		1917		
Norway	1887	1903	1898	34.1	1913	27.7	28.8
Spain	1879	1910	1907		1933		
Sweden	1889	1896	1907	28.9	1921	35.0	37.0
Switzerland	1887	1897	1848				
United Kingdom	1893[a]	1892[e]	1918		1928		

Note: Column headings are as follows: (1) Socialist Party formed; (2) first candidates elected to parliament; (3) universal male suffrage; (4) workers as a proportion of the electorate in the first elections after universal male suffrage; (5) universal suffrage; (6) workers as a proportion of the electorate in the last election before extension of franchise to women; and (7) workers as a proportion of the electorate in the first election after the extension.

[a] Major socialist or workers parties existed earlier and dissolved or were repressed.
[b] In 1884, approximate.
[c] In 1902.
[d] Under different borders.
[e] Keir Hardie elected.

The censitaire criteria discriminated against workers: before 1867 in the United Kingdom, before 1882 in Italy, before 1884 in Norway, and before 1887 in the Netherlands, property ownership was tied to the eligibility to vote. Where workers could qualify on the basis of income, tax, or rental value of their lodgings, their proportion in the electorate drifted upward with increases in wages. Nevertheless, most workers were probably excluded from the electorate until suffrage became almost universal for men. Even after extensive male suffrage was introduced, male workers continued to be underrepresented because of the age (typically twenty-five years and older) and residence (typically one year) requirements. In Sweden, for example, workers over fifteen years old constituted 33.2 percent of all males of the same age while workers who satisfied the age requirement introduced in 1907 made up 31.7 percent of those twenty-four years and older.

The timing of women's suffrage differed significantly from country to country. Simultaneous with the male suffrage in Finland, in France female franchise arrived seventy years after men acquired the right to vote. The effects of women's suffrage on the class composition of the electorate depended on its relation to industrialization. In Belgium and France, where the female franchise was introduced only after 1945, the proportion of workers in the electorate dropped sharply. In Denmark and Germany the effect was much less sharp, and in Norway and Sweden the proportion of workers among those eligible to vote increased in spite of the extension of voting rights to women.

Since workers and the adult dependents of workers were typically more numerous among males than were workers and dependents among women, the effect of extending the suffrage to women was always adverse to the workers' share of the electorate. In Sweden, for example, male workers and adult male dependents of workers made up 33.2 percent of adult males in 1910 and 41.7 percent in 1920 (see table 2.4). As women entered the electorate, workers of both sexes and their dependents constituted 35.3 percent of the adult population. Yet this was still an increase over the 1910 share of workers. The pace of industrialization in Sweden on the eve of World War I (Krantz and Nilsson 1975:173) was so rapid that the proportion of workers in the electorate rose even when women began to vote.

The size of the workers' share of the electorate (see table 2.5)

The Dilemma of Electoral Socialism

Table 2.4   The Swedish Working Class Electorate, 1910 and 1920

	1910	1920
Adult males/Adults	47.96	48.38
Male workers/Adults	14.99	19.67
Female workers/Adults	2.63	3.58
Adult male dependents of workers/Adults	0.93	0.48
Adult female dependents of workers/Adults	9.05	11.60
Adult male workers and dependents/Adults	15.92	20.15
Adult female workers and dependents/Adults	11.68	15.18
Adult male workers and dependents/Adult males	33.20	41.65
Adult workers of both sexes and dependents/Adults	27.60	35.33
The Electorate:		
Male workers and dependents, 24 years and older/males 24 years and older (1920 electorate)	31.65	
Workers of both sexes and dependents, 23 and older/Persons 23 years and older (1921 electorate)		34.65

Note: Workers include manual wage earners in mining, manufacturing, construction, transport, and agriculture as well as their inactive household members. Adults are all persons economically active and their dependents 15 years of age and older.

resulted from the combined effect of economic, demographic, and political transformations. The proportion of workers in the electorate did reach 50 percent in one country during a thirty-year period—in Belgium between 1900 and 1930. After 1930 the workers' share of the electorate declined slightly, and the extension of suffrage to women in 1948 reduced it to 20 percent by 1960. In Denmark workers made up about a quarter of the electorate from 1900 to the mid-1930s and about 28 percent since then. French workers held about 37 percent of the electorate until their numbers were reduced by the Great Depression to 34 percent in 1936 and subsequently to about a quarter of the electorate by female suffrage and further economic transformations. The proportion of workers climbed steadily in Germany from 1882 to 1907 and then dropped gradually to reach one-third of the electorate by 1933. This also has been the workers' share of the electorate in the Federal Republic. Norwegian workers were relatively most nu-

Table 2.5 Workers as a Proportion of the Electorate, Census Years

Year	Belgium	Denmark	Finland	France	Germany	Norway	Sweden
1882					29.5		
1895					34.8		
1900–1901	45.7	25.5		36.9		34.1	
1906–7				35.3	35.8		
1910–11	48.0	24.1	22.2	37.0		27.3	28.9
1920–21	50.0	24.7	23.6	36.8		30.0	35.0
1925–26				37.8			
1930–31	47.5	24.1	20.8	37.3	32.9	28.9	36.6
1933					33.1		
1936				33.7			
1940		27.7	21.2			29.4	37.5
1946–47	38.4					30.5	
1950		28.3	23.7	27.7[a]	32.2	31.5	40.1
1960–62	20.6	28.3	22.5	27.0	32.7	31.0	39.2
1968				24.8			
1970			20.3				

Note: Workers are defined in the same way as in table 2.2. The electorate consists of all persons who have the right to vote in the particular election. Our numbers take into account restrictions of voting rights based on sex, age, and dependence on public assistance but not residence and other minor impediments.

[a] 1954.

merous among the eligibles immediately after the introduction of universal male suffrage in 1898 when their share reached 34 percent. Finnish workers deviated very little from a 22 percent share of the electorate during the electoral history of that country. Finally, in Sweden the proportion of workers among the eligibles peaked around 1950 with slightly over 40 percent in the 1952 election.

Thus Marx's prediction, embraced almost universally by socialists around 1890, that the displaced members of the old middle classes would either become proletarians or join the army of the unemployed did not materialize. The old middle classes, particularly the small agricultural proprietors, have become less numerous in industrialized countries, but their sons and daughters were much more likely to find employment in an office or a store than a factory. Moreover, while the proportion of the adult population engaged in any activity outside the household has fallen drastically in the course of capitalist development, those excluded from participation in gainful activities did not become a reserve proletariat. Extended compulsory education, forced retirement, large standing armies, effective barriers to participation by women—all had the effect of reducing entry into the ranks of the proletariat. As a result, from 1890 to 1980 the proletariat has continued to be a minority of the population.

ALLIES

A majority composed of workers could not provide the mandate for socialism because workers never became a majority. Yet, even if socialist theoreticians were persuaded that the eventual proletarianization of the great masses is an inexorable tendency of capitalist development, they saw no reason to wait for history to take its course. Almost as soon as they decided to compete for votes, socialist parties sought electoral support from people other than workers.

Already in 1885, in a letter to an American friend, Engels expressed the view that "one or two million votes . . . in favor of a workers' party acting in good faith are actually infinitely more valuable than one hundred thousand votes obtained by a platform representing a perfect doctrine." That triumphant forecast made by Engels in 1895 (1960) which predicted that socialists would become an electoral force before which "all will have to bow" was conditional, in his view, on the success of the party in "conquering the greater part of the middle strata of society, petty bourgeoisie, and small peasants." His advice to the French party—advice which the French did not need—was the same: recruit small peasants. The Erfurt Programme of 1891 appealed explicitly to these old middle classes: their interests "paralleled" those of the proletariat, they were the "natural allies" of the proletariat. Guesdists in France began to advocate alliances as soon as Guesde was elected to the Parliament in 1893 (Derfler 1973:48). In Belgium, the first programme adopted in 1894 by the Workers' Party appealed to the lower middle classes and the intelligentsia (Landauer 1959, 1:468; Neimark 1976:25). In Sweden the multiclass strategy was debated as early as 1889 and fully embraced by 1920 (Tingsten 1973). The British Labour Party did defeat, in 1912, the proposal to open the membership, on an individual basis, to "managers, foremen, and persons engaged in commercial pursuits on their own account" (McKibbin 1974:85). But in 1918, as it took a programmatic turn to the Left, Labour opened its ranks to "workers by brain." Indeed, in his polemic with Beer (1969), McKibbin interprets the emphasis on socialism in the 1918 programme as an attempt to capture the "professional middle classes" (1974:97).

Revisionists everywhere asserted that workers were not a majority and that the party must seek support beyond the industrial working class. Bernstein, Jaurès, and McDonald came to this conclusion independently: once a party committed itself to electoral participation, they had to embrace this conclusion. By 1915, Michels could already characterize socialist strategy as follows: "For motives predominantly electoral, the party of the workers seeks support from the petty bourgeois elements of society. . . . The Labour Party becomes the party of the 'people'. Its appeals are no longer addressed to the manual workers, but to 'all producers', to the 'entire working population', these phrases being applied to all the classes and all the strata of society except the idlers who live upon the income from investments" (1962:254).

The strategy of searching for allies was directed during the early years to the old middle classes: small agricultural proprietors, craftsmen, artisans, shopkeepers, merchants, intermediaries. One of the central themes of Marx, developed at length by Kautsky, reasserted by Swedes (who actually used German examples), and widely shared long after Bernstein's revision (Haupt 1980:151–99), was that capitalism would destroy this middle class. Hence, these people had nothing to expect of capitalism; their meager property was doomed to be confiscated by the spontaneous development of the capitalist system; they or at least their children were already future proletarians; their interests were already those of the proletariat (Kautsky 1971). César de Paepe, who drafted the founding manifesto of the *Parti Socialiste Brabançon* in 1887, saw "big business and big property destroy small industry, small business and small property; and in this way the most numerous portion of the middle class finds itself in a painfully close position to misery and, if it understands its interests, will be led by them to make common cause with the proletariat" (Landauer 1959, 1:456–57).

Small farmers were the first target designated by most socialist parties. The "agrarian question" was at the center of preoccupations of European socialists at least until the Millerand affair. The difficulty which socialists faced stemmed from the fact that to offer protection to poor farmers meant defending private property of the means of production but to ignore them would have meant to seek electoral oblivion in several countries. Thus, as early as 1888 the Danish Social Democrats adopted a program in which they opposed forcible collectivization of land and proposed measures to provide agricultural workers with means to purchase land (Landauer 1959, 1:447). In 1892 in Marseilles French socialists adopted an agricultural program in favor of small farmers and extended it in 1894 in Nantes (Landauer 1961). Other parties soon followed suit and only Germans, theoretically minded as always, could not reconcile what they did with what they thought until deciding finally in 1927 that the law of concentration of capital does not apply to agriculture (Hunt 1970).

The position of socialists vis-à-vis craftsmen, artisans, and small merchants was not discussed as extensively as the peasant question. No elaborate recruitment strategy seemed required and most parties subsumed these people under references to the oppressed, the poor, or the exploited. The Swedish 1911 program was the first one to indicate that perhaps small-scale crafts can pass directly, that is, without being expropriated, to socialist production by associating together (Tingsten 1973:183).

The "new middle classes" were not originally a clearly specified target for recruitment for the simple reason that they were few in number and the theory of scientific socialism closed the eyes of party leaders to the process that was happening all around them. Around 1900, office and other manual employees constituted 4.8 percent of adults in Denmark, 5.4 in France, 2.9 in Germany (1895), and 3.0 percent in Sweden. And while socialist leaders noticed that some occupations were becoming proletarianized and a variety of new occupations were arising— Kautsky was particularly impressed by the post office—nevertheless the only terms in which they could understand these transformations were those based on the traditional conception of the proletariat. There was nothing to prepare them for the imminent explosion of all kinds of occupations in which people would only move papers and use only pens as instruments. Contrary to somewhat desperate recent attempts to discover a place for such people within Marxist theory (Nicolaus 1967; Urry 1973), it was thought that these occupations were not necessary for production, that they were not a lawful product of capitalist development but only an ephemeral invention of the poor people who tried to eke out a miserable existence by engaging in such flimsy pursuits. In the meantime, the most convenient posture was to treat these people simply as workers. They did fall under the theoretical definition of the proletariat and treating them as such meant that nothing special needed to be done to recruit them to the socialist ranks. Whenever salaried employees were mentioned at all, they appeared as "educated proletarians," "workers by brain."

This posture could no longer be maintained by the mid-1920s. In 1925 salaried employees made up 10.7 percent of German adults and 7.6 percent of the French adult population. By 1930 they were 9.3 percent of adults in Denmark and 7.2 percent in Sweden. The milestone in Germany was Theodor Geiger's 1925 study of the German class structure which confronted socialists with the empirical importance of the "new middle class." The SPD adopted a strategy oriented toward salaried employees in 1927 (Hunt 1970). The socialist quest for the new middle class was advocated in France by Marcel Deat, who, however, was expelled from the SFIO soon afterwards. The most influential prewar advocate of an alliance with the middle classes was Henrik de Man, whose Labor Plan was adopted by the Belgian *Parti Ouvrier* in 1933. In most cases, however, explicit strategies concerning salaried employees were adopted only after World War II. These strategies were couched in terms of wage earners, that is, once again all those who sell their labor services for a wage, whether they work in factories or offices (Tomasson 1970: xxiv; Heidar 1977:301; Paterson 1977:185).

There is a peculiar tendency among contemporary observers to see the strategy of appealing to a heterogeneous class base as a relatively recent effect of the deradicalization of socialist movements. The German *Mittelklassenstrategie* is seen as the prototype of this new orientation and Kurt Schumacher as its architect (Paterson 1977). In this view, socialists began to seek support from groups other than workers only after they had given up their socialist goals. This view is simply inaccurate. The post-1945 orientation of several parties is not a result of a new ideological posture but rather a reflection of the changing class structure of Western Europe. The proportion of the population engaged in agriculture declined during the twentieth century, more rapidly during the 1950s than any of the preceding decades. The new middle classes replaced the old ones (see table 2.6), since during this period the proportion of workers in the population did not change drastically. Party strategies reflected, with some lag, the numerical evolution of the class structure. But the search for electoral allies is inherent in electoralism. It was Bernstein, after all, not Schumacher, who claimed the party was a *Volkspartei*.

The major intervening transformation in class structure was a rapid increase of the adult population which was not engaged in any gainful activity, particularly students and retirees. Along with housewifes, these young and elderly people constitute the third strategic target of socialist parties. The traditional tendency was to perceive such groups through the prism of class membership. Although socialist parties organized women and youth in auxiliary movements, their targets were working-class women and youth, that is, those whose husbands and parents were workers. In Sweden, an autonomous women's organization has been associated with the party since 1920, and in several countries youth organizations developed into autonomous splinter groups. But the appeal to young people, women, and the elderly as categories which are not defined in class terms is a relatively recent phenomenon, forced upon socialist parties by the growth of the new social movements.

Table 2.6   Old and New Middle Classes as a Proportion of Adult Population, Census Years

Year	Denmark Old	Denmark New	France Old	France New	Germany Old	Germany New	Sweden Old[a]	Sweden New
1882					26.6	3.3		
1895					23.7	5.0		
1900–1901	25.4	7.1	18.7	6.6			30.6	6.1
1906–7			20.6	6.2	20.0	8.5		
1910–11	24.4	8.1	19.6	8.1			28.4	8.2
1920–21	22.0	8.6	17.2	9.2			23.8	9.8
1925–26			16.4	9.5	18.0	10.9		
1930–31	19.6	12.9	16.8	10.3			23.3	10.7
1933			16.8	10.0	16.0	15.5		
1936								
1940	16.7	15.7					22.1	14.5
1950	15.9	17.7			13.0	15.3	15.8	20.3
1954			16.4	16.1				
1960–62	14.0	19.5	12.8	18.8	9.1	21.7	11.5	25.3
1968			10.0	21.3				

Note: Old middle classes include adult members of households which constitute family farms and family operated nonagricultural establishments as well as self-employed professionals and their adult dependents. New middle classes here include clerical, technical, and sales personnel in private and public sectors and their dependents.

[a] All farms between 2 and 100 hectares were taken to constitute family farms.

This then is the effect of electoral participation on the relationship between socialist parties and classes. Having entered into electoral competition to win a majority of votes for socialism, these parties began to discover that the working class alone would not be sufficient to provide the necessary mandate. The search for allies became imperative if parties of workers were to be successful in the competition for the vote of the people. But could parties of the people continue to be parties of workers?

PARTY STRATEGY AND CLASS IDEOLOGY

By broadening their appeal, socialist parties dilute the general ideological salience of class and, consequently, weaken the motivational force of class among workers. When political parties do not mobilize individuals as "workers," but as "people," "masses," "poor," or simply "citizens," the people who are men or women, young or old, believers or not, city or country dwellers, in addition to being workers, are less likely to see the society as composed of classes, less likely to identify themselves as class members, less likely to see their interests as those of workers, and eventually less likely to vote as workers. As socialists appeal to voters in supraclass terms, they weaken the salience of class and either reinforce the universalistic ideology of "individuals-citizens" or leave room open for competing particularistic appeals of religion, ethnic or linguistic groups, regions, etc.

One fear that militated against socialist electoral participation before 1890 was that workers would become integrated as individuals into bourgeois society. As Bergounioux and Manin (1979:27) observed, "workers' autonomy outside politics, or political emancipation that would not be specifically workers', such were the two tendencies at the moment when Marx and Engels contributed to the founding of the International Workingmen's Association." Marx's decisive influence was the synthesis of these two positions—socialism as a movement of the working class in politics. The orientation Marx advocated was new— namely to organize a party, but one that would be made up distinctly of workers, that would constitute an organized class. The organization of the proletariat "into a class, and consequently into a political party" (Marx and Engels 1967:144) was necessary for workers to conquer political power and, in Marx's view, it should and would not affect the autonomy of the working class as a political force. "The emancipation of the working class should be," in the celebrated phrase, "the task of the working class itself."

We know why Marx and his fellow socialists expected workers to become the moving force for socialism. By virtue of their position within capitalist society, workers were simultaneously the class that was exploited in the specifically capitalist manner and the only class that had the capacity to organize production once capitalism was abolished. Yet this emphasis on the organic relation between socialism and the working class—the relation conceived of as one between the historical mission and its agent— does not explain by itself why socialists sought to organize all the workers and only workers during the initial period. The reasons for the privileged relation between socialist parties and the working class were more immediate and more practical than those that could be found in Marx's theory of history.

The emphasis on the distinct interests of the working class was necessary to prevent the integration of workers as individuals into bourgeois society. Under capitalism, capitalists naturally appear to be the bearers of future universal interests while the interests of other groups seem inimical to future development and hence particularistic. Capitalists are the investors, the employers, and the innovators. The part of societal product they appropriate is necessary for investment and that means necessary for continued production, employment, and consumption by anyone. Their particularistic interest in profit is a necessary condition for future improvement in the material condition of anyone else. Universalism becomes the natural ideology of the bourgeoisie, since as long as people are thought to have some general, common, or public economic interest, capitalists as a class are the embodiment of this interest. Hence, it is in the interest of capitalists as a class—although obviously not necessarily in the interest of each individual capitalist or firm—that society be pervaded by an ideology that portrays it as composed of individuals endowed with common economic interests. A classless vision of society is in the class interest of capitalists.

Moreover, the bourgeoisie is neither a caste, nor an estate—membership in it is open to anyone. Potentially anyone could become a capitalist. There are no barriers to entry other than the individual limitations of aspirants. Even the censitaire suffrage criteria and the plural voting systems did not mean that workers were excluded as individuals. They could become wealthy and join the ranks of citizens. The bourgeoisie portrayed itself as the future of the entire society—this was the revolution it introduced in the realm of ideology (Gramsci 1971:260).

Bourgeois legal norms distinguish the relations between people and things, which are institutionalized as property, from the relations among people which assume the form of contract. The relation of contract implies freedom to enter or not enter into binding agreements and responsibility to observe the contract once it is concluded. Owners of the means of production and sellers of labor power all appear in this vision of society as individuals-citizens. The relation between workers and capitalists is limited to a contract that is voluntary on both sides and limited in scope to the exchange of labor services for a wage. As a Swedish collective agreement explicitly specified in 1911, "Employers and workmen are not bound by one another longer than the period for which the agreement with regard to each particular piece of work is in force" (Guinchard 1913, 1:638).

At the same time bourgeois ideology postulates a basic harmony of interests among individuals-citizens. The market and representative political institutions allow self-interested individuals to find an optimum general interest. The collection of individuals-citizens constitutes a public and as a public it has an opinion, an interest, and opts for policies.

Bourgeois political institutions were to embody this vision of society. The parliament was to be the forum of rational deliberation in pursuit of the general good. Members of parliament were not to represent the social and economic interests of particular groups but the collective interests of society. Politics was to be an autonomous realm of reason.

This lengthy reminder of well-known origins is necessary to appreciate the ideological revolution introduced by socialists. Socialists juxtaposed to the abstract rationalism of pure politics an image reflecting the conflict of interests of a society divided into classes. In place of the ideal of rational individuals seeking the common good, socialists put forth the reality of men who are carriers of their class interests. The conception of society based on a harmony of interests was sharply denied by the ideology of class conflict.

Socialists claimed that the bourgeoisie not only has particularistic interests but also that these interests are in conflict with interests of workers. Workers are not individuals in bourgeois society. They are a distinct class in a society divided into classes. If their interests appear as particularistic within capitalist society, it is because this society is built on the conflict of the particularistic interests of classes. Only by separating themselves from other classes could workers pursue their interests and thereby fulfill their historical mission of emancipating the entire society, of abolishing classes. In his *Address to the Communist League* in 1850 (Marx and Engels 1969, 1:117), Marx maintained that workers "must themselves do the utmost for their final victory by clarifying in their minds as to what their class interests are, by taking their position as an independent party as soon as possible and by not allowing themselves to be seduced for a single moment by the hypocritical phrases of the democratic party bourgeoisie into refraining from the independent organization of the party of the proletariat.'' Rosenberg (1965:161) reports the tendency of German socialism in the 1860s to ''isolate itself and to emphasize these qualities that differentiated it from all the groups and tendencies of the wealthy classes. At this stage the radical proletarian movement tended particularly to see the nobility and the peasants, the manufacturers and the intellectuals as 'a uniform reactionary mass'.'' The same was true of the first labor candidates in the Paris election of 1863 (Rosenberg 1965:165). The notion of ''one single reactionary mass'' underlay the Gotha Program of 1875 and reappeared in the Swedish Program of 1889 (Tingsten 1973:357). Still in 1891, when Engels was asked to comment on an early draft of the Erfurt Programme, he objected to a reference to ''the people in general'' by asking ''who is that?'' (Engels n.d.:56). And with his typical eloquence Jules Guesde argued in Lille in 1900: ''The Revolution which is incumbent upon you is possible only to the extent that you remain yourselves, class against class, not knowing and not wanting to know the divisions that may exist in the capitalist world'' (Fiechtier 1965:258).

Indeed, to the extent that workers were not only economically but also culturally and politically isolated from the rest of society, socialists may have had no choice but to become a workers' party. Their initial difficulty in several countries was that workers were distrustful of any influences originating from the outside. Socialism seemed an abstract and an alien ideology in relation to daily experience. It was not apparent to workers that an improvement of their condition required that the entire system of wage labor must be abolished. Even workers who were organized and militant economically were not necessarily predisposed to accept socialist doctrines, at least not in the small French town of Mazamet (Cazals 1978). Bergounioux and Manin report that according to a study of French workers at the beginning of the Third Republic there was a resistance among workers to the socialist message, an emphasis on the direct conflict between workers and employers, and a neglect of politics (1979:25). In Belgium a party bearing a socialist label, *Parti Socialiste Belge,* was founded in

1879 but had difficulty persuading workers' associations to affili-
ate. According to Landauer (1959, 1:457–58), workers were mis-
trustful of socialist propaganda and de Paepe admitted that "the
word 'socialist' frightens many workers." Thus in 1885 the *Parti
Ouvrier Belge* was born, a workers' party in place of a socialist
one. If socialists were to be successful, theirs had to be a workers
party. In Sweden and in Norway, the first local cells of the party
were in fact called "workers' communes" (Fusilier 1954:29;
Martin 1972:34).

The quest for electoral allies forced socialist parties to de-
emphasize that unique appeal, that particular vision of society,
which made them the political expression of workers as a class, an
instrument of historical necessity. The concept of the proletariat
suddenly became unclear. Engels felt in 1889 that it required an
explicit definition. Kautsky in 1891 repeated this definition and
applied it in examining which groups would be vulnerable as
workers to socialist appeals. He included all kinds of people, obviously the industrial workers but also "employees of large
stores," who were becoming "genuine proletarians without pros-
pect of ever becoming independent," and a third category, "the
educated proletarians" (1971:36). Bernstein thought that such a
broad concept is useless for the purposes of political practice. "If
one counts in it," Bernstein argued about the proletariat, "all
persons without property, all those who have no income from
property or from a privileged position, then they certainly form
the absolute majority of the population of advanced countries. But
this 'proletariat' would be a mixture of extraordinarily different
elements . . . the modern wage earners are not a homogeneous
mass . . ." (1961:103). Bernstein's conclusion was that the party
should recognize this heterogeneity and it should turn to the people rather than to the proletariat.

And this is where socialist parties turn whenever and wherever
they seek broad-based electoral support. In 1911 the Swedish social democrats replaced the traditional reference to the working
class by an appeal to "the oppressed classes" (Tingsten 1973:184–
85). The socialist electorate became "all the oppressed," "the
exploited," "the poor," "the masses," "the people," "the nation." The linguistic slippage was almost unnoticed. From workers in the narrow sense of the industrial proletariat one step led to
what, in English, is "the working people," *das arbeitende Volk,* in

the language of the SPD Gorlitz Programme of 1921. In other languages it was even easier: from *ouvrier* to *travailleur, rabotnik* to *trudovnik*. "I thus appeal with confidence to all the working people (*tous les travailleurs*) . . . workers of the mine and the glass factory, of construction and of the railroad, agricultural daily laborers, share-croppers, peasant proprietors, small merchants, artisans"—this is how Jaurès saw his electorate in 1906 (Touchard 1977:58). Moreover, a yet broader set of terms was readily available—the masses, the people, the nation. "The people" in singular, "the people" of 1789, is a term that has traditional connotations of class. The flavor of these transformations is best caught in the speech by Palmiro Togliatti in Salerno in 1944: "The secret of our success rests in the fact that we have been faithful to the thought of Gramsci, who wanted the party of the working class and the laboring classes to be a profoundly national party, which would not separate the cause of workers, of peasants, of the working people from the cause of all classes which contribute to the life and the prosperity of the nation, which would know how to combine closely the struggle for the emancipation of the working people with the struggle for the renovation of the entire national life" (translated from a street poster dedicated to Gramsci).

The de-emphasis of class relations has a fundamental effect on the form of political conflicts since it strengthens the classless visions of politics. When socialist or communist parties become parties of the entire nation they reinforce the ideology in which politics is a process of defining the collective welfare of all individuals-citizens. "It is my personal and definite feeling," affirmed P. A. Hansson in a 1931 parliamentary debate, "that in the main it is never possible to create a happier state of affairs if at least the majority of the people are not joined in common labour for the general good" (Tingsten 1973:288; see also Hentilä 1978). Once again, society is portrayed as composed of individuals, and their interests are seen as potentially harmonious. Issues are presented as more important than identities, and political preferences are said to be a matter of choice, not destiny or even loyalty.

This general ideological transformation in turn affects workers. Workers see the society as composed of individuals, confessional groups, regions, or races. Class ceases to be the only conceivable source of self-identification: one can no longer recall, as Vivian Gornick did recently, that "before I knew I was a wom-

an and I was Jewish, I knew I belonged to the working class''
(1977:1). Political commitments are made on the basis of all kinds
of loyalties. Workers become Catholics, Southerners, Fran-
cophones. Political acts reflect immediate preoccupations and respond to ephemeral appeals. As socialists become parties like
other parties, workers turn into voters like other voters.

PARTY STRATEGY AND CLASS ORGANIZATION

The relation between political parties and workers is not only an
ideological one. The strategies oriented toward broad electoral
support have an effect on the relations among workers, on the
organization of workers as a class.

In search of electoral support, socialists must present themselves to different groups as an instrument for the realization of
their immediate economic interests, immediate in the sense that
these interests can be realized when the party is victorious in
forthcoming elections. As Enrico Berlinguer made explicit,
''Naturally, the point of departure for an alliance strategy lies in
the search for convergence between immediate economic interests
and prospects of the working class and those of other groups and
forces'' (1973:25). The party must offer credits to the petty bourgeoisie, pensions to salaried employees, minimal wages to workers, protection to consumers, education to the young. Since the
convergence of interests can rarely be perfect, some interests of
workers are likely to be compromised. When a party seeks the
support of owners of small businesses, it cannot simultaneously
propose to increase minimal wages or payroll taxes. When a party
seeks the vote of peasants it cannot advocate the nationalization of
land and not even low food prices. When it appeals to the higher
echelons of salaried employees, the party encounters narrow limits on the extent to which it can reduce salary differentials. Quite
often, when a party offers to promote or protect specific economic
interests of other groups it must sacrifice some interests of
workers.

But many issues do not require such compromise. There are
many interests which workers share with other groups. Honest
government is one; a decent transportation system another. Protection of forests, tolerable quality of television programs, a com-

petitive national team in the World Soccer Cup, and an efficient bureaucracy are as beneficial and as much desired by workers as by everyone else. Can socialists broaden their class appeal by turning to such issues, without sacrificing the interests of workers and thus without compromising their relations with workers?

A general increase of wages by ten percent is in the interest of all workers as is the availability of clean water and neither affects the relation among workers. However, a law establishing minimum wages, extending compulsory education, advancing the age of retirement, or limiting working hours does affect the relations among workers without being necessarily in the interest of each of them as an individual. Summary sketches of Swedish history often note that the second and the third Social Democratic governments fell over the issue of the magnitude of unemployment relief. In fact, on both occasions, the issue at stake concerned precisely the organization of workers as a class. "The controversy," according to Tingsten (1973:252, 261), "was concerned with the extent to which refusal to take the job offered in place of a worker engaged in a labour conflict should mean loss of compensation for the worker involved." What was involved was taking a job "in place of a worker," and Tingsten is correct to comment that "by resigning on this issue the government showed its desire to represent the interests of the working class."

Class interest is something attached to workers as a collectivity rather than a collection of individuals: it is their group rather than serial interest, to use the terminology of Jean-Paul Sartre (1960). The interests which workers have in common place them in competition with one another, primarily as they bid down wages in search of employment. Individual workers and particularly workers of a specific firm or sector have powerful incentives to pursue their particularistic claims at the cost of other workers. Some workers would prefer to work beyond their normal retirement age even if this were to exclude other workers from employment; some people who do not find employment would be willing to be hired for less than the minimum wage even if this were to result in a general fall of wages; some would be willing to be hired in place of striking workers even if this were to result in the defeat of the strike. Defecting from cooperation is frequently advantageous from an individual point of view even if it results in pernicious collective consequences (Shelling 1978). Some unions may prefer to cooperate with their employers to defend the monopolistic advantage of their firm or sector (de Menil 1971; McDonald and Solow 1981); some unions may collaborate with their employers even at the cost of their economic security as workers (Wallerstein 1983).

Solidarity among workers is not a mechanical consequence of their similarity. The competition among workers can be overcome only if some organization—a union confederation, a party, or the state directly—has the means of enforcing collective discipline. But when socialist parties look for convergence of interests across the lines of class they cannot find it in measures that strengthen the cohesion and combativeness of workers as a class against other classes. They cannot struggle for those interests that are attached to workers as a collectivity—those that constitute public goods to workers as a class—but only those which workers as individuals share with other individuals. This convergence can be found in honest government, in consumer protection, in liberalized divorce laws. These are interests which workers as individuals share with other citizens, consumers, or spouses.

Thus parties which appeal to the masses continue to represent interests of workers. Although the convergence is rarely perfect and some interests of workers as individuals are often sacrificed, such parties continue to promote those interests of workers which they share with other people. People's parties continue to be parties of workers as individuals. What they are not are organization of workers as a class—organizations which discipline individuals or groups of workers in their competition with one another by promoting confrontation with other classes. It is the principle of class conflict—of "stopping competition among the workers so that they can carry on general competition with the capitalist" (Marx n.d.:123)—that is compromised when class parties become parties of the people. The process of electoral mobilization of the masses is at the same time the process of disorganization of workers as a class.

As individuals, workers indeed share interests with other citizens, other consumers, taxpayers, parents, or renters. As individuals they are concerned about their interests, and when socialist parties offer policies to individuals, workers compare them with policies offered by other parties.

The Dilemma of Electoral Socialism

This is the manner in which the organization of society as a capitalist democracy molds the movements that seek to organize workers. The combination of a class structure in which workers are a minority with political institutions that call for a popular mandate imposes a particular logic on the choices available to socialist parties at any moment of history.

Some aspects of that history constitute, today, an irreversible past; other aspects constitute the recurrent reality of our own times. Whether or not it was inescapable, the decision to participate was made once and for all and its consequences have had by now almost one hundred years to impress themselves on the political parties of workers. The decision to compete in elections did not imply that socialists lost sight of their ultimate goals, and it did not foreclose the possibility of a socialist transformation of society. Perhaps there were few moments in history when workers alone could have brought about a revolutionary transformation through an insurrection of a minority. But once this strategy was rejected—either because one had to wait too long for power to be lying on the streets or because one believed that minority insurrections cannot result in socialism—once this strategy was rejected, the nature of all subsequent choices was irreversibly altered. For the decision to participate did preclude the possibility of bringing about socialism through the will of workers alone. To legislate a society into socialism, an electoral mandate of an overwhelming majority is necessary. Hence, an electoral party of workers could not be a revolutionary party. Once a party entered into electoral competition, class purity was no longer associated with a revolutionary posture and the strategy of broad recruitment with an abandonment of revolutionary goals. Socialist parties had to seek allies who would join workers under their banner if they were to be effective in elections at all, whether for ultimate or proximate goals.

The dilemma appears at this moment. When socialists seek to be effective in electoral competition they erode exactly that ideology which is the source of their strength among workers. To be effective they must organize the masses, and yet as they assume a supraclass posture they dilute their capacity to organize workers as a class. They cannot remain a party of workers alone, and yet they cannot broaden their appeal without undermining their own support among workers. They seem unable to win either way, and they behave the way rational people do when confronted with a dilemma: they bemoan and regret, change their strategies, and once again bemoan and regret.

3

The Stagnation of the Socialist Vote

The debate in the Ruhr has already provoked soul-searching within the Social Democrats' national councils. The party's so-called "ditch digger" wing, tied to the unions, blames leftist intellectuals in Bonn for having sought a nonexistent "new majority" of counter-culture youths, the pacifist movement and the workers.

James M. Markham
International Herald Tribune,
26–27 March 1983

THE ELECTORAL TRADE-OFF

Once they decided to compete for the votes of the middle classes, socialists were appealing to an overwhelming majority of the population. Branting's estimate that in 1889 "the people" constituted 95 percent of Swedish society was probably only slightly exaggerated. In the aftermath of World War I, *Labour and the New Social Order,* a programmatic document of the party, claimed the support of four-fifths of the whole nation (Henderson 1918:125). Today the working class and its allies are said to constitute 80 percent of the population of France (PCF 1971) or of the United States (Wright 1976). If, to industrial workers, one adds white-collar employees, service personnel, petit bourgeois, women, students, and the retired, almost no one is left to oppose socialism. Exploiters are but a handful: "the business man with a tax-free expense account, the speculator with tax-free capital gains and the retiring company director with a tax-free redundancy payment," in the words of the 1959 Labour Party electoral manifesto (Craig 1969:130; see also Birnbaum 1979 on the history of the concept of *les gros*). Even more sober counts will show that workers and allies together exceed at least two-thirds of the electorate in Europe.

And yet no party ever obtained the votes of that two-thirds of the electorate in any nation. Even where they are most successful, Socialists struggle to reach 50 percent of the votes cast. They have never won the support of one-half of those entitled to vote. Moreover, they cannot even win all the votes of workers. In several countries, one-fifth of the workers votes for bourgeois parties, in others one-third, and in some one-half of manual workers cast their votes against socialist candidates. Thus not only are socialists unable to win the support of all members of the middle classes, but they lose support among workers. They appear condemned to minority status when they are a class party of workers, and they seem relegated to the minority when they seek to be the party of the people. Is this not the quintessence of a dilemma?

Immediate interpretations are tempting. Socialism never was expressed as the will of an electoral majority because no majority ever wanted socialism—this is one way to dismiss the problem. Those more sympathetic to socialist goals are more likely to lament that workers are ideologically dominated under capitalism, that elections are unfair, or that socialist leaders are traitors. But the perplexing fact remains that if popular will is to be read from elections then it appears that nothing was ever willed by a majority. Working class parties perhaps had better reasons to expect majority support, but socialists are not alone in finding a clear mandate impossible to obtain in elections. We need to muster some capacity to be surprised by routine experiences, but is it not startling that no political party has ever obtained the support of 50 percent of those eligible to vote? That no party has ever won 60 percent of the votes actually cast in a free parliamentary election? Of the 337 elections that took place in nineteen countries with extensive suffrage before 1968, only twenty-three resulted in a majority of votes cast for a party, six of them in New Zealand. In each hundred elections, the plurality share was under 40 percent in forty-eight cases; in forty-five cases it was enough to win between 40 and 50 percent to become the largest party; only in seven cases out of each one hundred was a majority of votes cast for a party. In Western Europe, winning 51 percent of votes cast—the support of about 45 percent of the electorate—is a rare feat, one of which only Austrian and Swedish socialists seem capable.

Socialist parties did not win the electoral support of an overwhelming majority of the people, not even of those whom they viewed as potential supporters, because their efforts to extend the electoral appeal diminished the salience of class as a determinant of the political behavior of workers. When parties direct their efforts to mobilize the support of "the masses," they find it more difficult to recruit and maintain the support of workers.

Strategies of socialist and other left wing parties mold the manner and the degree to which class is a constituent element in the ideology with which workers understand the world and act upon it. As socialist, communist, and other parties diminish their emphasis on class, in their organizational practice as well as in their discourse, they make room for other ideologies. The fact that people follow the advice of their parish priest or that they opt for that party which is less likely to introduce new taxes is a consequence. Even the surge of nationalist feelings among workers on 1 August 1914 need not be viewed as an expression of some primordial sentiments. The possibility of finding in the nation a source of identification and object of loyalty was opened by the transformation of socialist discourse during the fifteen years preceding the war and by the failure of socialists to maintain the momentum of mobilization after 1912 (Haupt 1980: chap. 6).

Our claim is not that class is in some way privileged as a cause of the behavior of workers, not even that all ideological conflicts must involve class. At any particular moment multiple political forces compete to impose a specific causal structure on the political behavior of individuals. Class ideology is one of the potential competitors, along with the universalistic ideology of individuals-citizens, and various particularistic claims made on behalf of confessional persuasions, ethnic ties, linguistic affinities, regional, racist, or nationalistic values. Some of the most profound confrontations in European history did not involve class at all but rather juxtaposed confessional loyalties to universalistic conceptions of citizenship. The lines of conflict and the modes of individual behavior that emerge if and when class is not the force guiding the behavior of workers are beyond the scope of this analysis. Our analysis is a partial one: it concerns the causal importance of class as distinguished from everything else. What we insist on is only that the ascendency of motivations other than class is a consequence of strategies of political parties: when parties do not seek to organize workers as a class, class ideology is altogether absent from political life and other principles of organization and identification come to the fore.

If this hypothesis is valid, there should exist an electoral trade-off between the support a party obtains from the middle classes and its effectiveness in recruiting and maintaining the support of workers. Electoral trade-offs can perhaps be found between almost any two groups: if a party appeals to one constituency, it may suffer in its relation to some other constituency. Hence, a party may perhaps lose potential votes of miners when it emphasizes its roots among transport workers; it may lose opportunities among secretaries when it turns to managers; it may forsake votes among public employees when it directs appeals to shopkeepers. Yet the central trade-off facing socialist, social democratic, labor, and communist parties has concerned their opportunities among workers—workers in the narrow sense of the proletariat. Strategic deliberations of left-wing electoral parties focus on the choice between the support of any of a number of groups, including lower-level salaried employees, and their electoral success among manual workers. Thus, if this hypothesis is valid, one should be able to observe that whenever left-wing parties are successful in mobilizing large electoral support from anyone else they suffer a loss of opportunities among narrowly defined workers. If such a trade-off cannot be observed—for example, if workers are bandwagon voters, who support any party that wins many votes regardless of who casts them or if the trade-off is sharper when workers are defined broadly to include some layers of salaried employees— then this hypothesis is false.

A party may lose opportunities among workers in a number of ways. Young workers entering the electorate for the first time may be more likely to identify with other young people and less likely to respond to socialist appeals. Workers who become enfranchised by suffrage reforms may be less likely to enter the electorate as socialist voters. People who had voted before and who subsequently become workers, mainly peasants, may be less prone to become socialists. Finally, even workers who had voted socialist may be less likely to continue. Numerically most important under normal circumstances is probably the opportunity loss among young workers entering the electorate. Once workers vote socialist they are not very likely to change, even if party strategies do change. At least the overwhelming weight of evidence is that people who have voted for a party once are quite likely to keep supporting this party, and each decision already made reinforces the same choice in the future (Converse 1958; Przeworski 1975).

The workers who would have otherwise voted for a Socialist Party have three avenues open to them: they can vote for bourgeois parties, they can abstain from voting altogether, and in some countries, they can vote for other parties that appeal to them as workers. Where and when more than one party appeals to workers on the basis of class, workers can find escape in voting for one of the others when one abandons its class orientation. Communist competition is particularly important for social democrats since communist parties tended historically to pay special attention to the working class electorate. Hence in those countries where communist parties have been at all viable, notably in Weimar Germany, Italy, France, and Finland, workers have had an option of continuing to vote as workers by moving their support from socialists to communists. The Scandinavian left-socialist parties represent, however, a different competition. Workers, and particularly young workers, are likely to vote for such parties when social democrats de-emphasize class (Esping-Anderson 1985: table 3.11), but they do so as "youth" rather than as workers (Tarschys, 1977).

The trade-off facing each left-wing party has, therefore, a different origin than the trade-off facing the Left as a whole. When a socialist party meets communist competition, the opportunity cost of following supraclass strategies is high because workers can change their voting behavior without changing ideologies. But the Left as a whole faces a trade-off that results from general ideological transformations: the loss of support among workers reflects a society-wide weakening of class ideology.

Even if left-wing parties do face an electoral trade-off which divides narrowly defined workers from everyone else, this trade-off need not be evident at all times. Socialist vote can grow simultaneously among the middle classes and manual workers, as it did in several countries during some periods. Electorally motivated strategies to gain the support of private and public employees have been successful in West Germany where, according to surveys, the SPD vote among *Beamte and Angestellte* grew from 27 percent in 1953 to 50 percent in 1972, while the proportion of workers voting social democratic increased from 58 to 66 percent between 1969 and 1972 (Pappi 1973, 1977). In Sweden, the proportion of nonworkers voting for the SAP climbed from 23 percent in 1956 to 34 percent in 1968, while the proportion of workers voting social democratic hovered around 80 percent (Särlvik 1977; Esping-Anderson 1979).

The reason why the existence of a trade-off may not be evident, even suspected, during long periods is that the pool of workers still available for socialist recruitment may be large in comparison with the negative effects of the supraclass strategies on them. Even if any particular worker may be less likely to become a socialist, the party may be gaining votes of additional workers when there are many of them to be recruited. Thus, the socialist vote of workers may continue to grow visibly even if the supraclass strategy is in fact reducing opportunities: more workers would have voted for the party had it not diluted the appeal to class, but the number of workers who do become socialist voters may still be sufficiently large that no trade-off is observed by naïve inspection of aggregate numbers.

The mechanisms at work and their effects can be clarified with the use of a few symbols. The electorate for the tth election, where $t = 0,1, \ldots$ changes over elections, consists of all persons who have the legal right to vote at this time. A part of this electorate consists of workers, in the narrow sense of manual wage earners employed in mining, manufacturing, construction, transport, agriculture, and their adult dependents. Let $X(t)$ be the proportion of the electorate that consists of workers at the time of the tth election. Some workers vote for the major socialist party—a party that may bear a socialist, social democratic, or labor label—or other left-wing parties—the communist party or some minor socialist movements. Let $W(t)$ represent the proportion of the entire electorate which consists of workers who voted either for the major socialist party ("socialist") or for any left-wing party ("Left") during the tth election. In some cases our analysis concerns the largest socialist party separately and in those cases we will refer to $W(t)$ as the "socialist" vote: whenever we analyze the vote for all the left-wing parties taken together, we will refer to $W(t)$ as the "Left" vote. Thus $\Delta W(t)$ will denote the change between any two consecutive elections, from the tth to the $(t + 1)$st one, of the proportion of the electorate that consists of so-

cialist (or Left) voting workers. Our central hypothesis concerns
the effect of the cumulative success of a party among nonworkers
upon the change of its support among workers, that is, upon
$\Delta W(t)$.[1]

Given the above definitions, the pool of workers from which
additional socialist voters can be recruited for the $(t + 1)$st election consists of those workers who did not vote socialist during
the tth election or $[X(t + 1) - W(t)]$. Suppose that a particular
party (or the Left as a whole) recruits available workers with an
average effectiveness of p when it tries to recruit only workers. p
Under this assumption the proportion of the electorate consisting
of socialist (Left) voting workers would grow by the amount
$p[X(t + 1) - W(t)]$ between any two consecutive elections. But if
turning for support to nonworkers in fact diminishes the effectiveness of left-wing parties in recruiting workers, then the growth of
the socialist vote will be checked whenever the party adopts supraclass strategies.

As we have seen, left-wing parties have historically chosen
specific gtoups of nonworkers as targets for electoral mobilization; and they have adopted symbolic, programmatic, and organizational measures to win votes from these groups. We will refer
throughout to members of such groups as "allies" and denote
their proportion in the electorate by $L(t)$. While some members of $L(t)$
other classes at times vote for left-wing parties independently of
party strategies and while other parties compete for votes of the
allies, supraclass strategies eventually do result in some success.
We can thus view the proportion of the electorate that consists of
socialist (or Left) voting allies, a proportion which will be de-
noted as $N(t)$, as a cumulative result of supraclass strategies pur- $N(t)$
sued by a particular party or parties.[2]

Suppose then that as the cumulative effect of its efforts a party
has won some support among specific groups of nonworkers and

1. There are other people in the electorate besides workers, and there are other
ways to behave than to vote socialist (or Left). The reader who finds it difficult at
any stage to follow our partitioning of the electorate into social groups and into
political orientations may wish to consult the Appendix to this chapter, which
provides a formal recapitulation of the definitions and of the entire argument.

2. Thus the electorate is partitioned into three groups: workers, $X(t)$; allies,
$L(t)$; and others. In turn, socialist (Left) vote originates from workers, $W(t)$; allies,
$N(t)$; and from others.

electorate $X(t)$ $L(t)$

voters $W(t)$ $N(t)$

that in the course of this endeavor it weakened the salience of class as a motive for the political behavior of workers. As a simplification, let the loss of opportunities among workers be proportional to the strength of a party among the allies. Then the change in the socialist vote of workers between any two consecutive elections will be given by:

$$\Delta W(t) = p[X(t + 1) - W(t)] - dN(t), \qquad (3.1)$$

where the quantity $dN(t)$ indicates the opportunity loss in recruiting workers: it specifies how many votes, measured as a proportion of the electorate, the party would have won from workers had it not pursued strategies which resulted in recruiting $N(t)$ allies by the tth election.

Equation (3.1) shows that even if d is in fact positive, that is, if the support by allies does diminish the capacity of a party to win votes among workers, the socialist vote can still grow simultaneously among workers and other groups. Indeed, the proportion of the electorate consisting of socialist voting workers grows as long as the term $p[X(t + 1) - W(t)]$ is larger than the opportunity loss, $dN(t)$. This is clearly the case when socialist parties entered into electoral competition: workers constituted at that time a sizable proportion of the electorate in many countries and few of them voted socialist, since many did not vote at all. In Sweden in the 1911 election only about one half of the eligible male workers did vote (Särlvik 1977:391). In every country turnout fell after extensions of the suffrage, including those to male and female workers. As Rokkan and Valen observed, "new eligibles were mobilized after, rather than before extensions of suffrage" (1962:158).

The trade-off becomes apparent only when a party has achieved some success among workers and/or allies. When many workers vote socialist, the term $p[X(t + 1) - W(t)]$ is small; when many allies support socialists, the term $dN(t)$ is large. Under such conditions, continuing appeals to the middle classes may result in a net fall of aggregate socialist support among workers, thus provoking the kinds of discussions that accompanied the defeat of the Swedish SAP in 1976 (see Stephens 1981 for a summary) or preceded the debacle of the German SPD in 1983.

In fact a particular party may never reach the situation in which its support among workers would actually decline. Hence the trade-off may never be immediately evident. But as long as d is positive, the party pays an opportunity cost for winning the middle-class vote throughout its electoral history. If no allies voted socialist in the tth election, the party would have gained $dN(t)$ more votes of workers next time around.

The quantity $dN(t)$ measures the loss of opportunities among workers which a party suffers during the $(t + 1)$st election as a consequence of having had pursued strategies that attracted $N(t)$ votes of allies by the time of the tth election. Thus $dN(t)$ depends on the strategies a party pursued in the past, and it measures the actual cost which the party is suffering currently for its cumulative success among allies. In turn, the parameter d is a measure of conditions which are given to each party and under which parties make strategic choices. The value of this parameter indicates how sensitive workers are to the dilution of class ideology required to recruit allies; more precisely, the parameter d measures the number of potential votes lost among workers whenever a particular party succeeded in gaining the vote of one ally in the previous election. As long as the value of this parameter is positive, the party faces a situation in which it must lose opportunities among workers whenever it gains votes of allies. If workers were bandwagon voters, then the value of the parameter d would have been negative. The more allies, or nonworkers in general, would vote socialist, the more workers would follow them. Our theory would be false and the reasons for the stagnation of socialist vote would have to be sought elsewhere. Hence, the parameter d plays a crucial role in this analysis.

The value of the parameter d can be calculated in the following way. In a number of countries, we have enough information to measure the proportion of workers and allies in the electorate at the time of each election: this is true of Denmark, France, Germany, and Sweden. In some other countries we can count workers, but we are unable to distinguish among nonworkers to measure the size of the groups that particular parties considered as allies, namely, in Belgium, Finland, and Norway. In all seven countries there have been a sufficient number of elections to permit statistical analyses, and information about the distribution of the electorate into voters and nonvoters and of the voters among parties is easily available. Unfortunately, in other countries either the proportion of workers in the electorate could not be measured or there were not enough elections. Thus, although we believe that the argument presented here is general, our empirical analysis is limited to the seven countries listed above (see Appendix: The Data, for further details).

Once we know how many workers and allies (or simply nonworkers) there were in the electorate at the time of each election and how many people voted for each party, we can use this information to find the values of parameters such as d or p which best reconstruct the historical record of votes obtained by particular parties or the Left as a whole in each country. The combination of parameter values which best reconstructs the historical path of the vote for each party provides the best summary description of the conditions which this party encountered throughout its history (see Appendix: Calculations, for further details).[3]

Following this procedure yields values of d which everywhere confirm our central hypothesis. Although at times quite low, the values of the parameter d which best reconstruct the electoral history are positive in all the cases which we could analyze. Both the major socialist parties and the Left as a whole suffered a loss of support among narrowly defined workers (see table 3.1) whenever they pursued strategies of recruiting allies.[4]

Whenever a party succeeds in winning the vote of one nonworker in the current election, it suffers the loss of d votes of workers it would have recruited during the next election. Other than for the German SPD and the French Socialists, the values presented in table 3.1 may seem extremely low, almost negligi-

3. Unfortunately, recent censuses do not lend themselves to the kind of reconstruction of class structure that was required for this analysis and that was possible for earlier periods. Thus all the parameter values which are presented below were calculated on the basis of a time series which ended for Belgium and Denmark in 1971, Finland in 1972, France in 1968, Germany in 1933, Norway in 1969, and Sweden in 1964. The extrapolations based on these values predict quite well, however, the distribution of votes until the most recent elections, even in Germany, where we took the pre-1933 SPD values to extrapolate the post-1949 distribution of the vote in the Federal Republic.

4. The numbers were obtained in a slightly different way in Denmark, France, Germany, and Sweden, where we could measure the proportions of allies in the electorate, than in Belgium, Finland, and Norway, where we were forced to consider all nonworkers as allies. It turned out, however, that the results in the first four countries did not change much when we utilized the same procedure as in the latter three countries.

Table 3.1 The Immediate Trade-off between Support by Allies and Opportunity Loss among Workers, as Measured by the Parameter d

| | Value of Trade-off d for | |
Country	Total Left	Major Socialist Party
Belgium	0.137	[a]
Denmark	0.002	0.017
Finland	0.095	0.058
France	0.090	1.182
Germany	0.130	3.571[b]
Norway	0.009	0.001
Sweden	0.073	0.060

[a] The results for Belgian socialists are unusable. See Appendix: The Calculations for explanation.
[b] Before 1933.

ble. But the parameter d indicates only the immediate effect of the fact that one nonworker had been recruited by the party, and the effects last beyond the next election. Another way to think about the price the party must pay at any time for addressing its appeals to the middle classes is to examine the consequences that an infinitesimal increase in the socialist vote of allies has for all the subsequent support the party would obtain from workers. Suppose that one additional office employee is recruited as a socialist voter in the current election. What will be the effect of this marginal increase in the socialist vote of allies on the subsequent socialist vote of workers?

The fact that the party has succeeded in winning the vote of one ally at the present will have effects for several elections in the future. To recruit allies a party generates ideological and organizational transformations which continue to weaken the salience of class identification among workers. In the next election the party will have forsaken exactly d votes of workers per each nonworker recruited currently. As time goes on, the opportunity cost borne by the party tends to increase. Only after several elections does the effect on workers wear out. Thus, although the erosion of class ideology may be reversible in the long run, its effects persist over long periods.

As an illustration of this dynamic we present the trade-offs

Table 3.2   Opportunity Costs—Trade-offs Facing Major Socialist Parties:
Number of Workers' Votes Foresaken If the Party Recruited 100
Additional Middle-Class Voters h Elections Earlier

h	Denmark	Finland	France	Germany[b]	Norway	Sweden
1	1.70	5.80	118.20	357.10	0.10	6.00
2	2.45	8.99	142.39	60.00	0.17	9.76
3	2.69	10.63	123.69	219.28	0.22	11.90
4	2.65	11.33	91.40	71.98	0.27	13.04
5	2.48	11.48	60.09	140.55	0.29	13.41
6	2.26	11.31	35.41	65.78	0.31	13.28
7	2.01	10.97	18.39	93.39	0.32	12.87
8	1.77	10.53	7.82	54.23	0.32	12.18
9	1.55	10.05	1.99	63.83	0.32	11.42
10	1.36	9.55	−0.76	42.49	0.32	10.62
15	0.66	7.24	−0.64	22.54	0.27	6.81
20	0.32	5.43	−0.00	9.75	0.03	4.13
25	0.15	4.07	0.00	4.50	0.00	2.45
SUM[a]	33.14	504.63	595[c]	1031.13	9.37	319.98

[a] From zero to infinity.
[b] Before 1933.
[c] Approximate.

which confronted the major socialist parties in six countries at
every moment of history.[5] If at any time t a party decided to seek
electoral support outside the working class, it would have suffered
the consequences portrayed in table 3.2, which shows how many
workers each party would keep losing at all subsequent times ($t +
h$) as a consequence of having attracted one hundred additional
nonworkers h elections earlier. For example, when the Swedish
Social Democrats launched a campaign to recruit "all wage earners" in 1956, then for each 100 office employees they succeeded
in recruiting that year they forsook the votes of 6.00 workers in
1958, 9.76 workers in 1960, 11.90 workers in 1964, etc. The
most pronounced effect is delayed in Sweden: it occurs five elections later. And the effects linger—because of what the party had
to do to recruit each one hundred allies in 1956, 10.62 fewer
workers will vote for the SAP in the next Swedish election.

5. See the Appendix to this chapter for the explanation of how these numbers
were obtained.

The numbers presented in table 3.2 show pronounced differences among the socialist parties. In order to make international comparisons it is convenient to characterize the situation of each party in some summary fashion. Let us focus precisely on that moment when the trade-off would just become visible, because any increase in the vote of allies would result in a decline of support among workers. At this moment the efforts of the party to recruit workers are exactly offset by the effect of supraclass strategies on them: $p[X(t + 1) - W(t)] = dN(t)$. Hence, the proportion of the electorate consisting of socialist voting workers remains stationary: $\Delta W(t) = 0$. When the class structure is stable, so that X is constant, the stationary value of $W(t)$, which will be represented by W^*, is given by[6]:

$$W^* = X - (d/p)N. \tag{3.2}$$

We will refer to any value of $W(t)$ which satisfies equation (3.2) as the "carrying capacity" of the party among workers. Within a given class structure, a party can eventually conquer the electoral support of workers who constitute W^* percent of the electorate. Moreover, if at any time the proportion of the electorate consisting of socialist voting workers happens to be W^*, then this proportion will remain at W^* as long as the class structure does not change. In turn, any increase in W above W^* will not last, and the socialist vote of workers will return to its carrying capacity. Even if for some accidental reason—say a sensational scandal involving right-wing parties—socialists benefit during a particular election from an exceptional outpouring of workers' sympathies, eventually their vote among workers will fall to the level warranted by the class structure and the support they mobilized among allies. The carrying capacity is the proportion of the electorate a particular party can mobilize and hold.

The carrying capacity of a party among workers depends on the proportion of workers in the electorate and the support the party has mobilized among allies. A party which receives votes from N allies will never be able to win and retain votes of $(d/p)N$ workers, which means that no party which faces a trade-off ($d>0$) can ever hope to conquer the votes of all workers if it received the

6. Equation (3.2) is obtained by setting the change of $W(t)$ as equal to zero in equation (3.1) and solving for $W(t)$.

vote of a single ally. In equilibrium, as represented by equation
(3.2), the trade-off between the support the party can permanently
muster among workers and its success among allies is linear. The
intercept of the line is X, the proportion of workers in the electorate. The ratio (d/p) measures the severity of the trade-off confronting the party in equilibrium. This parameter shows how
sensitive the carrying capacity of a particular party is to the recruitment of allies and thus it defines the strategic situation the
party confronts. If the quantity (d/p) is greater than unity (or d is
greater than p), the party would lose votes in the electorate as a
whole for every nonworker it recruits since for each vote of an
ally it gains, the party would lose the capacity to retain the support
of more than one worker. If the value of (d/p) is such at $0 < d/p$
< 1, then the party would lose support among workers but gain
votes in the electorate as a whole by pursuing supraclass strategies. Hence, the parameter (d/p) is the best summary description
of the situation confronting each party in the long run. The values
of (d/p) are presented in table 3.3 for the major socialist parties
separately and for all the left-wing parties combined. As an illustration, figure 3.1 shows the equilibrium trade-off for the
Swedish Social Democrats under the 1964 class structure.

Our analysis shows that left-wing parties suffered a loss of
support among workers whenever they pursued a supraclass strat-

Table 3.3 Equilibrium Trade-off between Electoral Support by Workers and
Allies, as Measured by the Parameter d/p

	Value of the Trade-off d/p for	
Country	Total Left	Major Socialist Party
Belgium	1.10	a
Denmark	0.05	0.13
Finland	0.53	1.41
France	1.05	9.31
Germany	1.41	16.70[b]
Norway	0.27	0.02
Sweden	0.53	0.77

[a] The results for Belgian Socialists are unusable. See Appendix: The Calculations
for explanation.
[b] Before 1933.

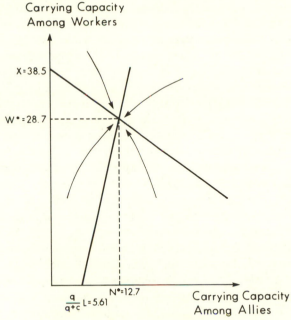

Figure 3.1 Carrying Capacities of the Swedish Social Democrats, Given the 1964
Class Structure, as Proportions of the Electorate

egy of electoral recruitment. But differences among major socialist parties are highly pronounced. Wherever social democrats
competed with a large communist party, the trade-off was extremely steep. For each middle-class voter it recruited, the German SPD faced, until the fall of the Weimar Republic, the loss of
16.7 workers. Throughout history, the French socialists faced a
loss of 9.3 workers. The reason the middle-class strategies were
so costly in Weimar Germany, in France, and in Finland is that in
these countries workers had the alternative of moving as workers
to the Communists. The German SPD could not afford to depart
too far from the stance of defending the narrowly defined corporate interests of workers when it faced the threat from the KPD but
could, and did, move to embrace the middle classes after the war
(Abraham 1982a; Green 1971:111; Hunt 1970:148). As a pure
party of workers, Social Democrats would have won, at most, the
support of one-third of the electorate: this is how many workers
there were in Weimar Germany. But any move toward the middle

classes would have meant that workers would vote communist *en masse*. In 1927 Social Democrats did decide officially to seek support outside the industrial proletariat, but in fact, they continued to behave as an electoral pressure group of unionized workers.

In France, communist competition became electorally significant after 1924. Until World War II, the Guesdist tradition prevailed and the SFIO persisted in its working-class orientation. The socialist language of the immediate postwar period was again highly *ouvrierist* but socialist strategies were much more opportunistic. Although the party was aware of losing votes among workers (Rimbert 1955), SFIO in fact conceded the hegemony over the working class to the communists. While no programmatic turn ever occurred, the language of socialist programmes seems to have become much less *ouvrierist* after 1962. While the words *"ouvrier"* and *"classe"* appeared very low on the list of socialist words throughout the postwar period, references to *travailleurs* and *lutte des classes* were much more frequent in 1945 than in 1969 (Gerstle 1979). As a result, socialists lost support among workers without gaining it elsewhere. Only after the break with the PCF in 1977 did socialists move in a concerted way to reconquer working-class support. This strategy was crowned with success in 1981 when the Socialist Party won many communist strongholds, thereby weakening the Communist Party, and made the left-wing coalition more palatable to the middle classes. Yet the Socialist Party continues to be pinched between the need for middle-class support and the threat that workers might defect to the Communists.

Social democrats in Sweden, Norway, and Denmark suffered from a much weaker trade-off. Communist competition was never significant in these countries. Communist parties were established in 1917 in Sweden, 1919 in Denmark, and 1923 in Norway; they were thoroughly proletarian in their composition and most of the time very small. The new left-socialist parties that emerged in the late 1950s drew on cultural and international issues rather than present themselves as stalwarts of the orthodoxy betrayed by the social democrats (Tarschys 1977). Hence the competition for workers' votes presented by these parties is not particularly threatening to the social democrats. In an ecological study Børre and Stehouwer (1970:243) found that the competition between left socialists and social democrats represented a positive sum game in Denmark: during the 1960s their vote shares were positively correlated.

The contrasts among equilibrium trade-offs facing major socialist countries can be attributed to the strength of the communist competition they confronted. Yet the trade-off for the Left as a whole also shows sizable cross-national differences. Almost negligible in Denmark and Norway, this trade-off is moderate in Finland and Sweden, and quite sharp in France, Belgium and in Germany until 1933. What accounts for these differences?

Unfortunately, with only seven countries which vary systematically in a number of ways, we find ourselves in the situation typical of comparative analysis, where competing explanations often cannot be eliminated. Denmark, Norway, Finland, and Sweden differ from France, Belgium, and Germany in more than one way relevant to the phenomena we seek to explain.

One is tempted to attribute these differences to some features of working-class culture which the parties confronted during their electoral history. Unfortunately, the field of working-class history has suffered from an empiricist bias and at its best produced intuitive understandings rather than analytical categories. Moreover, the categories which are used to characterize the working-class cultures during the nineteenth century no longer have a clear referent after political parties and trade unions began their struggle to mold this culture into conformity with political goals. "Radicalism," "classness," "antistatism," "autonomy," even "secularism" are no longer predicates of an autonomous working-class culture, but rather they are a product of interactions between spontaneous cultural processes and the activities of organized, purposeful, "centers of radiation," to use Gramsci's term. To impose a cultural interpretation on our findings we would have to find aspects of working-class culture that are independent of the strategies pursued by parties and other organizations. We do not believe that such aspects exist. But even if one overcomes these theoretical misgivings, *prima facie* empirical comparisons bode badly for any interpretation that would claim a similarity of working-class cultures in France and Germany.

A clue is provided by looking at the parties which competed for the loyalty of workers. The trade-off is steeper in those countries where some political parties appealed to workers on the basis of particularistic appeals other than class. Confessional parties have been more important in Belgium, France, and Germany than they have been in the Scandinavian countries. In Belgium regional-linguistic parties compete for the loyalty of workers, and a number of such parties existed in Germany before 1933. In Scandinavia only the Swedish People's Party in Finland achieved some stature as a regional party. These patterns seem to indicate that the trade-off facing the Left as a whole is weaker where class ideology competes mainly with the liberal ideology of individuals-citizens and the trade-off is stronger in those countries where confessional, linguistic, or ethnic parties appeal to workers. In this interpretation, the trade-offs facing the Left constitute a cumulative effect of the strategies of parties which compete for the political support of workers. From the point of view of just one group of participants in these conflicts—the left-wing political parties—the effect of other participants appears as a parametric constraint on their own actions, a cost to be borne if they de-emphasize class ideology. This cost turns out to be high when competitors campaign on behalf of particularistic identities but not as high when they offer only a universalistic ideology.

But the intensity of the trade-offs reflects not only the strategies of nonsocialist political parties, it also coincides with the role played by the trade unions in the process of organizing workers as a class (see table 3.4). Norway, Sweden, and Denmark are the countries where unions succeeded in combining a high density of membership with high concentration of members within a single federation along with a centralized bargaining system. Moreover, unions grew relatively early in relation to the growth of the socialist electorate. Although union density in 1910 was higher in Germany than either in Sweden or in Norway (but not Denmark), German unions were weak during the first forty years of socialist electoral participation. If we compare union density about forty years after socialist parties had entered into electoral competition—about 1930 for the Scandinavians and the French and 1910 for the Germans—the ratio of union members to the potential members turns out to be about 42 percent in Sweden, 34 percent in Denmark, 14 percent in Germany, and 11 in France. If we compare the end of the periods under consideration—about 1970 in the Scandinavian countries and France and 1933 in Germany—

the respective percentages are 90 in Sweden, 78 in Denmark, 65 in Norway, 31 in France, and 26 in Germany.

The French and the Finnish unions suffered from severe fractionalization during several periods. The rough guess made by the OECD in 1979 (1979:40) was that the largest French confederation, the CGT, had 58 percent of the membership in the five major federations. The 1974 election for bargaining representatives gave the CGT 42.7 percent, while survey studies show that about two-thirds of the manual workers belong to this federation. In Finland, unions supported by communists competed with those closest to social democrats. In 1970 the largest federation grouped 70 percent of union members but just five years earlier, before the two major unions merged, the larger of these, the SAK constituted only 45.4 percent of all unionists (Helander 1982:171).

Finally, collective bargaining is much more centralized in Denmark, Norway, and Sweden than in the remaining countries (Heady 1970). In Norway, Sweden, and at times in Denmark, central confederations negotiate binding agreements that leave only a circumscribed space for bargains by particular unions (Visser 1983:26), while in France and Germany collective bargaining tends to take place at the level of industry, region, or even firm. In terms of Visser's (1983:33) index of organizational centralization, Norway receives the score of 8.8 out of the maximum of 12 points, Sweden 8.4, Denmark 5.3, Germany 4.8, and France 4.2 (see also Windmuller 1981, 1975).

When they occur simultaneously, these three features—high density, high concentration of members of one federation, and high centralization of bargaining—make unions an effective mechanism of class organization. A single federation which includes most workers and bargains on behalf of them all is "an organ of class struggle which holds the entire class together in spite of its fragmentation through different employment": the task which Bernstein attributed to the party. Such a union is a class organization in the sense that it promotes and protects interests of workers as a class, their collective interests, and it enforces discipline on groups of workers that may be tempted by the advantages of pursuing particularistic interests (Schwerin 1980; Streeck 1984). Moreover, in the countries where a single union is the collective bargaining agent for most workers and where this

Table 3.4 Indices of Class Organization via Trade Unions

A. Unionized Manual Workers/Manual Workers

	1900	1910	1920	1930	1940	1950	1960	1970	1975
Denmark	13.9	16.2	37.0	33.8	44.3	54.4	64.3	72.1	77.7
Norway[a]								65.3	64.5
Sweden	8.7	12.2	32.4	41.7	64.3	75.2	83.4	89.6	92.3
Germany[b]	5.7	13.8	45.2	25.8		35.8	39.8	40.4	44.4
France		11.0[c]	38.0	9.5	45.0[d]	23.0[e]	17.3[f]	31.0[g]	31.0[h]

B. Manual Workers in the Largest Federation/Manual Workers Unionized

	1900	1910	1920	1930	1940	1950	1960	1970	1975
Denmark	76.8	81.0	73.0	72.6	93.3	96.3	95.6	98.5	98.5
Norway	23.9	100.0[j]	100.0	100.0	100.0	100.0	100.0	97.2	97.4
Sweden[i]	100.0	99.4	92.5	95.6	97.5	98.5	98.8	98.6	99.0
Germany[k]		82.8	85.8	85.4		100.0	96.5	98.5	98.5
France		36.4[l]						64.5[m]	71.0[n]

C. Manual Workers in the Largest Federation/Manual Workers[o]

	1900	1910	1920	1930	1940	1950	1960	1970	1975
Denmark	10.7	13.1	27.0	24.5	41.3	52.4	61.5	71.0	76.5
Norway								63.5	62.8
Sweden	8.7	12.1	30.0	39.9	63.0	74.1	82.4	88.3	91.4
Germany	4.6	11.4	38.8	22.0		35.8	38.4	39.8	43.7
France		4.0						20.0	22.0

Sources: For Danish, Swedish, and German union density and Danish pre-1950, Norwegian pre-1970, Swedish and German pre-1960 concentration, the sources is Bain and Price (1980). For recent concentration in Denmark, Norway, and Germany, Visser (1983). From France: Mitchell and Stearns (1971:68) for 1906; Sellier (1976) as cited by Adam (1983:45) for 1920, 1930, 1936, 1954, and 1962; Adam (1983:46) for 1970 and 1978.

[a] Until 1950 obtained by dividing LO and SAC members as given by Bain and Price (1980), by the number of manual workers as given by Przeworski et al. (1978). The 1950 figure derived in the same way would have been 77.8.

[b] Until 1933 these nubers slightly underestimate the total since they do not include minor and ephemeral unions.

[c] 1906.

[d] 1936.

[e] 1954.

[f] 1962.

[g] Survey response.

[h] 1978 survey response.

[i] Members of LO divided by members of LO and SAC. These numbers are slightly overstated because LO includes some nonmanual workers.

[j] Slightly overstated.

[k] Until 1933 these numbers slightly overstate the degree of concentration because they do not include minor and peripheral unions.

[l] 1906.

[m] Survey response.

[n] 1978 survey response.

[o] Obtained by multiplying A and B.

form of organization permeates most of political life, class continues to be repeatedly emphasized as a salient feature of society.
Under such conditions, socialist and other left-wing parties can
afford to pursue supraclass strategies without losing much support
among workers, since even if social democrats de-emphasize the
salience of class in their electoral strategies, this salience is being
continually reestablished by the role of the unions within the system of corporatist representation.

We are thus led to a particular interpretation of the effect of
corporatism on class organization, an interpretation close to Panitch (in his 1981 article) and Lembruch (1982). Our findings indicate that left-wing parties face a much weaker trade-off in the
countries with strong corporatist institutions. This should not be a
surprise. Parliaments are the quintessential mechanism of individualization. They are the forum of representation organized on
territorial bases. Parliaments individualize class relations precisely because they are based on principles that are deliberately
blind to all social and economic distinctions. Parliaments individualize and this is why in systems of parliamentary representation the salience of class as a determinant of political behavior is
so sensitive to the strategies pursued by political parties. But corporatism is a system of representation based on the recognition of
economic interests, and in the "neocorporatist" version (Schmitter 1974, 1984), it is a system based on recognition of class interests. Corporatism is a form of political institutionalization of
class relations.[7]

This interpretation of the crossnational differences in the intensity of electoral trade-offs facing the Left explains as well why
these differences tend to coincide with the intensity of competition among left-wing parties. This competition not only restricts
the freedom of maneuver of each left-wing party but increases the
trade-off for the Left as a whole. The reason is not directly electoral: political fractionalization leads to splits within the union
movement (Visser 1983), and without unity in the movement,
there is no organization to unite workers as a class in their relation
to other classes.

7. Thus Balibar (1970) and Poulantzas (1973) were mistaken when they maintained that individualization of class relations is a universal feature of capitalism in
any political form and that under capitalism the division of the society into classes
is never institutionally recognized.

The interpretation that focuses on the strategies of bourgeois parties and the interpretation that emphasizes the role played by trade unions are both theoretically homogeneous and complementary. They impose the same view of such trade-offs: the Left faces an electoral trade-off among workers because the salience of class as a cause of individual behavior is a product of interaction among multiple political forces. To the extent it meets political parties which appeal to workers in rival particularistic terms, the Left is highly vulnerable when it adopts supraclass strategies. To the extent that unions organize workers as a class, left-wing political parties can afford to pursue supraclass strategies at a relatively low cost to their support among workers.

Thus, the trade-off facing the Left as a whole should be lowest in those countries where unions are strong, concentrated, centralized, and where no political parties address workers in terms of confessional, ethnic, linguistic, or regional appeals. This trade-off should be very sharp where unions are weak and fragmented and where parties appeal to competing particularistic loyalties of workers. Unfortunately, among the seven countries we examined the two factors tend to coincide. This colinearity makes it impossible to weigh empirically the relative importance of the competition from other parties and of the functional equivalence of the unions in organizing workers as a class.

The existence of this trade-off constitutes one limitation of socialist growth. Faced with a working class which is a numerical minority, class-based parties seek electoral support from other groups. They often win this support, but in the process they dilute the salience of class as a cause of the workers' political behavior, and they erode their strength among workers.

PARTY STRATEGIES AND THE VOTE

The existence of the trade-off between support among the middle-classes and recruitment of workers does not explain, however, why socialists failed to win a larger share of the electorate. They had to lose the votes of some workers as they turned to other groups, but why did they not win enough votes from these groups to conquer clear majorities?

Clearly, other parties stood in the way, and whatever the socialists might have done, the counterstrategies of their competitors imposed limits on the socialists' success. But part of the reason must be internal—there are *prima facie* grounds to believe that socialist leaders have not been willing to seek the support of other groups at just any cost to their strength among workers. The socialist quest for electoral support was circumscribed by an autonomous concern for class loyalty. Socialists sought votes, but they seem to have valued the votes of workers above those of other supporters.

How do left-wing parties choose electoral strategies? Any strategy is a result of two decisions: the selection of the groups from which the party seeks support and the choice of a relative emphasis on a worker versus a mass constituency. A party might specify, for example, that small holders and the lower echelons of salaried employees constitute its natural base of support and that obtaining the votes of such people is the most urgent task for the immediate future. But a party may also treat such groups as potential supporters and nevertheless continue to emphasize its uncompromising dedication to the working class. The Norwegian Labour Party, for example, has recognized since the late 1950s that tertiary economic activities are causing an evolution in the composition of the labor force. Salaried employees in the tertiary sector have been identified as a potential source of support for the party. Yet the strategy is being debated. While the right wing of the party "wants to adopt an 'activist strategy' toward the new groups in searching for new issues and programmes with a multi-group appeal embracing all 'wage-earners', the latter [the left wing] represents a 'passive approach' by either leaving the enlarged bourgeois groups in peace as before or simply by defining them as new sections of the working class posing no qualitatively new questions" (Heidar 1977:301).

The identification of groups which a party considers as belonging to its base of support is not always as explicit and systematic as was Karl Kautsky's classic analysis of the German electorate in 1891. Often parties are satisfied with a global language that does not close too many doors. But the general conception of the socialist electorate evolved in a rather similar fashion in different countries, perhaps with the exception of the German Social Democrats' difficulties with the peasantry. Most parties decided quite early that artisans, craftsmen, small merchants, small agricultural proprietors, tenants, as well as other people who worked and were poor constitute a natural base of socialist support. True, Engels referred to artisans as "these people [who] are not born representatives of revolutionary socialism, like workers of large industry" (Engels and Marx 1975:164) but they were "oppressed and exploited" and hence potential supporters. White-collar employees were included among potential socialist voters without much controversy since they did not own the means of production at all. Supervisory personnel always created some difficulty for socialist theoreticians but not enough to occupy the attention of party congresses. The question about salaried employees was when they would become socialist voters rather than whether they have "objective" grounds for supporting socialists. Finally, left-wing parties often looked at their potential electorate in terms other than class. They often thought that women and young people naturally belong to their electorate. At times they saw people who held certain values, such as justice, as their potential supporters even when it originated from Christian inspirations or issues such as alcoholism (Andrae 1969). Most recently, left-wing parties discovered potential supporters among people already politicized as the "new social movements."

This description is somewhat schematic, but party documents do not reveal major differences among them. The private property of peasants, the ambiguous role of the supervisory personnel, and the bourgeois origins of some of the new social movements were at times cited by speakers at party congresses as reasons why socialists or communists should not fall into the trap of expecting support from such people. But in general, left-wing parties thought from the beginning that they could obtain the support of almost everyone with the exception of a handful of exploiters, and the designation of the particular groups reflected, even if sometimes with a significant delay, the evolution of class structure rather than of strategic conceptions.

Strategic decisions concerned emphases both in programs and in organizational efforts. A party might decide to dedicate itself to the competition for the vote of the people in general and it might decide to try to deepen its support among workers. The instruments of such strategies are both symbolic and organizational. Thus parties decide what to say and whom to organize, and these decisions are means toward an end. Moreover, while past history, including the mistakes committed earlier, weigh upon the present alternatives, such strategies are not chosen once and for all but are adjusted to changing circumstances. It is simply inaccurate to maintain that socialist parties progressively abandoned their working class orientation. Histories of particular parties are replete with strategic reversals, with changes of direction, with controversies and schisms. The German SPD returned to an emphasis on class in 1905; Swedish Social Democrats temporarily abandoned their first attempt to become a multiclass party in 1926; Communists in orchestrated unison passed from an alliance strategy of 1924–28 to the "class against class" posture; young German socialists launched a serious attack on the middle-class strategy a few years ago; the French Socialist Party decided to compete for hegemony over the working class in 1978; and today, conflicts between an *ouvrierist* and a multiclass tendency wrench apart several social democratic and communist parties.

Parties appeal to the middle classes, women, or ecologists by presenting themselves as representatives of their interests and values, by evoking appropriate symbols, and by offering specific policy proposals. They claim to represent the interests of all the poor people, not only in the future but also within present-day society. They offer, as the French Socialists did in 1905, a specific list of reforms that would be attractive to citizens, parents, farmers, and others. They "extend the hand," as did Maurice Thorez in 1936, "to you catholic, worker, employee, artisan, peasant," by "working for the union of the French nation against the two hundred families and their mercenaries . . . working for a true reconciliation of the French people" (Bodin and Touchard 1961:52). They maintain, as Schumacher in 1949 did, that "socialism is no longer the affair of the working class in the old sense of the word. It is the programme for workers, farmers, artisans, tradesmen, and the intellectual professions" (Paterson and Thomas 1977:184).

Socialists dissuade middle-class voters from voting for their party when they evoke their privileged relation to the working class, when they emphasize their special, or even exclusive, commitment to the defense of the interests of workers. When socialists talk about nationalizing land, they give up the votes of peasants; when they mention a general strike, they send the petite bourgeoisie into a panic. The issue of naval appropriations in 1907 was, for example, a moment when the SPD opted against a

Volkspartei strategy by refusing to use appeals to the nation. According to Söderpalm (1975:263), the attempts to develop unemployment assistance in Sweden, in 1923 and 1926, "strengthened the Social Democrats' grip on trade unionists but at the same time made the party seem even more a bastion for industrial workers and contributed to the loss of marginal votes in the rural population." Dr. Salvador Allende's inopportune quip that he was not the president of all Chileans contributed to the alienation of the middle classes from the Unidad Popular. The French Socialists' last minute decision to embrace the Communist demand for increasing the basic wage (SMIC) to 2500 francs on the eve of the 1978 elections scared away some potential middle-class supporters.

But programs, platforms, and pronouncements are examples of only one instrument of party strategy. The other is organization. Parties decide whom to organize and how to organize them. When socialists entered into the electoral competition, they were an organization of workers and their relation to other classes was limited to elections. Workers were tied to the party continually and in all facets of their lives. Not only party cells, but auxiliary groups, clubs of mutual aid, cultural circles, sporting teams, and even bars integrated workers with the party during every moment of their lives. As Bell described: "A working-class child, SPD model, could begin life in a socialist creche, join a socialist youth movement, go to a socialist summer camp, hike with the socialist *Wandervögel,* sing in a workers' chorus, and be buried in a socialist cemetery" (1968:511), and while socialist parties sought at the same time to conquer the votes of peasants and others, their relation to these groups was exclusively electoral (Söderpalm 1975).

Eventually the relationship between left-wing parties and workers became much more loose. To what extent the "electoralization" of the relation between political parties and the electorate is due to party strategies and to what extent to exogenous technological and social changes is a matter of long-standing debates (Duverger 1965; Neumann 1956). Television certainly seems to have something to do with this transformation (Thomas 1977). But what is clear is that parties do decide what organizational forms to develop and at whom they should be targeted. They can concentrate their efforts on membership campaigns, on developing subscriptions to party press, on youth branches, or on parasocialist voluntary associations. They can organize campaigns of mass education about party programs—millions of people were trained in economics by the Italian Communist Party when this party decided to follow a policy of austerity against the sentiment of its working-class base. They can organize bicycle races or support choirs. The Austrian Workers' Stamp Collecting Association continues to flourish (Sully 1977:221).

The strategies that parties adopt under particular circumstances depend on the degree to which the party leaders are concerned with the class composition of their electorate, that is, the degree to which they value the support of workers autonomously from electoral considerations. If leaders of left-wing parties were concerned exclusively with votes, wherever these come from, they would value the electoral support of workers only as much as of anyone else. But if they are concerned about the support of workers, they would orient party strategies depending on the class composition of the electorate.

A few symbols are again helpful. Suppose that party leaders value the votes of nonworkers at some fraction of the value they attach to electoral support by workers. Let this fraction be $k = N/W$, where N and W are defined as before as the proportion of the electorate consisting, respectively, of socialist voting allies and socialist voting workers. The ratio N/W indicates the class composition of the vote: it is the ratio of the middle-class to working-class socialist voters. Socialist leaders would like to maintain this ratio at k: this is the class composition they seek to achieve. If it happens at any time that the party is supported by a sufficient number of workers, so that $k > N(t)/W(t)$, and as a consequence $kW(t) > N(t)$ and $kW(t) - N(t) > 0$, then leaders will be free to pursue a supraclass strategy and recruit more nonworkers. The party is sufficiently working-class based and thus it can afford to dedicate itself to the middle-class electorate. But if there are not enough workers or too many allies among the party's supporters, so that $k < N(t)/W(t)$, $kW(t) < N(t)$, and $kW(t) - N(t) < 0$, then leaders will emphasize the commitment of the party to the working class, even at the cost of losing some votes among the middle classes. Thus, in this symbolic notation, a party would choose to pursue the votes of the middle classes whenever the actual composition of its support is such that the difference $kW(t) - N(t)$ is positive. A party would choose to restrict its appeal to the working class when this difference is negative.

The number k characterizes particular parties. Note that a party with leaders highly sensitive to class composition will be characterized by a low value of k. Indeed, a party with a $k = 0$ would always seek to discourage middle-class voters from voting socialist. Such a party attaches no value to the middle-class vote but cares only about the support of workers and the difference $kW(t) - N(t)$ is never positive for this party, regardless of its actual class composition. In turn, a party not concerned about party class composition would be characterized by a high positive k. Imagine in the extreme that k is a very large number. Then the difference $kW(t) - N(t)$ will always be positive, regardless of the actual composition of the vote, and the party will always seek to recruit more middle-class voters.

The value of the parameter k which belongs to the set of parameter values that best reconstruct the historical path of the vote received by a particular party is the summary description of the strategies which party leaders must have followed in the past. The values of k indicate the average value which leaders of each party must have attached to the votes of allies as compared to the votes of workers throughout the period on which our calculations are based. The numbers we calculated—using the procedure described above with regard to the parameter d—indicate that the value which the leaders of the Norwegian Labour Party attached to votes of nonworkers exceeded that of workers ($k = 1.11$). The leaders of the Danish ($k = 0.22$) socialist parties valued the votes of allies much less than those cast by workers. And the German SPD, at least before 1933, persisted in an orthodox laborist stance ($k = 0$).[8]

Perhaps these numbers are more telling if we look at them in a slightly different manner. Since $k = N/W$ is the class composition of the electorate which party leaders want to maintain, their de-

8. Again, the numbers for Finland and Norway were calculated somewhat differently than those for Denmark, France, Germany, and Sweden. In Finland and Norway, k represents the value party leaders attached to votes of nonworkers, while in the remaining countries they measure the value they attached to votes of specific groups of nonworkers, whom we designate throughout as "allies." Nevertheless, here as before, using the same procedure in the latter four countries has only minor consequences.

sired supporters would consist of $N = kW$ allies whenever the support of the party among workers is W. Hence, the total vote for the party would be $Y = kW + W$, and the target proportion of workers among socialist voters would be $W/Y = 1/(1 + k)$. Viewed in this way, the calculated values of k indicate that Norwegian Labour Party leaders chose strategies to maintain a party in which workers would constitute 47.4 percent of supporters; Danish Social Democratic leaders sought a party in which workers would provide 70.8 percent of the vote; Swedish SAP leaders maintained as their target a party in which workers would furnish 77.5 percent of their electoral support; Finnish Social Democrats opted for 80 percent; French Socialists for 82 percent; and the German Social Democrats (always pre-1933) for 100 percent.

This is what parties do with regard to their actual and potential supporters. But the effects of the strategy chosen by any one party depend on the competition offered by other parties. Socialists are not the only political force in search of middle-class support and neither is the Left as a whole. Left-wing parties may decide to dedicate all of their efforts to the conquest of the middle classes but may find that this electorate is insensitive to their appeals. On the other hand, socialist parties which decide to abandon the middle-class electorate may also find that their strategic choice is not reflected in the behavior of the nonworkers who continue to vote for the party. Let c stand for the effectiveness of a party in recruiting or discouraging additional nonworkers depending on all competitive factors. Then the effect of party strategies on the change of socialist support among nonworkers will be $c[kW(t) - N(t)]$, so that a party that decides to seek some additional middle-class voters ends up only with a part, c, of the desired increase. The Norwegian middle-class electorate seems least sensitive to the strategic decisions of the Labour Party according to our calculation ($c = 0.20$). The respective numbers for the other parties are 0.25 for the Swedish Social Democrats, 0.36 for the Finnish Social Democrats, 0.43 for the Danish party, 0.67 for the French Socialists, and, note, 1.55 for the pre-1933 German SPD. The German middle-class electorate amplified the strategic choices of the party by running away from Social Democrats at an even faster pace than party leaders would have wished. But in general, these numbers indicate that party strategies are moderately effective and most parties do win between 20 and 67 percent of the additional middle-class voters they set out to recruit.

Some people, however, vote for left-wing parties independently of the strategies these parties pursue with regard to the middle-class electorate. Many nonworkers vote left as a "protest vote" (Engels and Marx 1975; Braga 1956; Allardt 1964, 1970)—an expression of a general dissatisfaction with the political system but not necessarily of support for the programs offered by the parties which benefit from this vote. Let $L(t)$ represent the proportion of the electorate that consists of people other than workers to whom the party may turn for support in the current election. Then the quantity $L(t + 1) - N(t)$ measures the pool of nonworkers available for socialist recruitment—all the potential middle-class socialist supporters less those who support the party already. To represent protest vote, we simply assume that if a party did not formulate any specific strategies oriented to encourage or discourage nonworkers from voting socialist, its vote among nonworkers would change proportionately to the size of this pool, where q represents this proportion. Empirically, q plays a rather minor role. Its value turns out to be approximately zero for socialists in Denmark, Norway, and France, and not more than 0.06 in Sweden, Finland, and Germany. Only for the left-wing parties together, does the value of q exceed 0.10 in France and Belgium. These results are consistent with the general finding that it is Communists who generally benefit from the protest vote and who have therefore a more volatile electorate (Särlvik 1974:388; Hill 1974:74).

If some nonworkers drift toward left-wing parties in protest and if these parties choose the strategies in the manner and with the effects described above, then the change of the proportion of the electorate consisting of socialist voting nonworkers will be given by

$$\Delta N(t) = q[L(t + 1) - N(t)] + c[kW(t) - N(t)]. \quad (3.3)$$

The first term of (3.3) shows the influx into the ranks of voters resulting from the protest vote while the second term shows the effects of party strategies.

Following the procedure used with regard to workers, we can now ask what is the level of support among nonworkers that a particular party or the Left as a whole can recruit and hold? Setting $\Delta N(t) = 0$, we solve equation (3.3) for N^*, the carrying capacity of the party among the allies, to obtain

$$N^* = \frac{q}{q + c} L + \frac{c}{q + c} kW. \tag{3.4}$$

Note that if there is no protest vote then the carrying capacity of the party among the allies is simply $N^* = kW$.

Barring the one case of extreme sensitivity to class composition, the German SPD before 1933, the slope of the line given by equation (3.4) is positive (see fig. 3.1). While the carrying capacity of a party among workers depends negatively on the support from the middle classes, the carrying capacity among the middle classes depends positively on the strength among the workers. The reason is that efforts to recruit nonworkers, the willingness to engage in middle-class strategies, are conditioned by the support the party enjoys among workers. Only if a party has sufficient strength among workers can it devote itself to the mobilization of allies.

Causes of Stagnation

The causes of stagnation of the socialist vote are thus twofold. First, workers are less likely to vote socialist when parties accumulate electoral support from other groups. Second, socialist leaders are willing to pursue supraclass strategies only if they enjoy sufficient support among workers.

These two limitations interact. Suppose that at some moment a party enjoys substantial support among workers and not much among the middle classes, so that its actual class composition permits the leaders to embark on a supraclass strategy. As the party continues to conquer the middle classes, it suffers costs in opportunities to recruit or maintain the support of workers. Its growth among workers slows down or even reverses. And as the support among the middle classes grows and the mobilization of workers tapers off, the class composition of the voters becomes a source of concern among leaders. The party adopts a strategy emphasizing its ties with the working class, even at the cost of scaring off some of the recently won support among nonworkers. As a result, the support for the party among workers now begins to increase, its class composition tilts again in favor of workers, and the leaders once more are willing to embark on the chase for middle-class voters.

Support from nonworkers decreases the rate at which the socialist vote grows among workers while support from workers increases the rate at which the party recruits nonworkers. Workers are more likely to vote socialist when the party has mobilized only a few middle-class voters, and party leaders are more willing to recruit middle-class voters when many workers vote socialist. But workers are less likely to vote socialist when many middle-class people vote for the party, while party leaders are less willing to pursue middle-class voters when fewer workers vote socialist. Thus, the reaction of workers to supraclass strategies ultimately restricts the willingness of party leaders to pursue such strategies.

Under normal circumstances, and in all the cases we examined, the result is that the socialist vote tended to stop growing over time. During the early period, when few workers and few allies still voted socialist, the growth was rapid, often simultaneously among workers and allies. When the party achieved the support of a large part of the working-class electorate, it could dedicate itself to the recruitment of middle-class voters and still continue to grow. But eventually this growth slowed down.

Since the carrying capacity of each party among workers depends on its strength among allies, and the carrying capacity among allies is a function of its strength among workers, both carrying capacities and eventually the carrying capacity of the party in the electorate as a whole are determined uniquely. The carrying capacity among workers, W^*, is a function of the proportion of workers in the electorate, X, and the proportion of socialist voting allies in the electorate, N (see equation [3.2]). The carrying capacity among allies, N^*, depends in turn on the proportion of allies in the electorate, L, and the proportion of socialist voting workers in the electorate, W (see equation [3.4]). The intersection of these two functions—$W^* = f(X,N)$ and $N^* = g(L,W)$—specifies a unique point which gives the carrying capacity of the party among workers and allies. Figure 3.1 shows an illustration of the carrying capacities of the Swedish Social Democrats under the 1964 class structure. The sum of these two carrying capacities is the carrying capacity of the party in the entire electorate, $Y^* = W^* + N^*$. If class structure remained the same for a long time, that is, if X and L were fixed, then the support of the party among workers and allies would eventually approach the carrying capacity, following the path of one of the arrows in figure 3.1. Moreover, if some unusual event—a major crisis or a minor scandal—happened to give a jolt to the party system, then the socialist vote would again begin moving in the direction of this point after the event had passed into history.

Since class structure does change, even if quite glacially, the carrying capacities of the party change as well. The carrying capacity of each party depends on the proportions of workers and allies in the electorate. These proportions constitute the intercepts of the lines shown in figure 3.1. If the proportion of workers in the electorate, $X(t)$, decreases, then the entire line $W^* = f(X,N)$ shifts downward, and the carrying capacity of the party decreases both among workers and allies. The capacity to recruit and hold workers decreases because there are fewer of them; the capacity to recruit and hold allies falls because the party is less willing to recruit allies when there are fewer workers. If the proportion of allies in the electorate increases, then the line $N^* = g(L,W)$ moves to the right and the carrying capacity of the party to retain workers falls, the latter because the party now has more allies. Thus transformations of the class structure always simultaneously effect the capacity of the party to hold onto workers and allies.

The actual history of the socialist vote is thus a result of two movements occurring simultaneously: the growth of the vote from some initial level toward the carrying capacity and the changes of the carrying capacity which result from transformations of the class structure (see fig. 3.2). The first movement is relatively fast; the second as slow as the transformations of the class structure. But as time goes on, the actual vote begins to approach the carrying capacity and the changes become much less accentuated. Party strategies dominate the dynamic of the vote during the first period; transformations of class structure mold the path of the socialist vote in the longer run of electoral experience. No particular dates divide these periods sharply, particularly since discrete events, such as border changes or extensions of suffrage, do not always affect the carrying capacities and the actual vote in the same way. But some lines can be drawn. The vote for the German Left turned in the direction of its carrying capacity in 1919 and had almost converged to it by 1933; it turned in that direction

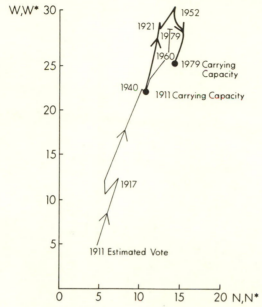

Figure 3.2 Class Specific Carrying Capacities and Estimated Vote Shares for the Swedish Social Democratic Party (in Proportions of the Electorate)

again in 1976 after the rapid growth of the 1957–72 period. The vote for the French Left began tracing the carrying capacity after 1953. Only in Denmark, where the carrying capacity has always been exceedingly high, does the Left vote still seem to change quite independently of transformations in the class structure.

The capacity of the Left to recruit and hold voters peaked quite a long time ago in most countries—in 1903 in Germany, in 1912 in Belgium, 1928 in France, during the early 1950s in Finland, Sweden, and Norway, and most likely around 1970 in Denmark (see table 3.5). In some countries the loss has been important. The Belgian Left in 1912 could have carried 48.7 percent of all those who had the right to vote if the country had remained as industrialized and if the suffrage had continued to be restricted to men. By 1971, most of the industry which had made Belgium the most industrialized country in Europe toward the end of the nineteenth century either closed or was modernized to save labor. In the meantime, in 1949, all women entered the electorate, decreasing the proportion of workers among the potential voters. The result is

Table 3.5 Carrying Capacities for Total Left among Workers, Allies, and the Electorate at Its Peak and for the Last Election Estimated

	Peak In	Carrying Capacity			Year	Carrying Capacity		
		Workers	Allies	Electorate		Workers	Allies	Electorate
Belgium	1912	35.1	13.6	48.7	1971	1.6	15.8	17.4
Denmark	a				1971	26.7	32.4	59.1
Finland	1951	9.6	26.9	36.5	1972	5.5	27.1	32.7
France	1928	22.3	15.4	37.7	1968	12.0	12.3	24.3
Germany	1903	19.5	12.3	31.8	1969	17.6	11.1	28.7
Norway	1953	18.0	50.3	68.3	1969	17.2	48.1	65.3
Sweden	1952	35.8	8.8	44.6	1964	34.1	8.4	42.5

a In Denmark, 1971 was most likely the peak.

that by 1971 the Left in Belgium could retain only 17.4 percent of the electorate if the class structure remained frozen at 1971 proportions. In France the Left was able to hold 37.7 percent of the electorate by 1928—assuming a turnout rate of about 70 percent, this translates into 54 percent of the votes actually cast. By 1968 there were fewer workers and after 1946 women finally won the right to vote. By 1968 the French Left could carry only 24.3 percent of the electorate—with a turnout rate of 85 percent this would mean about 29 percent of the votes cast. In other countries this erosion of the carrying capacity has been less dramatic—in Germany from 31.8 percent of the electorate in 1903 to 28.5 percent in 1933 and 28.7 percent in 1969; in Norway from 68.3 percent in 1953 to 65.3 percent in 1969; in Finland from 36.5 percent in 1951 to 27.1 percent in 1972; and in Sweden from 44.6 percent in 1952 to 42.5 percent in 1964. But if the trends of the 1950s and early 1960s continued through the 1970s, and there is every reason to believe that they did, then the carrying capacities must have fallen even further since 1970. Reduction in the proportion of workers and an increase in the proportion of employees in the tertiary sector combine to reduce carrying capacities: there are fewer workers from whom to draw and more effort is needed to mobilize the allies, thus further reducing the salience of class. A simple extrapolation of the French 1962–68 trends would result in a 1980 carrying capacity of 21.4 percent; a similar extrapolation in Sweden would show a 1980 carrying capacity of 39.9 percent. In Denmark the proportion of workers in the population grew through 1960, and thus an extrapolation of earlier trends would show a 1980 carrying capacity slightly higher than that of 1971. But if we rely on the changes in the proportion of workers in the labor force, we will discover that this proportion has indeed fallen in Denmark as well, and actually at a faster pace than our linear extrapolations for Norway and Sweden would indicate (Børre 1977a). Using survey data to calculate the carrying capacities gives Denmark a figure of 54.8 percent in 1975.

All of these percentages represent the proportion of the electorate, that is, of all people who have the right to vote in a particular election rather than those who turn out and cast their votes. This means that in several countries there was a moment when the Left had a carrying capacity of more than one half of the votes actually cast. In Belgium and France, it was the exclusion of women which led to the overrepresentation of workers, but even in those countries the Left would have become majoritarian among voters if the class structure of the period of labor-intensive industrialization had lasted longer. In Sweden, the carrying capacity among voters slightly exceeded 50 percent in 1952, and in Denmark and Norway it still exceeds one half of the votes cast. Given the prevailing turnout rates, even the German SPD could have carried more than one half of the voters if the class structure had remained what it was in 1903. Thus there was a moment in the history of all these countries when the class structure was such that the Left could have become permanently majoritarian among voters if this class structure had remained frozen for a long time. But by the time left-wing parties had secured a large part of their potential electorate, this electorate began to dwindle. The idea had its time, but time worked against it.

In different countries, however, the outcomes are far from the same. The Norwegian Labour Party continues to be able to recruit and hold more than one half of those entitled to vote and so does the Left as a whole in Denmark. On the other hand, the French and the Finnish socialist parties do not seem to have radiant electoral futures. And even if the numbers we present are inaccurate, the relative differences among countries and parties are so large that they do call for an explanation (see table 3.6).

The differences among the major socialist parties seem again to be attributable to the split within the Left. The carrying capacities of the French Socialists, pre-1933 German Social Democrats, and the Social Democrats in Finland are much lower than the carrying capacities of the social democratic parties in the three Scandinavian countries where the leftist, particularly communist, competition is weaker. Among the three socialist parties which faced communist competition, the German party had the steepest trade-off to confront, but it had the most ouvrierist strategy as well. The French Socialists faced a very costly trade-off; Finnish Social Democrats were able to exchange middle-class and working-class voters almost one for one. Our French estimate of carrying capacity among the allies is most likely much too low, so one should not make too much of these differences. The contrast with the remaining three Scandinavian countries is, however, quite sharp. Note that the difference between these two groups of countries does not stem

Table 3.6 Class Structure, Electoral Trade-offs, Party Strategies, and Their Carrying Capacities Based on 1970 Class Structure

	Workers/ Electorate X	Allies/ Electorate L	Electoral Trade-off (d/p)	Party Strategy k	Carrying Capacity		
					Workers W*	Allies N*	Electorate Y*
			Major Socialist Party				
Denmark	28.4	33.8	0.13	0.41	26.9	11.1	38.0
Finland	20.3	b	1.41	0.25	5.2	10.4	15.6
France	24.8	47.9	9.31	0.22	8.1	1.8	9.9
Germany[a]	33.1	29.2	16.70	0.00	19.4	0.8	20.3
Norway	30.3	b	0.02	1.11	29.7	33.1	62.8
Sweden	37.5	40.9	0.77	0.29	27.5	12.9	40.5
			Total Left				
Belgium	19.1	b	1.10	0.14	1.6	15.8	17.4
Denmark	28.4	33.8	0.05	1.02	26.7	32.4	59.1
Finland	20.3	b	0.53	0.37	5.5	27.1	32.7
France	24.8	47.9	1.05	0.63	12.0	12.3	24.3
Germany	33.3	38.9	1.41	0.63	17.6	11.1	28.7
Norway	30.3	b	0.27	2.80	17.2	48.1	65.3
Sweden	37.5	40.9	0.53	0.24	33.2	8.3	41.4

[a] Class structure and carrying capacities are for 1933; parameters are for the pre-1933 period.
[b] No exact information available, see Appendix: The Data for details.

from the class structure—there were more workers in Germany in 1933 than in Denmark or Norway in 1970 and more allies in France than anywhere else. This difference seems due mainly to the intensity of the electoral trade-offs confronting particular parties when they embark on a quest for middle-class support.

The cross-national differences for the Left as a whole are again more difficult to explain. In those countries where unions are large, concentrated, and centralized, and where no other parties appeal to workers on particularistic bases, the Left confronts milder trade-offs when it engages in the pursuit of middle-class votes. But here party strategies seem to account for some of the cross-national differences. The trade-off faced by the Danish Left was weaker than that confronted by the Left in Norway, and yet the carrying capacity in the electorate is higher in the latter country. The reason is that the Left in Denmark seems to have been more concerned about class. The same is true of Sweden, where the Left appears to be highly concerned about class composition, and as a result the carrying capacity is quite low given the relatively mild trade-off.

Thus, whether or not the stagnation of socialist voting is due to the trade-offs which the socialist and other left-wing parties encountered or to the strategies which these parties have chosen remains questionable. Was history unkind to the notion of conquering the overwhelming majority, or did socialists wish the disappointment on themselves?

Appendix to Chapter 3

The deductive reasoning in the main body of the text is based on the properties of the model given by:

$$\Delta W(t) = p[X(t + 1) - W(t)] - dN(t), \qquad (3A.1)$$

$$\Delta N(t) = q[L(t + 1) - N(t)] + c[kW(t) - N(t)], \qquad (3A.2)$$
and

$$W(t) + N(t) = Y(t) \qquad (3A.3)$$

where $W(t)$ is the proportion of the electorate composed of socialist voting workers, $N(t)$ is the proportion of the electorate composed of socialist voting nonworkers, $Y(t)$ is the proportion of the electorate voting socialist, $X(t)$ is the proportion of the electorate composed of workers, $L(t)$ is the proportion of the electorate composed of allies, and $t = 0,1, \ldots$ is counted in elections.

The electorate consists of all those who have the right to vote in a particular election. This electorate is partitioned in two ways: by class and by voting behavior. In terms of class the electorate consists of workers, allies, and others, so that $X(t) + L(t) +$ Others $(t) = 1$.

In terms of voting behavior, this electorate consists of people who vote for left-wing parties (or the major socialist party, depending on the analysis to be conducted) and people who either vote for other parties or do not vote at all. In turn, left-wing (or socialist) voters are distinguished by class between socialist voting workers and allies. Thus, the electorate is partitioned as follows:

$$W(t) + N(t) + \text{Others}(t) + \text{Everyone who does}$$
$$\text{not vote socialist}(t) = 1.$$

A graph may be helpful as a reference:

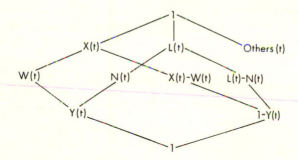

The system given by (3A.1) through (3A.3) can be rewritten for each of the state variables $W(t)$, $N(t)$, $Y(t)$ as

$$Z(t + 2) + BZ(t + 1) + CZ(t) = f(t), \qquad (3A.4)$$

where Z stands for any of the state variables, $W, N,$ or $Y; B = -(2 - p - q - c); C = (1 - p)(1 - q - c) + cdk,$ and $f(t)$ is a function of $X(t)$ and $L(t)$, different for each state variable W, N, Y.

Equation (3A.4) represents a second order linear difference

equation with constant coefficients (Goldberg 1958). The homogeneous solution to this equation is given by

$$Z(t) = C_1(m_1)^t + C_2(m_2)^t, \qquad (3A.5)$$

where the roots m_1 and m_2, real or complex, are given by

$$m_{1,2} = \frac{(2 - p - q - c) \pm [(p - q - c)^2 - 4cdk)]^{1/2}}{2},$$

and C_1 and C_2 are constants to be determined by the initial conditions $W(0)$ and $N(0)$ for each of the state variables W, N, Y.

Note that the roots are the same for all the three variables W,
N, Y, but the constants by which they are weighted are different
since they depend differently on $W(0)$ and $N(0)$.

The system given by (3A.1) through (3A.3) is stable, that is,
all three vote shares converge over time to some values if neither
root is larger than 1 in absolute value. It can easily be shown that
as long as all the parameters are nonnegative, this condition will
be satisfied for real roots. In turn, all the parameters other than d
are restricted to be nonnegative for theoretical or descriptive reasons while the parameter d, which could have conceivably been
negative, is positive in all cases. Thus if the system has real roots
then it is stable.

The equilibrium values to which this system converges from
any initial conditions $W(0)$, $N(0)$ are obtained by setting $\Delta W(t) = \Delta N(t) = 0$ and solving for W^*, N^*. These values are:

$$W^* = X - (d/p)N^*, \qquad (3A.6)$$

$$N^* = qL/(q + c) + ckW^*/(q + c). \qquad (3A.7)$$

Since X and L change over time, the time path of these equilibria
will depend on the values of parameters and the exogenous variables $X(t)$, $L(t)$. Solving (3A.6) through (3A.7) to obtain the explicit dependence yields:

$$W^*(t) = \frac{p(q + c)}{p(q + c) + cdk} X(t) - \frac{dq}{p(q + c) + cdk} L(t), \quad (3A.8)$$

and

$$N^*(t) = \frac{pq}{p(q + c) + cdk} L(t) + \frac{ckp}{p(q + c) + cdk} X(t). \quad (3A.9)$$

As the proportion of workers in the electorate falls, both W^* and N^* fall; as the proportion of allies augments, W^* falls and N^* increases.

Finally, the values of the trade-offs presented in table 3.1 are the successive derivatives $\partial W(t + h)/\partial N(t)$. It can be shown that

$$\frac{\partial W(t + h)}{\partial N(t)} = -d\frac{m_1^h - m_2^h}{m_1 - m_2}, \qquad (3A.10)$$

where m_1, m_2 are the roots given by (3A.5). These derivatives show the change in $W(t + h)$ due to an infinitesimal change in $N(t)$, h elections earlier, $h = 0,1,\ldots$. Given the lag structure of the model, $\partial W(t)/\partial N(t) = 0$, $\partial W(t + 1)/\partial N(t) = -d$, $\partial W(t + h)/\partial N(t) < -d$ for a few subsequent elections, and eventually this derivative tends to zero. The sum of all such derivatives, that is, the cumulative shift of the time path of workers' socialist vote due to an infinitesimal change in the allies' vote at t, is given by:

$$\sum_{h=1}^{\infty} \frac{\partial W(t + h)}{\partial N(t)} = \frac{-d}{p(q + c) - cdk}. \qquad (3A.11)$$

Note that this measure of trade-off is ahistorical; it depends only on h but not t. If the proportion of socialist voting allies changes infinitesimally at any time, then the consequences for the subsequent vote of workers will be those given by (3A.10) and (3A.11). The actual cost a party pays is $dN(t)$ and this cost depends on the strategies which this party did in fact follow in all the elections preceding t. The trade-off values given by (3A.10) represent therefore the costs facing the party if at any time it would embark upon the recruitment of allies, rather than the costs the party did actually suffer.

4

Are Socialist Leaders Vote Maximizers?

Social Democracy views historical development from the standpoint of necessity, and its own activities as a necessary link in the chain of those necessary conditions which combined make the victory of socialism inevitable.

Georgij V. Plekhanov

CHOICE AND NECESSITY

If history is not determined uniquely, if under given historical conditions men and women have some room for choice and their choices have consequences, then historical analysis cannot be limited to that unique sequence of events that happens to have transpired. A theory must rediscover opportunities that were lost, possibilities that were inherent at each junction, and alternatives that remain open.

Class structure and the intensity of the trade-off between the support of workers and allies constitute, for party leaders, conditions which, at least within a short time span, are independent of their actions. These conditions impose limits on political opportunities. But within the limits party leaders do choose, and their choices have consequences for socialist performance at the polls.

At least this is what party leaders must have thought when they fought over the "peasant question" or when they debated whether to make any special efforts to recruit office workers. They argued over strategies, they betrayed some of their personal loyalties, they delayed some programmatic steps because they thought it was necessary for electoral success. They did experience successes as well as defeats, and in the postmortems they

often asked what was wrong with their strategies. But perhaps
they were wrong; perhaps these strategic choices were without
consequence. Perhaps it did not matter whether the party turned
for support to office employees, to the new social movements, to
workers, or to citizens. Once this possibility is considered a new
array of questions is presented.

One question concerns the range of choice that was available to
party leaders at particular historical moments. This is a question
about historical determination, about the degree to which socialist
electoral performance was shaped by forces independent of anyone's will. In a world in which socialist parties are just a necessary link in the chain of necessary conditions, political behavior is
determined by class position, and the history of socialist electoral
performance is reduced to the history of class structure. But one
does not have to reach the extremes of social democratic
Hegelianism to find deterministic views of history. Indeed, as
Goldthorpe et al. (1969:17) were perhaps the first to observe, today it is those who argue against marxist empirical assertions who
tend to be economic determinists. "Embourgeoisement" and
"deradicalization" are as inevitable, according to many contemporary social scientists, as the victory of socialism was to
Plekhanov. "Economic development," to cite an influential
book, "producing increased income, greater economic security,
and widespread higher education, largely determines the form of
'class struggle', by permitting those in the lower strata to develop
longer time perspectives and more complex and gradualistic
views of politics" (Lipset 1963:45). There is no room for choice
or strategy when the fate of "class struggle" is determined by the
irresistible economic progress of capitalism. But perhaps these
limits are not so narrow; can it be, perhaps that what leaders want,
see, and do has some effect on class struggle as well?

If leaders do have alternatives, the question becomes whether
or not they did exploit the opportunities presented by these
choices. While analyzing the causes of the stagnation of the socialist vote we assumed that leaders of left-wing parties are not
indifferent to the class composition of their electoral support. But
perhaps this assumption is false: perhaps leaders of the parties we
studied were in fact preoccupied exclusively with winning votes,
regardless of where these would come from. Indeed, unless we
know what the party leaders were able to do, we cannot even

judge whether the strategies they have chosen were those that would have maximized the vote or those that would preserve support from workers.

Are socialist leaders vote maximizers? Or are they driven by an autonomous concern with class, a concern that restricts their willingness to compete for votes? And if they did not seek to maximize the socialist share of the electorate, how costly was it to their electoral performance? How much better could socialist parties have performed in elections if their leaders were concerned exclusively with electoral success and all it brings? Have socialist parties missed historic opportunities, moments when people in general were ready to give their support to socialism if only socialist parties had been willing to abandon their working-class roots?

THE REALM OF CHOICE

To answer such questions we need some instruments of analysis. Let us look at party strategies again, but instead of taking the criterion of class composition, k, to be fixed once and for all for each party, assume now that party leaders are free to choose a new criterion at any and every election. Having recovered from the last campaign, socialist leaders meet to decide what strategy of electoral recruitment to follow in the next round. First they choose the criterion of class composition to be observed in the next electoral campaign—they pick a number $k(t)$ which is the value they attach to the votes of allies as compared to the votes of workers. They can pick a low value of k, opting for the support of workers, or they can decide on a high k, indicating their concern over middle-class support. Once having decided what they want to achieve, leaders compare the criterion they chose with the actual composition of their electorate. As before, if they discover that there are enough workers in the socialist electorate—the difference $k(t)W(t) - N(t)$ is positive—they orient their efforts toward the recruitment of allies. If this difference is negative they turn to workers, with the effect of reducing their recruitment of allies. Thus the choice of a strategy to be followed for the next election involves two steps which are at least analytically distinct: a choice of a criterion for the class composition and a comparison of the desired with the actual state of affairs. But we will now focus only on the choice of the criterion $k(t)$ and we will use the word "strategy" to refer to the chosen values of $k(t)$.

Parties can try to mobilize workers, allies, or both. They can follow a strategy of maintaining the proletarian outlook, addressing all the efforts and appeals to workers, emphasizing their distinctiveness and their conflict with other groups. In the extreme, a party may seek to keep its electorate free of the "petty bourgeois element." Such a party would seek to maximize the proportion of workers in its electorate, or the ratio $W/(W + N)$. It would pick a value of k, which we will call k^c, for "class-only," that would have the effect of maximizing this ratio for the next election. But since to maximize the proportion of workers in the electorate is to reduce the ranks of nonworking class supporters, $k^c(t)$ can be defined as the criterion of class composition that would dissuade all nonworkers from voting for the party if party strategies were perfectly effective. Hence, $k^c(t)$ would be a number which would satisfy at the time of the tth election the criterion that

$$\Delta N(t) = -N(t), \text{ when } c = 1. \tag{4.1}$$

Alternatively, parties may devote all of their efforts to the recruitment of nonworkers. They would address themselves to the whole of society; they would portray themselves as "the party of the small and the many," they would appeal to the rural population by emphasizing existing inequalities; to small businessmen by attacking big business and finance; to fishermen by blaming big finance again; to white-collar workers by emphasizing the deep-seated clash of interests between employees and employers; to young people by advocating democratization of education and even of military services; to Christians by stressing cooperation and solidarity as virtues of the good society. This description is based almost verbatim on the summary by Sainsbury (1980:107) of the Swedish Social Democrats' campaign of 1946 (see also pages 74–76 for 1944 and 140–41 for 1948). In the extreme, a party may choose a strategy which, if perfectly effective, would result in the recruitment of all allies during the next election. Such a party would choose a value of k which we will call k^s, for "supraclass," which would satisfy the criterion that

$$\Delta N(t) = L(t + 1) - N(t), \text{ when } c = 1. \tag{4.2}$$

If party leaders choose $k^s(t)$, it means that they want to recruit all the allies who do not yet vote socialist into the ranks of the socialist electorate.

The strategies defined as pure "class-only" and pure "supraclass" are the most extreme courses of action on which any party can embark at a particular time. Pure supraclass strategy is defined by the criterion of recruiting all the allies in a perfectly noncompetitive environment; the pure class-only strategy is defined by the criterion of recruiting all the workers when party strategy is perfectly effective. A party cannot recruit more than all the allies or more than all the workers, at least outside Chicago and in that city socialist parties are not very strong. Naturally a party may choose, at any time, a strategy that lies between these pure extremes by picking a value of k such that $k^c < k < k^s$. It may address itself to white-collar employees, farmers, small businessmen, persons with small incomes, and apartment tenants promising to defend their economic and social freedom, but at the same time the party may find a different language for workers. According to Sainsbury (1980:140–41), in the 1948 campaign of the SAP, "The main ideological theme in the appeal to the workers involved neither a statement of goals nor means. Rather the appeal emphasized divisions of class and wealth in society and bordered on invoking the class struggle. The appeal addressed labor as the working class. . . ."

If party strategies are at all effective, then the courses of action chosen by leaders have consequences for the future electoral support parties may draw from workers, nonworkers, and the electorate as a whole. If a party chooses after the tth election to embark on a pure supraclass strategy for the next round, then during the ($t + 1$)st election that party will win $Y^s(t + 1)$ percent of the electorate, $N^s(t + 1)$ from allies and $W^s(t + 1)$ from workers. If a party chooses class purity as its strategic objective, then during the next election it would win $Y^c(t + 1)$ percent of the electorate, of which $N^c(t + 1)$ comes from allies and $W^c(t + 1)$ from workers.

Now, we already know that k^s and k^c are the extreme strategies a party can adopt. It happens to be also true that the vote shares in the electorate, Y^s and Y^c will be the largest and the smallest possible (not necessarily in this order) under these assumptions. Hence the difference $D = Y^s - Y^c$, whether positive or negative, is the range within which a party can affect its electoral performance by choosing strategies k. This is then the realm of choice; the difference that is in principle available; the range of historical opportunity.

Thus at any time t a party can make a difference of $D(1) = Y^s(t + 1) - Y^c(t + 1)$ for the next election. But suppose that once a party settled on a strategy it follows this strategy indefinitely. Then again one of the extreme strategies will be electorally the best and the other one the worst after any number of elections. The greatest difference a particular party can make by the time of the $(t + h)$th election by having chosen its strategy after the tth election and following this same strategy faithfully, will be again $D(h) = Y^s(t + h) - Y^c(t + h)$, the difference between the two pure strategies.

Finally, under our assumptions, we know that if a party settles on a strategy and pursues it repeatedly, its share of the vote will eventually stabilize and become a function only of class structure. If the strategic choice is to seek votes of the middle class, then the carrying capacity of the party in the electorate will be Y^*_s; if the party prefers to keep its electorate class pure, its carrying capacity in the electorate will be Y^*_c. These carrying capacities represent as before the proportions of the electorate a party can recruit and hold. Since it is again true that one of the pure strategies will maximize and the other one will minimize the carrying capacities, the difference between them, $D^* = Y^*_s - Y^*_c$ shows the range within which a party can affect its long-term electoral future.

To recapitulate, during each election party leaders face a choice of strategies. The extreme directions they can opt for are the pure supraclass and pure class-only strategies. These are the strategies that would, respectively, lead the party to recruit all the allies or all the workers in a perfectly noncompetitive environment. Each strategic choice affects the subsequent shares of the vote the party obtains from workers, from nonworkers, and the electorate as a whole. The difference between the shares resulting from pursuing pure strategies is the range of choice that a party faces when it decides which course of action to adopt.

Suppose then that after the tth election a party chooses the supraclass strategy and continues to adhere to it in the future and compare the share of the electorate the party would win in this manner with the share it would have won had it pursued, with equal persistence, strategies designed to keep the electorate class-pure. If party strategies are at all effective, then the choice of the

supraclass strategy after the *t*th election will give the party in the
next election some more votes, exactly $cL(t + 1)$, than would the
class-only strategy. But as time goes on a number of consequences may ensue: (1) the difference between the vote shares
associated with the supraclass and the class-only strategy can
grow forever (case A in fig. 4.1 and table 4.1); (2) this difference
can reach a maximum and then decline, the permanent gain being
larger than the initial one (case B); (3) the difference can reach a
maximum and decline below the initial gain (case C); and finally
(4) the supraclass strategy may turn out to be perverse after some
time and the party may end up electorally worse off than it would
have been had it persistently pursued the class-only strategy.

If our numbers are at all reliable, a caveat we do not repeat
only to avoid repetitiousness, then for the Left in Belgium and in
France strategic choices made almost no difference in the long

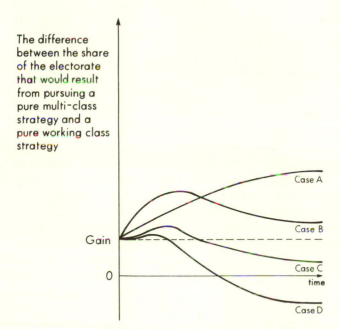

Figure 4.1 Analytically Distinguished Typical Cases of Long-term Consequences
of Pursuing Pure Strategies: The Time Path of the Difference in the Shares of
the Electorate That Would Result from Pursuing Pure Strategies in Every
Election

Table 4.1 Long-term Differences between Vote Shares Resulting
from Supraclass and Class-pure Strategies, Recent Class Structure

Country	Number of Elections during Which Difference Will Increase	Number of Elections When Difference Will Equal Zero	Long-term Difference[a]
	Total Left		
Belgium	2	19	−0.2
Denmark	99	never	7.0
Finland	always	never	5.7
France	9	36	−0.9
Germany	7	21	−9.8
Norway	12	never	50.7
Sweden	14	never	17.6
	Socialists Only		
Denmark	7	never	29.2
Finland	5	32	−1.9
France	1	2	−22.1
Germany	1	1	−13.0
Norway	31	never	68.4
Sweden	6	never	7.3

[a] Difference is calculated as $Y^s - Y^c$. Hence positive sign indicates that supraclass strategy is superior in the long run.

run. The long-run difference in both countries is less than one percent of the electorate. In Finland, Denmark, and Germany, the Left as a whole could have done better or worse depending on the strategic choices, but the margin is less than 10 percent of the electorate. In Sweden and particularly in Norway, the choice was wide open to the Left. If the Swedish or the Norwegian leaders had opted for one or another pure strategy from the time they entered into elections and if they had pursued this strategy persistently ever since, they would have engineered a sizable difference in their vote. Looking at particular parties, we find the Finnish and the Swedish Social Democrats to have been quite constrained while other parties, again notably the Norwegian Labour Party, enjoyed a wide margin of choice. Outside of Norway not everything was possible but most parties did have some difference to make in the long run. If they had tried to win votes, it was in their power to do better or worse.

But elections are not a goal in themselves and the stakes are not simply "winning" or "losing." Political mandates are much more continuously dependent on election results than notions of winning coalitions often presuppose. At least when we think of major social transformations, Berlinguer (1973) understands mandates better than Riker (1962). Such transformations require an overwhelming mandate and every additional vote counts, even those that are 50% plus two. Thus the strategic choice that was available to the Danish and Norwegian Social Democrats seems particularly important. As a preliminary glance at table 4.2 will indicate, these two parties could have conquered a large part of the electorate if they had entered on the path of a pure supraclass strategy from the beginning. But other parties also had a political difference to make. The Swedish Social Democrats had a choice between a strategy that would keep them almost permanently in office and one that would not. This is not an unimportant difference, as Martin (1975) has shown. The French Socialists and the pre-1933 German Social Democrats faced a less attractive alternative since for them the strategy choice was a matter of electoral survival. Thus the electoral choices translated into different political alternatives in different countries. In some they involved electoral survival of the party, in some they held the stake of control over the government, in yet others they represented an opportunity for winning an overwhelming popular mandate. But in general, electoral strategies mattered. Party leaders did have some difference to make. Their strategies had consequences and these consequences, although not unlimited, were politically, not only electorally, important.

Vote Maximizing Strategies

What should socialist leaders have done if they had wanted to win as many votes as possible, regardless of all other considerations? The obvious answer turns out to be electorally risky. Turning for support to nonworkers would not have been always advantageous from the purely electoral point of view. From Michels' observation in 1915 onward, interpreters tend to assume that socialist parties are always better off electorally if they turn for support to the middle-class electorate. But there exist conditions under which the pure class-only strategy would deliver more votes than any degree of flirtation with people other than workers.

Table 4.2 Comparison of Carrying Capabilities Associated with the Actual, Supraclass, and Class-only Strategies—1970 Class Structure

Strategy: Country	Actual[a] Carrying Capacity	Actual[a] Workers/ Socialist Voters[c]	Limited Supraclass Carrying Capacity	Limited Supraclass Workers/ Socialist Voters[c]	Full Supraclass [d]	Class-only[b] Carrying Capacity
			Total Left			
Belgium	17.4	87.8	17.3	0	max	17.5
Denmark	59.1	49.5	60.4	44.0		53.4
Finland	32.7	73.0	37.7	0	max	32.0
France	24.2	61.3	23.7	0	max	24.6
Germany	28.5	61.4	23.6	0	max	33.3
Norway	65.3	26.3	81.0	14.1		30.3
Sweden	42.5	80.7	56.3	33.5		37.8
			Socialists Only			
Denmark	38.0	72.5	57.6	41.4		28.4
Finland	15.6	80.0	14.1	0	max	16.0
France	9.9	81.8	2.7	0	max	24.8
Germany[e]	15.0	100.0	2.0	0	max	15.0
Norway	62.8	47.3	98.7	29.4		30.3
Sweden	41.4	77.6	47.1	20.6		39.8

[a] Actual strategy is the strategy estimated to best fit the model.

[b] In the case of the class-only strategy, the desired proportion of workers among socialist voters is always 100 percent.

[c] This is more precisely the proportion of workers among socialist voters which would result from following the particular strategy.

[d] A max in this column indicates that the allies are more numerous than the proportion of the electorate a party can win with either the limited supraclass or class-only strategies.

[e] As of 1933.

Since we are considering counterfactuals, assumptions become very important. One can think in more than one way about the possibilities that were open to socialists. Analyzing their actual behavior, we assumed that socialist leaders would be willing to turn for support to nonworkers only to the extent to which they enjoy support among workers. They did choose strategies by deciding the relative emphasis they would place on the recruitment of nonworkers, but their efforts with regard to allies were thought throughout to bear at least some relation to their success among workers. If we continue to think in this fashion, we will conclude that socialist recruitment of the middle-class must stop at least at the point when no workers whatsoever vote for the party. The differences shown in table 4.1 and the carrying capacities associated with the "limited supraclass strategy" in table 4.2 are based on this assumption, namely that the recruitment of nonworkers is limited by the support the party obtains from workers and stops when the socialist vote of workers dwindles to nothing.

If we assume that the mobilization of allies is limited by success among workers, then a pure class-only strategy is best in winning votes as long as the party faces a steep equilibrium trade-off, specifically, as long as $(d/p) > 1$. This is not a surprise—for each additional middle-class voter, the party loses (d/p) working-class voters in equilibrium. Thus if $d/p > 1$, the party loses net votes by turning for support to the nonworkers. But if the trade-off is milder, $d/p < 1$, the party is best off following a pure supraclass strategy, all the way to the point where no workers vote socialist, if necessary. Moreover, this result concerns not only the share the party can recruit and hold in the long run. The same will be true if party leaders seek to win as many votes as possible during all elections, from now onward, by following a persistent strategy. They will again discover that the supraclass strategy is indeed the one that gives them the most votes if the trade-off they face is mild.

Since socialist parties faced constraints other than those which we are now discussing—constraints that originated both from the class background of their militants and from their mutual dependence upon trade unions—the notion that socialist leaders could go as far in their strategy choice as to generate an electorate without workers seems indeed counterfactual. But if we are willing to ignore some actual historical conditions, and particularly if we want to examine the alternatives that face left-wing parties today, as they make strategic choices for the future, then there is no reason to maintain that socialists could not abandon their attachments to workers as a class altogether. If party leaders want to maximize their share of the vote regardless of where these votes come from, they would not condition their strategies on the support given by workers. If they could win more votes by abandoning any considerations of class in their organizational practice and in their discourse, they would do so. And then the carrying capacity associated with the supraclass strategies may be as large as the proportion of those nonworkers who are conceivably vulnerable to the socialist appeal.

Which strategy is best when socialist leaders are willing to abandon considerations of class altogether depends on class structure as well as the intensity of the trade-off. As long as the ratio of workers to allies in the electorate is larger than the trade-off, $X/L > d/p,$ the party is best off pursuing a class-only strategy if the trade-off is steeper than 1 and best off with a supraclass strategy if the trade-off is milder. But if there are more allies than workers in the electorate and if party strategies are somewhat effective in recruiting allies, the party may be electorally best off to seek middle-class voters even if the trade-off is very steep.

Table 4.2 shows carrying capacities associated with the strategies that best reconstruct the actual experience of socialist voting compared with the carrying capacities that would have resulted from the pure supraclass and the pure class-only strategies. These numbers indicate what proportions of the electorate each major socialist party or the left-wing parties together would be able to recruit and hold if the class structure were frozen at its 1970 levels. The column associated with the "full supraclass strategy" indicates whether the party would maximize its vote share if it pursued a strategy of mobilization of nonworkers independently of support from workers. Since such a strategy would alter the logic of socialist electoral competition, we hesitate to provide specific numbers to identify the potential pool of nonworker socialist support. Orders of magnitude are sufficient, however, to compare this strategy with the supraclass posture in which mobilization of allies is limited by the success of the party among workers. Wherever a "max" appears in the "full supraclass" column, the strategy that would involve a complete abandonment of class is electorally superior both to the limited supraclass strategy and to class-only strategy. The remaining columns in this table indicate the resulting class composition that would characterize the particular strategies—the actual strategy and the pure ones. Instead of presenting the values of k, however, we have translated these values into proportions indicating how many workers would be found among party supporters if the party adopted the particular strategy.

The Finnish, French, and the pre-1933 German major socialist parties faced an equilibrium trade-off which was steeper than unity, as did the Left as a whole in Belgium, France, and Germany. The Finnish Left faced a milder trade-off, but workers constituted only about 19 percent of the Finnish electorate in 1970. In all these cases the unlimited supraclass strategy is best electorally. In the cases where the trade-off is steep, the pure class-only strategy is second best and the supraclass strategy which limits the recruitment of allies on the success among workers is the worst. These parties thus faced a bifurcation in their road—they had to decide to abandon all concerns with class or alternatively to struggle to keep the party class pure. A half-hearted middle-class orientation was the worst from the electoral point of view. They had to decide whether to have a party in which there would be no workers or one in which there would be only workers.

In Denmark, Norway, and Sweden the limited supraclass strategy would maximize the vote. The Left as a whole and the major socialist parties in these countries would get most votes by turning for support to nonworkers and they could get this support and still retain a sizable support among workers. They did not face an all-or-nothing choice as far as class is concerned. They would have to tolerate electorates in which workers were a minority, but they could choose continuously between having more workers and fewer votes or fewer workers and more votes. In all these cases the pool of the potential middle-class supporters was, by 1970, larger than the proportion of workers in the electorate. Thus, the pure class-only strategy was electorally the worst.

WAS THE STAGNATION OF THE SOCIALIST VOTE INEVITABLE?

Within the realm of available choice, leaders of left-wing parties disappoint those who believe that their exclusive concern is, or should be, to maximize the vote. Among the parties which would maximize their vote share by abandoning workers altogether, none has accepted this option. This is not surprising given all we know about the view of the future with which socialist leaders analyzed their choices eighty years ago. Most of them certainly did not expect that the strategy that would require abandoning the proletariat altogether would eventually be the one that would win the most votes. Bernstein had the correct intuition but, as we have seen, there was in fact little empirical support for his arguments. There were many more reasons why socialist leaders could not have adopted this strategy, and the fact that they did not should not be taken as the evidence that they did not want to maximize their future votes.

But the evidence against pure vote maximizing goes further. If our numbers can be believed, only the pre-1933 SPD leaders did the second best, by keeping the party as pure in terms of class as they could. The leaders of the Finnish Social Democrats had little choice and placed themselves somewhat closer to their better strategy, again the class-pure one. At least during the period under consideration, that is, until 1970, the French Socialists seem to have chosen almost the worst electoral strategy. They tried to conquer middle-class voters without losing workers and did not succeed in either. The German Left, which includes the post-war SPD, placed itself again exactly halfway between the second best strategy, which would have been class pure and the worst strategy which turned in a halfhearted way toward the middle classes.

The three Scandinavian parties for which the supraclass strategy is electorally superior, by quite a wide margin in Norway and Denmark, nevertheless have opted to pursue strategies that have kept them closer to their working-class base. To maximize votes, the Danish Social Democrats would have to tolerate an electoral support in which workers would have constituted 41.4 percent. In the light of our calculations, they have opted for a class composition in which workers would make up 72.5 percent—a strategic decision which placed them closer to the electorally inferior class-only strategy. The Norwegians would have maximized their share of the vote with an electoral base in which workers would constitute 29.4 percent; they have opted for one in which workers would make up 47.3 percent. Finally, the Swedes would have been electorally best off by bringing the workers share in their electoral support to 20.6 percent. Instead, they chose to compete with a party of which 77.6 percent of the electoral support would be from workers.

All these parties did embark on strategies designed to recruit the middle classes. Danes turned for support of peasants as early as 1888 and always kept the party open to nonworkers. Swedes made their first deliberate move to extend the electorate beyond the working class in 1911 and formalized this move in 1921. Norwegians began in the same way as the Danes, then adopted a working-class posture, but by 1933 joined the other two parties in turning to "the people" (Martin 1972:48). The Swedish party decided to turn to office employees in the late 1950s, when it embarked on the wage earners' solidarity policy. Yet our analysis indicates that none of these parties has gone even half of the way they could have to recruit the middle classes. Even the Norwegian Labour Party, which was willing to tolerate more middle- than working-class supporters in its electorate, could have gained by becoming more supraclass oriented.

At this time we must return to the causes of the stagnation of the socialist vote, for the conclusions we drew from the analysis of trade-offs are implausible. On the one hand, we argued that the social democratic parties faced a relatively mild trade-off in the three Scandinavian countries because the trade unions played an important role in organizing workers as a class. But we passed over, on the other hand, numbers that might have been seen as showing that these parties are quite free from any attachment to the working class when they choose electoral strategies. The actual values of the criterion of class composition, k, with which parties chose strategies, were higher for the Danish and Norwegian Left and for the Social Democrats than for the other parties. Thus it might have seemed as if the Scandinavian Left benefited from their symbiotic relation with the unions without being at all constrained by them. This would have been the best of all possible worlds.

We see now, having analyzed the alternatives that were open, that social democratic leaders in these countries pursued strategies which were in fact far from optimal from the purely electoral point of view. In Denmark, Norway, and Sweden, the Social Democrats could have permanently conquered a majority of the electorate—all those who had the right to vote—and repeatedly won elections with an overwhelming majority if they had only embarked from the beginning and persevered unswervingly in a strategy of electoral recruitment that would distance them permanently from workers as a class. Just examine figure 4.2 which compares the share of the vote the Danish and the Swedish Social Democrats could have obtained with the actual historical record of their electoral performance. And yet neither the Norwegians, nor the Danes, nor the Swedes did pursue the course of action that would have been most successful in winning elections at the cost of abandoning the working class.

The reason why these parties could have made this much of a difference by following supraclass strategies is that they faced relatively mild trade-offs among workers when they diluted the emphasis on class in their organization and propaganda. But the reason, at least in part, why the abandonment of class by these parties would have had relatively little effect on the voting behavior of workers was that workers were organized as a class by large, concentrated, and centralized unions. And here the circle closes rather viciously, for it is precisely because of their interdependence with the unions that Social Democrats in Denmark, Norway, and Sweden could not adopt strategies that would have maximized their vote.

Since their foundation, all three parties were closely related to the unions. Indeed, before 1900 the two organizations were almost indistinguishable, particularly at the local level. While the Danish party had already abolished collective membership in the 1870s, in Norway and particularly in Sweden the collective membership of union members in the party continued to be important. As of 1974, 40 percent of the membership of the Norwegian Labour Party and 73 percent of the Swedish SAP consisted of union members affiliated collectively. Unions provided, however, not only members but also finances for electoral campaigns. The leadership of the unions and parties often overlapped, and in Denmark several union leaders became Social Democratic prime ministers (see Elvander 1979; Esping-Anderson 1985).

Unions are necessarily class organizations, in two senses of this term. Their potential membership is defined only in class terms; unions are not and cannot become organizations of Catholics, women, or citizens; they can associate only workers or at most wage earners. Hence their constituency is necessarily more restricted than that of electoral parties for whom the ultimate pool

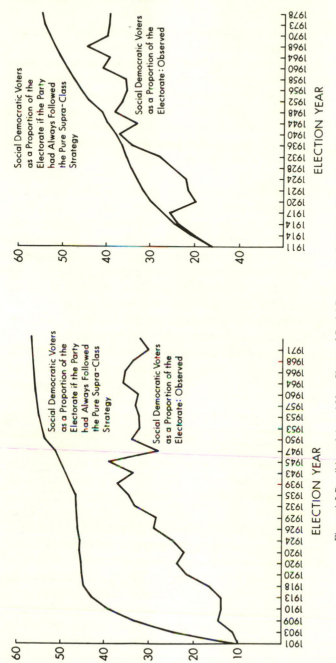

Figure 4.2 Possible and Actual Vote Shares of Social Democratic Parties in Denmark and Sweden

of support consists simply of citizens, whoever they may be otherwise. But perhaps more importantly unions are organizations
whose principal task is to protect their members from competition
with one another; to prevent workers from bidding their wages
down in exchange for employment. And this means that the union
organization constitutes a collective good only for those people
who may conceivably find themselves in competition for the same
kinds of employment, not for everyone. Thus unions represent
interests narrower than those that can be organized by political
parties.

The trade unions in Scandinavia often resisted the adoption of
supraclass strategies (Hentilä 1978:331–32; Scase 1977:323; Elvander 1979:18). Heidar reported (1977:300) that in Norway
there were "strong counterforces to this process of breakdown in
the 'organic' link between party and class. In the forefront here is
the trade union movement which is still a potent force in resisting
the trend towards a purer political mandate for the working-class
vote." Martin (1972:15, 168ff) showed that most leaders of the
Norwegian Labour Party had thought that if the party were to
actively pursue the white-collar electorate it would have had to
weaken its organizational ties to the trade unions, specifically, to
abolish collective affiliation.

Belgium, Finland, France, and at least the pre-1933 Germany,
on the one hand, and Denmark, Norway, and Sweden, on the other
hand, constitute two different types of situations. In the first group
of countries unions did not remove the burden of organizing workers as a class from the shoulders of political parties. They did not
play this role because they were apolitical, or because they were
politically fractionalized, or because they were organizationally
decentralized, but they could not and did not. The result was that
class ideology and class organization were highly vulnerable to
socialist electoral strategies. The electoral trade-off the left wing
parties encountered in these countries was so steep that any major
turn for support to the middle classes would have been disastrous
for their vote-getting power. The best the Left could have done
from the purely electoral point of view was indeed to abandon the
working-class electorate altogether, but that option was not feasible for reasons of ideology as well as for fear that the union movement would become completely independent and apolitical
(Schorske 1972; Gay 1970:136–37; Fiechtier 1965:148–52). In-

deed in 1925 when the SPD drafted a program which asserted that "the struggle of the working class against capitalist exploitation is necessarily a political struggle," party leaders were soon taught by the ADGB that it is "not only an economic one, but also necessarily a political struggle" (Hunt 1970:175–76). And the second best option—a pristinely *ouvrierist* stance—was not good enough to win majorities and mandates because the development of the "great industry" turned out to be much less labor-intensive than socialists had expected and workers never became the majority.

The Danes, Norwegians, and Swedes were in a different predicament. The trade unions in these countries grew rapidly and unified at an early stage. Class relations became institutionalized by a nationwide collective bargaining system. As a result, Social Democrats in these countries could pursue middle-class oriented strategies at a tolerable or even negligible cost. But that very same partner which took from the parties most of the burden of organizing workers as a class imposed constraints on the degree to which these parties could freely pursue their electoral opportunities.

ARE SOCIALIST LEADERS VOTE MAXIMIZERS?

The interdependence between socialist parties and trade unions is not the sole constraint which binds strategic alternatives. Internal relations within each party are likely to provide another constraint. Party members may have preferences distinct from party leaders and leaders may be unable to wage campaigns which do not have the support of members. Many people become party activists because they have strong beliefs about issues and such militants may be unwilling to follow the leaders in an opportunistic pursuit of votes. Unfortunately, while Schorske's (1972) study of the SPD between 1905 and 1917 highlighted the tension between party leaders and the rank and file, we could not find direct evidence of members' resistance to leaders' electoral strategies. We remain persuaded, nevertheless, that internal relations within the party must restrict the strategic freedom of the leadership.

Thus the issue is not whether leaders of electoral parties seek to maximize the vote or follow ideologies. Leaders of electoral parties prefer to win more votes rather than fewer: this we do not doubt. The question is under what constraints they maximize votes, and the issue may be at most whether there is any room for choice left after all the constraints are considered. To ignore such constraints, to assume that party leaders can pick any strategy, address themselves to any group with any program, reduces the study of parties and elections to empty formalisms. To conclude that party leaders who do not maximize must be victims of the irrationalism of ideology is to forget how many obstacles stand in the way of those who would very much like to win elections.

One of these obstacles is intertemporal. Once we look at party strategies in historical perspective, as a process, we cannot view each election as an event that had no antecedents and would have no subsequent consequences. We must understand how the past choices have shaped the current alternatives, and we must ask how far into the future party leaders look when they examine the eventual consequences of their strategic choices.

The analysis of long-term consequences placed an unfair burden on party leaders. The question we asked above was whether leaders of left-wing parties sought to maximize the vote in the long run, trying to get as many votes as possible in all future elections, from now to eternity. But while the Catholic Church is perhaps able to see the future in millennia and Communist ideologues were able to think in centuries, it is unreasonable to expect leaders of electoral parties to pay much attention to anything but the proximate future. Politicians who maximize for the long run end up writing memoirs within a very short one, even socialist politicians. We should ask, therefore, whether party leaders tried to win all the votes they could in the proximate elections, regardless of the consequences the particular strategy might have for the longer run.

Two parties are particularly interesting since they represent the clearest contrast, although each is representative of others in the same situation. The Swedish Social Democrats, as well as the Danish Social Democrats and the Norwegian Labour Party, could have improved voting performance by adopting a strategy that would distance them further from the working class. The French Socialists, as well as the Social Democrats in pre-1933 Germany, were in a situation in which their best strategy was to break all ties with the working class. Their second best strategy, however, was to maintain the electorate pristinely pure in terms of class, and the SPD did all it could in this direction. But the French Socialist Party adopted a strategy of mixing appeals to workers with the

organization of the middle classes and the effect was quite subop-
timal electorally.

These were the conclusions of the analysis of long-run maximizing. But the consequences of the different conditions these
two parties faced during their electoral histories manifest themselves also in the short run. Figure 4.3 shows what would have
been the consequences if the French Socialists and the Swedish
Social Democrats chose, at any moment, either of the pure strategies and followed this strategy during just two consecutive elections. The point of origin—the bigger dots—at each election time
represents the vote share which the party had actually obtained.
The two lines which originate from each point represent the vote
shares the party would have obtained had it adopted at the time the
pure supraclass and the pure class-only strategy. For example, the
French Socialist Party won 10.1 percent of the electorate in the
1962 elections. Had the Socialists adopted at this moment the
pure supraclass strategy, they would have gained 15.5 percent in
the 1967 elections. Had they persevered with the same strategy
for the 1968 elections, they would have won the votes of 8.9
percent of the electorate. In turn, if the Socialists had opted for the
pure class-only strategy, they would have obtained 13.3 percent
in 1967 and 13.5 in 1968.

The analysis of alternatives available in the short run to the
leaders of the Swedish Social Democratic Party confirms the conclusions derived from the long-run analysis. At each moment of
history, Social Democrats would have improved their electoral
performance by embracing a pure supraclass strategy. Until the
battle for universal male suffrage, about 1905, the trade unions
resisted any opening on the part of the Social Democrats (Hentilä
1978:331–32). But having learned about the importance of alliances, the party gingerly opened its ranks in 1911, when it
changed the clause by which it identified itself from the working
class to "all the oppressed" (Tingsten 1973). Nevertheless, this
first strategic turn was far from a pure supraclass strategy. Had the
party gone the full way in its appeal to the middle classes, it
would have won in the two successive elections of 1914 first 25.3
and then 32.9 percent of the electorate, instead of the 20.9 and
23.9 percent it did win. Since the party would have obtained 19.4
and 20.5 percent with the pure class-only strategy, the 1911 turn
to the middle classes seems halfhearted indeed. The quest for

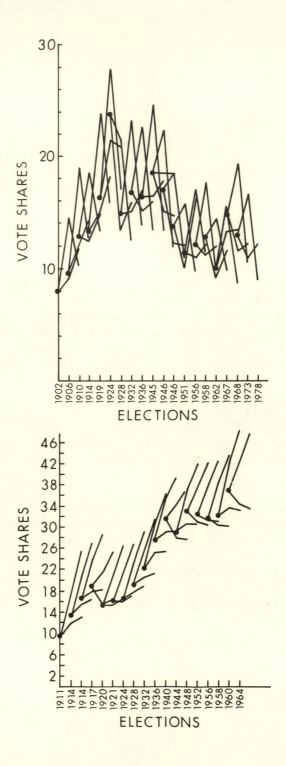

VOTE SHARES

1902 1906 1910 1914 1919 1924 1928 1932 1936 1945 1946 1951 1956 1958 1962 1967 1968 1973 1978

ELECTIONS

VOTE SHARES

1911 1914 1914 1917 1920 1921 1924 1928 1932 1936 1940 1944 1948 1952 1956 1958 1960 1964

ELECTIONS

middle-class voters was extended in 1921 after Social Democrats had suffered their first electoral reversal and formed the first minority government. But again the strategy adopted in 1921 was far from the pure supraclass orientation—unreserved pursuit of the middle-class electorate would have resulted in a share of 26.8 percent in 1924 and 32.7 percent in 1928, a pure working-class stance would have brought 21.2 percent in 1924 and 23.1 in 1928, while in fact that party won 21.7 and 24.9 percent in these two elections. Even the wage-earner campaign of the late 1950s did not constitute a vote maximizing strategy. Had the party embarked upon such a strategy in 1958, it would have won 46.4 percent in 1960 and 51.9 percent in 1964. In fact, it won respectively 40.9 and 39.4 percent of the electorate, still closer to the pure class-only and electorally inferior strategy which would have brought 37.8 percent by 1960 and 36.8 percent by 1964.

This analysis merely confirms, therefore, the conclusions derived from the examination of the strategies oriented toward long-run objectives. A similar dissection of the behavior of the Danish Social Democracy and the Norwegian Labour Party would have brought the same results. In these countries, as table 4.1 has already shown, there is no intertemporal trade-off between that which is best in the short and in the long run. Supraclass strategies are electorally superior in the short run and the longer a party perseveres the more votes it would win. If party leaders did not opt for the vote maximizing supraclass strategies, it is because they cared about the class orientation of the party, not only about votes.

The notion that party leaders seek to maximize votes for votes' sake is not only ad hoc, but it also conjures a strange world in which everyone derives utility from consumption until and unless they become leaders of electoral parties (Hirschleifer 1976; Pizzorno 1983). Our evidence demonstrates that even when socialist parties could indefinitely increase their vote shares by mov-

Figure 4.3 The Choices Facing French Socialists and Swedish Social Democrats

The dots represent the estimated vote share. The lines originating from them at each time represent the vote shares the party would have obtained had it followed pure strategies during the two next elections. Vote shares as a proportion of the electorate.

ing away from their working-class roots, socialist leaders had other reasons to care about the class orientation of their parties. Hence our analysis joins the line of empirical findings which support the assumption that party leaders maximize the expected utility rather than votes (see Wittman 1983, for a recent review). Votes are worth only as much as the mandates they embody.

The French socialists always have been in a much tighter spot. Note in figure 4.3 that the limited supraclass strategy invariably became electorally inferior within the span of two elections. The party could always improve its electoral performance in the next election by moving toward the middle-class electorate, but during every moment of history such a move would have had perverse effects if it lasted two consecutive elections. Until 1924, before the Communist Party became a serious contender, the limited supraclass strategy was only mildly inferior after two elections. Had Socialists chosen the pure supraclass strategy in 1902, they would have suffered two elections later the loss of 1.5 percent of the electorate as compared to the result they would have had with a pure class-only strategy. Had they made this choice in 1906, after the unification, they would have foreseaken 2.3 percent two elections later, by 1914. But after the Tour Congress, the cost of the flirtation with the middle class increased. If Socialists had opted for the pure supraclass strategy in 1914, they would have received by 1924 almost 4 percent less than would have resulted from a pristinely *ouvrierist* stance. These costs continued to be high during the interwar period, but the difference between the result of the two pure strategies decreased after 1945. Only in 1968 did the strategic choice made two elections earlier, in 1962, matter: the difference was 4.6 percent of the electorate. And in 1978 the decisions made in 1968 could make a difference of 3.2 percent of the electorate.

While the two world wars roughly mark the periods in the strategic choices of the French socialists, the intertemporal trade-off was present during their entire electoral history. After two elections socialists would have always won more votes had they pursued working-class oriented strategies. But for the next election the supraclass strategy was always superior, and often by a sizable chunk of the electorate. In 1902 socialists could have looked forward to winning in the next election 5.5 percent more with the pure supraclass than with the pure class-only strategy; indeed they could have won 5 percent more than they did in 1906. This was probably not the time, however, to flirt with the middle classes since the pressing issues concerned the unity of the socialists themselves and their relation to the trade union movement. Decided on in 1919, the pure supraclass strategy would have made SFIO by far the most important force in the Cartel des Gauches of 1924—its share of the electorate would have been 31.7 percent, which translates to almost one half of the votes cast. Chosen in 1936, the supraclass strategy would have resulted in a significant gain by 1945. Chosen in 1967, it would have prevented the beating socialists received in 1968.

Thus the limited supraclass strategy was always superior for the next election while the class-only strategy was superior electorally for one election later. French socialists were caught between short-run maximization, which tempted them to flirt with the middle classes around 1890 and again in the 1930s and which reduced them to a party of teachers in the 1950s, and the longer-run superiority of the *ouvrierist* stance. During the interwar period, under pressure from the communists, the SFIO maintained a working-class oriented stance and even expelled the main advocate of the supraclass strategy, Marcel Deat (Touchard 1977). After the war, the party moved toward the middle-class constituency and the electoral results were rather pathetic. It is therefore significant that the newly reconstructed Socialist Party sharply improved its electoral performance after it decided, in the aftermath of the 1977 split with the PCF, to wrest hegemony over the working class from the communists (Daniel 1978).

Thus in the case of the French socialists, as well as the SPD, where strategies which maximize the vote for the next election were electorally inferior soon afterwards, it is just impossible to speak of vote maximization ahistorically. The fiction of elections as a series of unconnected events is no longer tenable. If the votes cast in each election are indeed a cumulative consequence of past strategies, then party leaders cannot every few years begin history anew, picking for their parties the strategy that would place it best electorally in a known distribution of public opinion. The assumption that public opinion is exogeneous to party strategies is absurd, whether one thinks that party leaders maximize votes (Downs 1957), substantive goals (Wittman 1973), or a mixture of both (Schlesinger 1975). Parties mold the "public opinion": they present the public with images of society, evoke collective identifications, instill political commitments. Thus the distribution of preferences parties encounter in each electoral campaign is, as Gramsci emphasized, a result of past actions; the conditions which parties encounter at the present are a product of strategies they chose in the past. And many of today's objective conditions are the errors of yesterday. Therefore, when party leaders choose strategies for the next election they must worry about the conditions they will encounter when they will be making their future strategic decisions.

The reason the socialist vote stagnated after an initial burst of growth, the reason socialist parties did not win the mandate of an overwhelming majority of the electorate, is not that party leaders were blinded by their ideology to existing electoral opportunities. The reason is that their choices were constrained. They were constrained by class-structure—the fact that workers never became a majority. They were constrained in Belgium, Finland, France, and Germany by the electoral trade-off they encountered among workers as they sought to win the votes of the middle classes. They were constrained in Denmark, Norway, and Sweden by their symbiotic relation with the organizations of workers as a class, the trade unions. They probably made strategic mistakes. People do make strategic mistakes and socialists did find it difficult to throw off the blinders imposed by the "scientific socialism" of the Second International. But these mistakes pale when placed within the context of constraints. Ultimately, it probably mattered relatively little whether socialist leaders did everything they could to win elections. Their choices were limited.

Appendix to Chapter 4

This appendix contains formal definitions and explanations of some terms used in the analysis, proofs of the more important assertions, and a discussion of alternative assumptions. Most of the material involves only elementary conceptual and algebraic operations and should be accessible to anyone who wishes to inquire more deeply into the analysis. The only section which is mathematically more difficult is the last one, concerning maximization.

The order of this appendix does not follow the body of the text. We begin by defining the pure strategies and proceed immediately to the analysis of the short tun. Only then limits are taken and the discussion concerns the carrying capacities. Two alternative models are presented subsequently to show the robustness of the results. Finally, the last section contains the proof of the assertion that vote maximizing strategies depend on the intensity of the equilibrium trade-off.

As a reference, the model is given by:

$$\Delta W(t) = p[X(t + 1) - W(t)] - dN(t), \tag{4A.1}$$

$$\Delta N(t) = q[L(t + 1) - N(t)] + c[k(t)W(t) - N(t)], \tag{4A.2}$$

$$Y(t) = W(t) + N(t). \tag{4A.3}$$

The steady-state values are (see the Appendix to chapter 3):

$$W^* = X - (d/p)N^*, \tag{4A.4}$$

$$N^* = qL/(q + c) + ckW/(q + c), \tag{4A.5}$$

$$Y^* = W^* + N^*. \tag{4A.6}$$

Pure Strategies

A pure supraclass strategy is a course of action that would result in the recruitment of all the allies in the next round of voting if party strategies were perfectly effective, that is, if parties could always get what they wanted. Thus a pure supraclass strategy at time t is defined by a number $k^s(t)$ such that

$$N(t + 1) = L(t + 1) \text{ when } c = 1. \tag{4A.7}$$

Another way to write the same criterion is that the party would want to recruit the remaining allies, or

$$\Delta N(t) = L(t + 1) - N(t), \text{ when } c = 1. \tag{4A.8}$$

A pure class-only strategy is a course of action that would maximize the ratio of workers to socialist voters. Hence this strategy can be defined by a number $k^c(t)$ which is the solution to the problem given as

$$\max_{k} W(t + 1)/[W(t + 1) + N(t + 1)]. \tag{4A.9}$$

Since in our model the only state the party can modify during the next election is $N(t + 1)$, maximizing the ratio of workers in the socialist vote is equivalent to minimizing the proportion of nonworkers voting socialist. Thus, the alternative way to define the pure class-only strategy is by $k^c(t)$ such that

$$N(t + 1) = 0, \text{ when } c = 1, \quad (4A.10)$$

or, which is still the same,

$$\Delta N(t) = -N(t), \text{ when } c = 1. \quad (4A.11)$$

Note again that since k is taken to be the strategic variable the state $N(t + 1)$ is accessible at t but the state $W(t + 1)$ is not. The party can influence only $W(t + 2)$, and indirectly, by affecting $N(t + 1)$. Short-term consequences of our analysis are obviously sensitive to this lag structure but longer term consequences are not.

To calculate $k^s(t)$ we proceed as follows: first, substitute the objective (4A.8) as the left-hand side of (4A.2), setting $c = 1$. Then $L(t + 1) - N(t) = q[L(t + 1) - N(t)] + [k^s(t)W(t) - N(t)]$. Solving for $k^s(t)$ yields

$$k^s(t) = \frac{(1 - q)L(t + 1) + qN(t)}{W(t)}, \quad (4A.12)$$

subject to the constraint that $W^s(t + 2)$, which eventually depends on $k^s(t)$, be nonnegative.

Analogously, $k^c(t)$ can be obtained by substituting the objective (4A.11) in (4A.2), and setting $c = 1$ to obtain

$$-N(t) = q[L(t + 1) - N(t)] + [k^c(t)W(t) - N(t)],$$

and solve for $k^c(t)$:

$$k^c(t) = -q\frac{L(t + 1) - N(t)}{W(t)}. \quad (4A.13)$$

Any value of k such that $k^c(t) < k(t) < k^s(t)$ is not a pure strategy.

Time Paths of the Vote Under Pure Strategies

If a party adopts the strategy S (for supraclass) at time t, by picking as its value of nonworkers' vote the number $k^s(t)$, then its vote from allies will change during the subsequent period according to

$$\Delta N^s(t) = q[L(t + 1) - N(t)] + c[k^s(t)W(t) - N(t)].$$

Substituting the value of $k^s(t)$ from (4A.12) and remembering that $\Delta N(t) = N(t + 1) - N(t)$, the proportion of the electorate consisting of socialist voting allies when the party adopts the pure supraclass strategy at t will be given by

$$N^s(t + 1) = N_t + [q + c(1 - q)][L(t + 1) - N(t)]. \tag{4A.14}$$

Note that if $c = 1$, then the criterion (4A.7) is fulfilled by (4A.14).

The vote of workers at $(t + 1)$ is not affected by the strategy chosen at t. Hence this vote is $W(t + 1)$, as implied by (4A.1). The total socialist vote, always as a percent of the electorate, is thus:

$$Y^s(t + 1) = N^s(t + 1) + W(t + 1). \tag{4A.15}$$

If a party adopts the strategy C (for class-pure) at time t, by picking $k^c(t)$, then its vote from allies will change according to

$$\Delta N^c(t) = q[L(t + 1) - N(t)] + c[k^c(t)W(t) - N(t)],$$

and by the next election it will be

$$N^c(t + 1) = q(1 - c)L(t + 1) + (1 - q)(1 - c)N(t). \tag{4A.16}$$

Note again that if party strategies were perfectly effective, $c = 1$, the criterion of (4A.10), and of (4A.9), would be fulfilled by (4A.16).

Since the vote of workers at $(t + 1)$ will be still $W(t + 1)$ as implied by (4A.1), the total vote associated with the pure class-only strategy will be

$$Y^c(t + 1) = N^c(t + 1) + W(t + 1). \tag{4A.17}$$

The range of choice which the party enjoys at time t with regard to the next election is the difference $D(1)$, given by

$$D(1) = Y^s(t + 1) - Y^c(t + 1) = N^s(t + 1) - N^c(t + 1) = cL(t + 1). \tag{4A.18}$$

To simplify the exposition, we assume throughout this section that $W^s(t + 2)$ associated with the $k^s(t)$ given by (4A.12) is nonnegative. The numerical analyses presented in the main body of the text were all based on this constraint, which means that in some cases $k^s(t)$ was smaller than the value given by (4A.12).

This is the immediate gain from the supraclass strategy. This gain occurs because of the lag structure of our model and is therefore quite arbitrary. We could have a model in which instead of $-dN(t)$ equation (4A.1) would contain $-dN(t + 1)$, making the effect of strategies on workers instantaneous. The immediate difference in such a case would be $c(1 - d)L(t + 1)$, which would be less than $cL(t + 1)$ but still a gain as long as $d < 1$, which is true in all but two cases analyzed. In the present structure, the model recovers the effect on workers one period later.

Just to provide more intuition and to explain the procedures used to obtain figure 4.3, consider what would happen if the party repeats one more time the same strategic choice, now at $t + 1$ for the $t + 2$ election. The party chooses $k^s(t + 1)$ if it opted for $k^s(t)$; it follows $k^c(t + 1)$ if it picked $k^c(t)$.

Examine first the supraclass strategy. At $(t + 1)$ the party has obtained $W(t + 1)$ from workers, $N^s(t + 1)$ from allies, and $Y^s(t + 1)$ from the electorate as a whole. It chooses $k^s(t + 1)$ and obtains:

$$W^s(t + 2) = W(t + 1) + p[X(t + 2) - W(t + 1)] - dN^s(t + 1),$$

$$N^s(t + 2) = N^s(t + 1) + q[L(t + 2) - N^s(t + 1)] + c[k^c(t + 1)W(t + 1) - N^s(t + 1)],$$

$$Y^s(t + 2) = N^s(t + 2) + W^s(t + 2). \qquad (4A.19)$$

Note that the vote from workers at $(t + 2)$ carries the superscript "s" because it is a consequence of the strategic choice S made at time t.

Analogously, if the party follows the strategy C it will win at time $(t + 2)$ the share of $W^c(t + 2)$ from workes, $N^c(t + 2)$ from allies, and $Y^c(t + 2)$ from the electorate as a whole. The algebra is trivial and messy so we will not reproduce it. Just note that since $N^s(t + 1) > N^c(t + 1)$, and since $W(t + 2)$ depends negatively on $N(t + 1)$, $W^s(t + 2)$ will always be smaller than $W^c(t + 2)$. The party pays opportunity costs among workers. Whether it will have gained votes at $(t + 2)$ as the result of having had pursued the supraclass strategy during the two preceding periods depends on the difference

$$D(2) = c[(1 - c)(1 - q) - d]L(t + 1) +$$
$$cL(t + 2). \qquad (4A.20)$$

This difference represents again the realm of choice party leaders have at time t in influencing the result of elections two periods later. Note that this difference is always negative for the French Socialists and the pre-1933 German Social Democrats.

Figure 4.3 is based on the values calculated in this manner, with $k^s(t)$ constrained in the French case to assure nonnegative votes among workers. Wherever the two lines in figure 4.3 cross after two elections, $D(2) < 0$.

One can go on with this analysis by asking what would happen if the party had persisted during 3,4,. . . ., etc. elections with the same pure strategy. The difference $D(h)$ would change according to

$$D(h) = B_1[(1 - q)(1 - c)]^{h-1} \qquad (4A.21)$$
$$+ B_2(1 - p)^{h-1} + [1 - (p/d)]\frac{c}{q(1 - c) + c} L,$$

where B_1 and B_2 are constants as is the proportion of allies, L. Since the expressions under the exponent are smaller than 1.00 in their absolute value, the difference converges to the last term of (4A.21). Thus this difference is positive if $(d/p) < 1$; otherwise it is negative. Figure 4.1 and table 4.1 are based on (4A.21), with L assumed to be constant around the 1970 level.

Carrying Capacities Associated with Pure Strategies

If a party follows the pure supraclass strategy then its vote from allies changes according to (see equation [4A.14])

$$\Delta N^s(t) = [(q + c(1 - q)][L(t + 1) - N^s(t)]. \qquad (4A.22)$$

When would this share of the vote remain stable? Setting the difference at zero and solving for $N^s(t)$ yields

$$N^*_s(t) = L(t + 1). \qquad (4A.23)$$

This is the carrying capacity of the party among allies, associated with the pure supraclass strategy. Using (4A.4) we can deduce immediately that the carrying capacity among workers associated with this strategy will be

$$W^*_s(t) = X(t) - (d/p) L(t + 1). \qquad (4A.24)$$

The problem we encounter at this moment is that (4A.24) does not guarantee that W^* will be nonnegative. One way to proceed would be to constrain N^* in such a way that $W^* \geq 0$. This would imply that

$$X(t) - (d/p)N^*_s(t) \geq 0, \qquad (4A.25)$$

and

$$N^*_s \leq (p/d)X(t). \qquad (4A.26)$$

Hence, N^*_s would be given by (4A.23) if the constraint (4A.25) is observed and by (4A.26) otherwise. Every time N^*_s assumes the value given by (4A.26) we say that the mobilization of allies is limited by the success of the party among workers. The values associated with the supraclass strategy in table 4.2 are based on (4A.26) whenever the constraint (4A.25) is not satisfied by (4A.23). These cases are distinguished by the fact that the proportion of workers to socialist voters associated with the supraclass strategy is then zero, as shown in the appropriate column of table 4.2.

As discussed in the text, this constraint may seem unreasonable. Hence, the alternative is to assume that if the constraint (4A.25) is violated by (4A.23), then $W^*_s = 0$ and $N^*_s = L$. The "Middle Class" column of table 4.2 indicates whether L would be larger than the shares of the electorate associated with the pure class-only strategy as well as with the pure supraclass strategy in which the mobilization of allies is limited by the success of the party among workers, the latter condition being true by definition.

The shares of the electorate the party could recruit and hold under the pure supraclass strategy are given as follows:

$Y^*_s = L(t + 1) + [X(t) - (d/p)L(t + 1)$, if W^*_s
    $= X(t) - (d/p)L(t + 1) \geq 0$; otherwise,
$Y^*_s = (p/d)X(t),$ (limited mobilization of allies)

or

$Y^*_s = L(t + 1),$ (full mobilization of allies)
if $X(t) - (d/p)L(t + 1) < 0.$ (4A.27)

Note for future reference that this inequality condition also can be written as

$$X(t)/L(t + 1) < d/p. \qquad (4A.28)$$

The steady-state associated with the pure class-only strategy can be obtained by setting to zero the expression (from equation [4A.16])

$$\Delta N^c = q(1 - c)L(t + 1) - [q(1 - c) + c]N^c(t) \quad (4A.29)$$

to obtain

$$N^*_c(t) = \frac{q(1 - c)}{q(1 - c) + c} L(t + 1). \quad (4A.30)$$

For future reference, it will be convenient to define $Q = q(1 - c)/[q(1 - c) + c]$. Note that if party strategy is perfectly effective or if there is no protest vote, that is, if $c = 1$ or $q = 0$, then $N^*_c = 0$.

The carrying capacity among workers associated with the class-only strategy is

$$W^*_c(t) = X(t) - (d/p)QL(t + 1). \quad (4A.31)$$

Hence,

$$Y^*_c(t) = QL(t + 1) + [X(t) - (d/p)QL(t + 1)]. \quad (4A.32)$$

The difference in the carrying capacities associated with the pure strategies is given by

$$D^*(t) = [1 - (d/p)](1 - Q)L(t + 1), \text{ if } X(t)/L(t + 1) > 0,$$

otherwise

$$D^*(t) = [1 - (d/p)][(p/d)X(t) - QL(t + 1)],$$
$$\text{(limited mobilization)}$$

or

$$D^*(t) = [L(t + 1) - X(t)] - [1 - (d/p)]QL(t + 1)$$
$$\text{(full mobilization).} \quad (4A.33)$$

Since $(1 - Q) = c/[c + q(1 - c)]$, the difference between carrying capacities when $X(t)/L(t + 1) > 0$ equals the limit of the difference between vote shares as given by (4A.20), assuming L is constant.

Would Different Assumptions Make Much Difference?

In order to be able to answer some questions more generally, we first introduced modifications of the model. These modifications are intended to demonstrate that the conclusions presented in the text are valid even if the model is altered to accommodate some reasonable objections that may be raised with regard to the particular assumptions. We will work only with the steady states.

First, suppose that there is no protest voting. Protest voting was defined as that part of socialist voting by allies which is independent of party strategies. Note that in the statistically estimated model it may also turn out that people who are neither workers nor allies would vote socialist. Such votes are of no interest to us here; indeed, they have been ignored in all the theoretical analyses. The protest voting to which we are referring now is the socialist vote of allies, due to the term $q[L(t + 1) - N(t)]$ in (4A.2). Since this vote was defined as independent of party strategy, an argument can be made that it should not enter into the analysis of strategies. We did not remove it in the main body of the text because the absolute magnitudes of socialist vote shares are politically important. Two parties may have a range of choice of 30 percent but one may be getting 25 percent in protest vote and the other no protest vote whatsoever. Their alternatives will be electorally the same but politically quite different, and this is why protest votes were included in the analysis. But we could remove it.

Note that in many cases the parameter q turned out to be zero anyway—for the German and Norwegian Left and the Danish, French, and Norwegian socialist parties. In several other cases this parameter is almost negligible. Hence, removing protest vote from the analysis would not have made much of an empirical difference in most countries. But let us first examine some analytical consequences.

If we let $q = 0$, then the carrying capacities will become

$$N^* = kW^*. \tag{4A.34}$$

$$W^* = X - (d/p)N^*. \tag{4A.35}$$

Substituting (4A.34) into (4A.35) and solving for W^* yields

$$W^* = \frac{1}{1 + (d/p)k} X. \tag{4A.36}$$

Consequently,

$$N^* = \frac{k}{1 + (d/p)k} X, \tag{4A.37}$$

and

$$Y^* = \frac{1 + k}{1 + (d/p)k} X. \qquad (4A.38)$$

These results are theoretically interesting and we will have a chance to return to them in another context.

Now if a party followed the pure supraclass strategy, then its carrying capacities would be as before

$$Y^*_s = L + [X - (d/p)L], \text{ if } X/L > d/p; \text{ otherwise}$$

$$Y^*_s = (p/d)X \text{ in the case of limited mobilization, and}$$

$$Y^*_s = L \text{ in the case of full mobilization.} \qquad (4A.39)$$

The carrying capacities will be different, however, when the party pursues pure class-only strategies. With no protest vote, the carrying capacity among allies becomes zero and the party can recruit and hold all workers, so that

$$Y^*_c = X. \qquad (4A.40)$$

The difference between carrying capacities now is

$$D^* = [1 - (d/p)]L, \text{ if } X/L > d/p; \text{ otherwise}$$

$$D^* = [1 - (d/p)](p/d)X \text{ in the case of limited} \\ \text{mobilization and}$$

$$D^* = L - X \text{ in the case of full mobilization.} \qquad (4A.41)$$

Another reasonable criticism of the model would run as follows. We argued that parties lose opportunities among workers because they decrease the salience of class as they adopt supraclass strategies. But we used $N(t)$ to measure the cumulative effect of these strategies in equation (4A.1), while in fact $N(t)$ contains protest vote which is not an effect of strategies at all. Thus we should have excluded the part of $N(t)$ due to protest voting from having an impact on workers. Our defense is that one might also argue reasonably that if there are people who vote for the socialists, it is because the party is wishy-washy in its class orientation, because it is a party of generalized discontent rather than of the working class endowed with a project for the future. But since both arguments seem quite plausible, let us examine the consequences of assuming that the protest vote has no effect on workers.

In this case, we would have, as in the full model:

$$N^* = \frac{q}{q + c} L + \frac{c}{q + c} kW^*,$$

but the carrying capacity among workers would become

$$W^* = X - (d/p) \frac{c}{q + c} kW^*,$$

or

$$W^* = \frac{1}{1 + k(d/p)[c/(q + c)]} X. \qquad (4A.42)$$

$$N^* = \frac{k\left(\frac{c}{q + c}\right)}{1 + k(d/p)[c/(q + c)]} X \qquad (4A.43)$$

and, to rewrite more simply,

$$Y^* = \frac{p(q + c) + ckp}{p(q + c) + ckd} X. \qquad (4A.44)$$

If a party followed the pure supraclass strategy, its carrying capacity would be

$$Y^*_s = L + \left[X - (d/p) \frac{c}{q + c} L \right] \text{ , if } X/L > (d/p) \frac{c}{q + c}$$

$$(4A.45)$$

and they would be the same as under other assumptions otherwise.

If the party followed the pure class-only strategy, its carrying capacity would include all the workers and the protest vote of allies

$$Y^*_c = X + QL, \qquad (4A.46)$$

Q defined by (4A.30). The difference between carrying capacities would be

$$D^* = [1 - (d/p) \tfrac{c}{q+c} - Q]L, \text{ if } X/L > (d/p) \tfrac{c}{q+c},$$
$$\text{otherwise}$$

$$D^* = [1 - (d/p)](p/d)X - QL \text{ in the case of}$$
$$\text{limited mobilization,}$$

$$D^* = (1 - Q)L - X, \text{ in the case of full}$$
$$\text{mobilization.} \qquad (4A.47)$$

Tables 4.3 and 4.4 show the information contained in table 4.2 in the main body of the text under the alternative assumptions now discussed. Table 4.3 shows carrying capacities in the case protest voting is ignored altogether. Table 4.4 shows carrying capacities when protest vote is assumed to have no effect on workers. A comparison of these three tables will show that none of our qualitative conclusions depends on the assumptions which were just reviewed. Even numerical differences are few. The most interesting finding is that once workers are not affected by protest voting, the pure class-only strategy turns out to be actually the

Table 4.3 Comparison of Carrying Capacities Associated with the Actual, Supraclass, and Class-only Strategies—1970 Class Structure Without Protest Voting ($q = 0$)

Strategy	Actual[a]	Limited Supraclass	Full Supraclass[b]	Class-only
Country		Carrying Capacity		
		Total Left		
Belgium	18.9	17.3	max	19.1
Denmark	50.7	60.4		28.4
Finland	23.2	37.7	max	20.3
France	24.3	23.7	max	24.8
Germany	28.5	23.6	max	33.3
Norway	65.3	81.0		30.3
Sweden	41.3	56.3		37.5
		Socialists Only		
Denmark	38.0	57.6		28.4
Finland	18.8	14.1	max	20.3
France	9.9	2.7	max	24.8
Germany[c]	33.1	2.0		33.1
Norway	62.8	98.7		30.3
Sweden	39.5	47.1		37.5

[a] Actual strategy is the strategy estimated to best fit the model.
[b] A max in this column indicates that the middle classes together are more numerous than the proportion of the electorate a party can win with either of the two alternative strategies.
[c] As of 1933.

Table 4.4 Comparison of Carrying Capacities Associated with the Actual,
Supraclass, and Class-only Strategies—1970 Class Structure
Protest Voting by Allies Has No Effect on Workers

Strategy	Actual[a]	Limited Supraclass	Full Supraclass[b]	Class-only
Country		Carrying Capacity		
		Total Left		
Belgium	34.6	21.4	max	23.7
Denmark	60.7	61.8		54.7
Finland	48.0	56.7	max	45.6
France	30.0	26.8	max	25.3
Germany	28.5	23.6	max	33.3
Norway	65.3	81.0		30.3
Sweden	41.7	57.1		37.8
		Socialists Only		
Denmark	38.0	57.6		28.4
Finland	28.1	16.2	max	26.4
France	9.9	2.7	max	24.8
Germany[c]	9.9	2.1		33.1
Norway	62.8	98.7		30.3
Sweden	45.5	51.7		42.3

[a] Actual strategy is the strategy estimated to best fit the model.
[b] A max in this column indicates that the middle classes together are more numerous than the proportion of the electorate a party can win with either of the two alternative strategies.
[c] As of 1933.

vote maximizing one for the pre-1933 SPD. If protest voting by allies is included but assumed to have no effect on workers, then it will turn out that the Belgian and the French Left as well as the Finnish Social Democrats have actually gone some way toward the full supraclass strategy. But otherwise neither the ordering of the strategies with regard to their vote getting effects nor the comparisons of the optimal and the actual strategies are affected by the variations of these assumptions. Hence, our conclusions are quite robust empirically.

Vote Maximizing Strategies

Altogether we can subject the model utilized in the main body of the text to the following variations:

1. When W^*_s is negative at $N^*_s = L$, we can use either the assumption that the mobilization of allies is limited by the support the party draws from workers and then $N^*_s = (p/d)X$ or that the party continues to fully mobilize the allies and then $N^*_s = L$

2. We can assume that the party has no control over protest vote and exclude it completely from consideration

3. We can assume that workers are not affected by the protest vote

Without going into details, which are only laborious, we can assert the following about vote maximizing. The condition that the equilibrium trade-off, as measured by (d/p), is steeper than unity, $d/p > 1$, is sufficient to guarantee that the pure class-only strategy maximizes the carrying capacity of the party in the electorate as a whole in all cases, with the exception of protest voting with no effect on workers and full mobilization of allies, when the condition is slightly more strict, namely, $(d/p) > (q + c)/(q + c - qc) > 1$. Formally, $Y^*_c > Y^*_s$ if $(d/p) > 1$ or, when protest voting has no effect on workers and allies are fully mobilized,

$$(d/p) > (q + c)/(q + c - qc). \tag{4A.48}$$

Otherwise the pure supraclass strategy maximizes the carrying capacity.

This result shows that there are conditions under which the pure class-only strategy is the one that maximizes the steady-state share of the electorate and that these conditions hold with a minor modification independently of particular assumptions which sometimes may be called into question.

What remains is to prove that the condition $(d/p) > 1$ is also sufficient in the main model to guarantee that the pure class-only strategy will maximize the time path of the socialist share of the electorate. The results presented above concerned only the carrying capacity, but it may be possible, in principle, that in order to get to the higher carrying capacity a party would have to experience a period in which it would have to pursue a strategy inferior for this period. We will now show that this will not be the case— the strategy which maximizes the carrying capacity also maximizes the sum of the votes the party would obtain throughout its history. This proof is more difficult than the rest of this appendix.

   The theorem to be demonstrated is the following: If party leaders seek to maximize the sum of the future shares of the electorate by pursing the same strategy throughout the entire period, and if the voting process obeys equations (4A.1) through (4A.3), then k^c is the maximizing strategy as long as $(d/p) > 1$ and k^s is the maximizing strategy otherwise. The leaders program is to:

$$\max_{k} \sum_{t=1}^{t=\infty} (W(t) + N(t)), \qquad (4A.49)$$

subject to (4A.1) and (4A.2). The Lagrangian is:

$$\mathcal{L} = \sum_{t=1} \Big\{ [W(t) + N(t)] \qquad\qquad (4A.50)$$

$$+ \mu[X(t + 1) + (1 - p)W(t) - dN(t) - W(t + 1)]$$
$$+ \Omega[L(t + 1) + (1 - q - c)N(t) + ckW(t) - N(t + 1)] \Big\}.$$

Since both the objective function and the constraints are linear, the derivative of the Langrangian with regard to the strategic variable will be either positive or negative:

$$\frac{\partial \mathcal{L}}{\partial k} = c \sum_{t=1} \Omega(t)W(t) \lessgtr 0. \qquad (4A.51)$$

This implies that the maximizing strategy will be one of the extreme strategies, that is, either k^s or k^c. Since it is always true that $k^s > k^c$, what we need to prove is that

$$\text{SIGN} \frac{\partial \mathcal{L}}{\partial k} = \text{SIGN} [1 - (d/p)]. \qquad (4A.52)$$

The remaining first order conditions are

$$\frac{\partial \mathcal{L}}{\partial W(t)} = 1 + \mu(t)(1 - p) - \mu(t - 1) + \Omega(t)ck = 0, \quad (4A.53)$$

$$\frac{\partial \mathcal{L}}{\partial N(t)} = 1 - \mu(t)d + \Omega(t)(1 - q - c) - \Omega(t - 1) = 0.$$

$$(4A.54)$$

   Since we are interested only in the sign of $\Sigma\Omega(t)W(t)$, note only that the equations (4A.53) and (4A.54) can be solved to obtain $\Omega(t)$ as an explicit function of time. $\Omega(t)$ will be of the form:

$$\Omega(t) = C_1 m_1^t + C_2 m_2^t + \Omega^* \qquad (4A.55)$$

where the m_i's are real or complex roots of (4A.53 = 4A.54), C_i's are constants which depend on initial conditions $\Omega(0)$ and $\mu(0)$, and importantly it can be shown that

$$\Omega^* = [1 - (d/p)] \frac{p}{p(q + c) + cdk}. \qquad (4A.56)$$

Note that the sign of Ω^* is the same as the sign of $[1 - (d/p)]$.

5
The Voting Behavior of Individuals

The counting of 'votes' is the final ceremony of a long process.
Antonio Gramsci

CONFLICTS OVER CLASS AND THE VOTING BEHAVIOR OF INDIVIDUALS

Through a variety of means, ideological as well as organizational, conflicting political forces impose images of society on individuals, mold collective identities, and mobilize commitments to specific projects for a shared future. Collective identity, group solidarity, and political commitments are repeatedly forged, destroyed, and molded anew. Thus the causes which lead individuals to vote in a particular way during each election are a cumulative consequence of the competition which pits political parties against one another as well as against other organizations which mobilize and organize collective commitments. The strategies of these organizations determine, as their cumulative effect, the relative importance of potential social cleavages on the voting behavior of individuals. Religion, language, class, or individual self-interest each may become at various times the dominant motivational force of individual behavior as a consequence of the strategies pursued by parties, unions, schools, and churches. The causes of individual voting behavior are produced in the course of history by conflicting political forces. This is why discussions of whether class, religion, region, party identification, or the pursuit of individual self-interest are most important in determining voting behavior are not theoretically enlightening. Causes are but a product of reciprocal interactions and hence should be expected to vary across countries and to change over time.

But if the behavior of individuals is not ruled by fixed natural causes, it is nevertheless lawful. We have seen that the salience of class as a cause of individual voting behavior is a consequence of the strategies pursued by political parties of the left, by trade unions, and by other parties and organizations that may seek to organize workers on the basis of identities and commitments other than class. We now examine the effect of this process on the voting behavior of individuals, specifically, on the historical patterns of class voting.

Patterns of class voting vary across countries and change over time depending on the strategies pursued by political parties of the Left, on the severity of the trade-off these parties encounter as they move to mobilize nonworkers, and on transformations of the class structure. To clarify the consequences of our theory for patterns of class voting, it is convenient again to revert to the analysis of comparative statics. Note that our argument about the way in which workers join and defect from the ranks of socialist voters entails the following assumption about the way in which individual workers make voting decisions: they are indifferent between voting and not voting socialist whenever exactly $W^*(N)$ workers vote socialist in response to N allies voting for the party, where, to remind the reader,

$$W^*(N) = X - (d/p)N.$$

Another way to state the same hypothesis is that workers are indifferent to socialist mobilization when the class composition of the socialist electorate equals

$$N/W = (X/W - 1)/(d/p). \tag{5.1}$$

We know, however, that party leaders are indifferent whether additional allies vote socialist or leave the ranks when the class composition of the electorate is such that

$$N/W = k. \tag{5.2}$$

Workers and party leaders are thus simultaneously inert in their actions when $(X/W - 1)/(d/p) = k,$ or when the proportion of workers voting socialist is

$$\frac{W^*}{X} = \frac{1}{1 + k(d/p)}.$$ (5.3)

Under these conditions it also will be true that the proportion of allies voting socialist will be given by (5.2) and (5.3) as

$$\frac{N^*}{L} = \frac{k}{1 + k(d/p)} \frac{X}{L}.$$ (5.4)

Since we know the proportions of workers and allies voting socialist on the basis of the empirically estimated theoretical model, we can characterize the entire electorate by making the kind of a table that is normally generated by surveys. It is also possible to compute various indices that measure the degree of class voting in the electorate as a whole. One established way to measure the general prevalence of class voting, due to Alford (1963), is to compare the proportion of workers and nonworkers (or some more narrowly specified class) voting socialist. At equilibrium, Alford's index based on the carrying capacities becomes

$$\frac{W^*}{X} - \frac{N^*}{L} = \frac{1 - k(X/L)}{1 + k(d/p)} = A.$$ (5.5)

The intuition on which this index is based is that in a society in which class would exclusively and completely determine the voting behavior of individuals all workers and no nonworkers would vote left. Under those conditions this index takes the value 1. In turn, in a society in which class is not an important cause of voting, workers and nonworkers might be equally likely to vote left and the value of the index would be in the vicinity of zero. Thus this index is not free of prior assumptions. What is important, however, is to distinguish class voting among workers from the degree of class voting in the electorate as a whole (as measured by Alford's index or some alternative coefficient). Under some circumstances most workers may vote socialist but the value of Alford's index will be low because many nonworkers will also vote for the socialist party. Under other circumstances the value of this index may be low because neither workers nor allies vote socialist.

With these instruments we can now examine the implications of our theory. The degree of class voting among workers, allies, and the electorate as a whole depends in the long run on the strategy pursued by the socialist (left) party and on the electoral trade-off this party encountered. The proportion of allies voting socialist as well as the extent of general class voting depends additionally on the class structure, specifically, on the ratio of workers to allies. When the trade-off is mild and the party is highly concerned about class composition, almost all workers will vote socialist. Under such conditions few allies will vote socialist, and the degree of class voting in the electorate as a whole will be high. When the trade-off is mild and the party is less concerned about the class origins of its support, the proportion of workers voting left will still be high but so will be the proportion of allies. When the trade-off is steep but the party is very concerned about class composition, the proportion of workers voting socialist will be low and the proportion of allies will be moderate. These conclusions are conveniently summarized in figure 5.1. These are, then, the long-run consequences of the strategies pursued by political organizations for the voting behavior of individuals. The result of the activities of trade unions and of bourgeois political parties is the trade-off which socialists encounter among workers when they dilute the salience of class. Faced with this trade-off, socialist and other left-wing parties choose their strategies for electoral recruitment. The salience of class as a cause of the voting behavior of individuals depends in the long run on the combinations of the

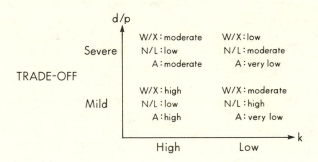

Figure 5.1 Theoretical Analysis of Class Voting

severity of the trade-off and the criterion of class composition chosen by the party.

ELECTORAL HISTORY AND THE ACT OF VOTING

The decision made by each individual in each particular election is a cumulative consequence of strategies pursued by political parties and other organizations during the entire history of parties, classes, and elections. Socialist parties entered electoral competition when workers were already numerous, when they were quite distinct socially and culturally, and often when they were discriminated against and oppressed politically as in Germany. Socialist parties participated in the competition for votes, they sought support from the middle classes, formed alliances with other parties, formed governments, and administered their respective societies. In this entire process and throughout the entire history of electoral politics, socialist and other left-wing parties, in their interaction with trade unions and other political parties, have molded the importance of various factors that cause individuals to behave in a particular way on that special day when they are called on to make a political choice.

Thus the fact of voting, recorded in the official statistics, reported or announced in response to pollsters, cannot be treated as a result of a decision made by each individual separately and independently from the past each time. Individuals do decide; they behave strategically and probably quite rationally. But the framework of these decisions—what people want, know, and can do—changes in the course of history. Hence, the patterns of voting reported recently should be predictable on the basis of the process that began when socialist parties entered electoral competition.

Indeed, the most convincing way to validate the theoretical principles that underlie our analysis of electoral socialism is to compare the predictions derived from the model with reports of surveys, conducted many years after the entire proces had begun. If the voting acts of each individual in particular elections are indeed a consequence of the long-term process, then they should be predicted by this process. From the model, we can derive predictions concerning the proportions of workers and allies voting socialist during each election, from the beginning until now. And to evaluate these predictions empirically we can compare them with the reports of survey studies during the period, typically after the mid-1950s, when such reports are available.

We must begin, however, by warning the reader not to expect a perfect, even a good, fit. There are several reasons to expect that at best the predictions derived from the model and the results of surveys will not be completely independent from each other. One group of reasons is internal to surveys. Surveys are replete with error, sampling error is one obvious source. Most importantly, surveys report either intentions or recollections, not the vote itself. And we know both that people sometimes change their voting decisions at the last moment and that they tend to overreport having voted for the winners. Indeed, the survey results reported in table 5.1 often differ substantially from each other because they were conducted at different moments in relation to the election itself. The resulting differences between or among surveys are often larger than the differences between some of the surveys and the predictions derived from the theoretical model. Moreover, while surveys do tend to predict the actual election results somewhat more accurately than the model, the error of prediction is often quite large for the surveys or the information necessary to reconstruct the error is not presented. In general, as one examines survey reports in some detail, it becomes apparent that we are not contrasting the predictions of a model of unknown validity against surveys which present the true state of affairs. We are comparing two ways of discovering what people really do, both imperfectly valid.

We harbor no illusions that the predictions of the model are error free. The model is far too simple to account for the rich historical variety of electoral behavior, and this is the most important source of the error in our predictions. This source of error is inherent in the logical form of the model. The data we used are often far from reliable, and some of the procedures we had to adopt involved guesses. These technical sources of error are discussed in the appendices, so we do not dwell on them here. It is sufficient that some error in model predictions should be expected.

Finally, the lack of fit between model and survey results is due to definitional differences. Workers were defined for the purposes of the model as manual wage earners employed in mining, manufacturing, construction, transport, and agriculture, as well as

their adult dependents who do not exercise a gainful activity outside the household and, where possible, people retired from these
occupations. Survey studies use a number of definitions which do
not always correspond to the one we chose for our theoretical
purposes. Indeed, quite often survey reports refer to "workers"
without specifying how the term was defined at all. Many surveys
define workers as "manuals," that is, manual wage earners in all
sectors, including workers in the service sector and day workers
where they become employed. But even the notion of "manual"
is not very sharp and "shop assistants" are sometimes defined as
workers and at other times as "lower white-collar employees."
These definitions of workers as "manuals" are somewhat broader
than ours, by about 20 percent on the average. In turn, some surveys do not include among workers the manual laborers in agriculture. This difference is not a major source of error since
agricultural workers are not very numerous by the time our comparisons begin, and the rate at which they vote left is not very
different from that of industrial workers (Pappi 1977:217;
Pesonen 1974:294).

Allies were defined for the purposes of the model as manual
workers in services and commerce, the lower and middle echelons
of white-collar employees, and those self-employed who do not
employ anyone outside their family, as well as their adult dependents and people retired from such pursuits. Surveys differ widely
in their categorization of nonworkers. To compare the two types
of results, we recomputed the survey results whenever possible to
obtain a category similar to our definition.

With all these caveats we present the results. Table 5.1 shows
the proportions of workers and allies voting left and table 5.2
gives the socialist results both according to the model and to survey studies. Also shown are the proportions of the electorate consisting of workers and allies according to the model and the
proportions of the particular survey samples that consisted of
workers or of categories which would be defined as allies according to the model. Finally, the error compares the share of the vote
predicted by the model or the surveys with the actual results of
elections, whenever the published reports allow us to compute the
survey prediction.

There are two ways of looking at the comparisons. One is to
examine whether the model and the surveys agree about orders of

Table 5.1   Comparison of Model and Survey Results About Class Voting
for the Left

	W/X	N/L	X	L	Error
Belgium					
1968 Model	53	20	20		0.5
Hill 1977:48	47	23	38	40	
Denmark					
1960 Model	67	73	28	33	−5.8
Esping-Anderson 1985:3−4	85	62			
1964 Model	66	69	28	33	1.5
Berglund and Lindstrom 1978:108	85	65	42		
1966 Model	69	63	28	34	−1.7
Esping-Anderson 1985:3−4	86	58			
1968 Model	61	63	28	34	6.3
Esping-Anderson 1979:276	79				
1971 Model	67	70	28	34	−3.3
Børre 1977a:15	75	33	49	39	2.4
Damgaard 1974:121	69	30	36	26	−4.3
Uusitalo 1975:39	77	49	40		−4.5
Esping-Anderson 1985:3−4	78	60			
1973 Model	51	53	27	34	11.1
Børre 1977a:15	65	29	28	35	9.2
Esping-Anderson 1985:3−4	51				
1975 Model	57	59	27	34	−2.6
Børre 1977b	64	26	27	21	0.3
Berglund and Lindstrom 1978:180	61	43			
Esping-Anderson 1985:3−4	59	43			
1977 Model	64	68	27	34	−3.9
Børre 1977b	67	32	25	20	−0.7
1979 Model	66	70	27	34	−0.8
Esping Anderson 1985:3−4	65	56			
Finland					
1958 Model	73	23	23		1.3
Allardt and Pesonen 1967:342	68	14	49	15	−10.8
1966 Model	87	31	21		−5.3
Pesonen 1974:294	80	23	48	16	3.2
1972 Model	68	28	20		−2.1
Allardt and Wesołowski 1978:63	74	21	41	23	−0.1
France					
1956 Model	63	35	28	43	−0.9
Sondages 1960:18−19	56	35	31	59	

Table 5.1 (*Continued*)

	W/X	N/L	X	L	Error
1958 Model	52	29	28	44	4.9
Sondages 1960:18–19	45	35	28	61	
1967 Model	65	34	25	47	−7.3
Braud 1973:32	44	29	31	54	
Rabier 1978:362	41	28	28	65	
Jaffré 1980:41	54				
Sondages 1973:18–19	43	29	32	62	
1968 Model	60	29	25	48	1.9
Braud 1973:32	43	29	31	54	
Sondages 1973:18–19	38	26	32	62	
1973 Model	67	33	25	48	−4.2
Sondages 1973:18–19	53	27	32	62	
Jaffré 1980:41	68				
Le Monde 1973[a]	63	28	24	62	
1978 Model	73	35	25	48	−4.3
Le Matin 1978	47	30	29	62	
Jaffré 1980:69–71	67	53			
Germany[b]					
1953 Model	51	31	32	29	1.2
Pappi 1973:199	48	27	35	21	
Pappi 1977:217	58	29	45	27	0.0
Klingeman 1983	36	20	45		−0.7
1961 Model	63	34	33	33	−5.0
Pappi 1973:199	56	30	37	21	
Klingeman 1983	45	21	51		−1.7
1965 Model	66	35	33	36	−2.5
Pappi 1973:199	54	34	38	30	
Klingeman 1983	48	29	47		−0.9
1969 Model	69	36	33	39	−2.9
Pappi 1973:199	58	46	38	27	
Klingeman 1983	48	41	48		2.0
1972 Model	77	40	34	41	−5.5
Pappi 1973:199	66	50	32	37	
Klingeman 1983	59	44	44		4.3
1976 Model	70	36	34	43	1.5
Pappi 1977:217	53	39	32	48	0.0
Klingeman 1983	44	34	37		−2.6
Norway					
1957 Model	39	44	31		2.1
Valen and Martinussen 1977:51	77				

(*continued*)

Table 5.1   (*Continued*)

	W/X	N/L	X	L	Error
1965 Model	40	44	31		−0.5
Valen and Martinussen 1977:51	77				
Martin 1972:92[c]	71	30	44		−2.4
Esping-Anderson 1985:3–4	77				
1969 Model	42	46	30		1.9
Valen and Martinussen 1977:51	75				
Uusitalo 1975:41	80		35		−1.5
1973 Model	35	38	30		6.5
Valen and Martinussen 1977:51[d]	69	32	45		1.9
1977 Model	36	40	30		−0.2
Esping-Anderson 1985:3–4	70				
Sweden					
1956 Model	76	19	40	30	1.5
Särlvik 1966:217	85[e]	48[e]	23	53	−0.7
Särlvik 1974:398	73				
Särlvik 1977:95	76[f]	23[f]			
Esping-Anderson 1985:3–5	77[g]				
1960 Model	77	20	39	35	−5.3
Särlvik 1966:217	84[e]	54[e]	26	51	−0.2
Särlvik 1967:169	73	45	30	52	2.2
Särlvik 1974:398	78				
Särlvik 1977:95	80[f]	25[f]			
Esping-Anderson 1979:276	87[g]				
Esping-Anderson 1985:3–5	81[g]				
1964 Model	88	20	39	37	0.7
Särlvik 1974:398	75				
Särlvik 1977:95	77[f]	30[f]			
Petersson and Särlvik 1975:88	84[f]	44			−2.0
Esping-Anderson 1985:3–5	81[g]				
1968 Model	99	23	39	37	−5.6
Särlvik 1974:401	75	47	44	36	
Särlvik 1977:95	76[f]				
Esping-Anderson 1979:276	81[g]				
Esping-Anderson 1985:3–5	79				
1970 Model	93	22	39	37	2.5
Särlvik 1977:95	72[f]	32[f]	38	45	
Esping-Anderson 1979:276	76[g]				
Esping-Anderson 1985:3–5	75[g]				
1973 Model	93	23	38	38	−0.3
Särlvik 1977:95	73[f]	29[f]	38	45	
Petersson and Särlvik 1975:88	79[g]	37			
Esping-Anderson 1985:3–5	75[g]				

Table 5.1   (*Continued*)

	W/X	N/L	X	L	Error
1976 Model	92	23	38	38	−0.6
Esping-Anderson 1985:3–5	73g				
Stephens 1981:167	76e		29		
1979 Model	93	23	38	38	−0.9
Esping-Anderson 1985:3–5	75g				

a Includes *extrême gauche.*
b Vote for the SPD predicted by extrapolating results for total left.
c Also reported by Converse and Valen (1971).
d Using additional information reported by Berglund and Lindstrom (1978:180).
e Survey definition narrower than model definition: typically industrial workers only (mining, manufacturing, and construction) and allies without nonagricultural self-employed.
f Survey definition broader than model definition: typically shop assistants counted as workers and all persons other than manual workers are counted as allies.
g No definition.

magnitude characteristic of particular countries. The other is to examine the changes over time within each country. These two procedures need not and do not yield the same result. Note, for example, that the model drastically underpredicts the survey results concerning the left vote of Norwegian workers. Yet the predictions of the model and the results of surveys consistently change together over time. (The correlation between them is 0.90; see table 5.4.) On the other hand, the model predicts quite accurately the magnitude of the survey results for the left vote of Swedish workers but over time the results of the model and of the surveys change quite independently. (The correlation is 0.25.)

   The results for workers are excellent in the case of the Belgian Left, the Danish left-wing parties since 1971, the Left in Finland, and the major socialist parties in Finland and Norway. In these cases both the orders of magnitude are close and the predictions of the model and surveys covary over time. In the cases of the left-wing parties in France, Germany, and Norway, as well as the Danish Social Democrats, the model overpredicts survey results systematically but the two change quite closely together over time. Note that in all these cases survey workers are more numerous than model workers. Since the more detailed data concerning

Table 5.2   Comparison of Model and Survey Results about Class Voting
for Major Socialist Parties

	W/X	N/L	X	L	Error
Denmark					
1960 Model	91	31	28	33	−2.6
Esping-Anderson 1985:3–4	84				
1964 Model	90	30	28	34	0.6
Berglund and Lindstrom 1978:108	73		42		
1966 Model	85	29	28	34	2.2
Esping-Anderson 1985:3–4	65				
1968 Model	77	26	28	34	3.9
Esping-Anderson 1979:276	65				
1971 Model	82	27	28	34	−1.1
Børre 1977a:15	65	29	49	39	7.2
Damgaard 1974:121	59	25	36	26	1.6
Uusitalo 1975:39	65		40		
Esping-Anderson 1979:276	60				
1973 Model	57	19	27	34	10.3
Børre 1977a:15	48	20	28	35	7.3
Esping-Anderson 1985:3–4	38				
1975 Model	68	21	27	34	−2.2
Børre 1977b	47	18	27	21	0.0
Berglund and Lindstrom 1978:180	46				
Esping-Anderson 1985:3–4	45				
1977 Model	83	25	27	34	−4.6
Børre 1977b	55	24	25	20	−4.4
1979 Model	83	26	27	34	−0.5
Esping-Anderson 1985:3–4	52				
Finland					
1958 Model	34	12	23		3.2
Allardt and Pesonen 1967:342	34	6	49		−3.6
1966 Model	46	17	21		−5.9
Pesonen 1974:294	42	15	48		1.5
1972 Model	45	15	20		−1.8
Allardt and Wesołowski 1978:63	45	15	41		2.0
France					
1956 Model	30	4	28	43	−0.9
Sondages 1960:18–19	39	28	31	59	
1958 Model	32	4	28	44	4.9
Sondages 1960:18–19	30	26	28	61	
Dupeux ICPSR #7278	10	5	28	14	3.2
1967 Model	41	4	25	47	−7.3
Sondages 1973:18–19	15	15	32	62	
Braud 1973:32	16	15	31	54	
Rabier 1978:362	16	15	28	65	

Table 5.2 (*Continued*)

	W/X	N/L	X	L	Error
1968 Model	37	4	25	48	1.9
Sondages 1973:18–19	14	13	32	62	
Braud 1973:32	14	13	31	54	
1973 Model	50	6	25	48	−4.5
Sondages 1973:18–19	17	14	32	62	
Le Monde 1973	22	13	24	69	
Rabier and Ingelhart, ICPSR #7330	35	40	42	24	3.3
1978 Model	58	8	25	48	−5.1
Le Matin 1978	19	18	29	62	
Jaffré 1980:69–71	27				
Norway					
1957 Model	64	26	31		0.7
Valen and Martinussen 1977:51	75				
1965 Model	62	25	31		1.5
Valen and Martinussen 1977:51	69				
Martin 1972:92[a]	63	27	44		−0.4
Esping-Anderson 1985:3–4	69				
1969 Model	67	27	30		−0.9
Valen and Martinussen 1977:51	69				
Uusitalo 1975:41	73		35		−3.0
1973 Model	48	20	30		11.8
Valen and Martinussen 1977:51[b]	55	25	45		3.0
1977 Model	60	24	30		−5.4
Esping-Anderson 1985:3–4	64				
Sweden					
1956 Model	57	27	40	33	2.1
Särlvik 1974:398	69				
Esping-Anderson 1985:3–5	74[e]				
1960 Model	67	31	39	35	−4.1
Särlvik 1967:169	69	44	30	52	4.2
Esping-Anderson 1979:276	83[e]				
Esping-Anderson 1985:3–5	77[e]				
1964 Model	66	29	39	37	1.6
Petersson and Särlvik 1975:88	78[d]	43			2.8
Esping-Anderson 1985:3–5	75[e]				
1968 Model	81	36	39	37	−7.6
Särlvik 1974:401	73	46[c]	44	36	3.0
Esping-Anderson 1979:276	79[e]				
Esping-Anderson 1985:3–5	77[e]				
1970 Model	73	32	39	37	4.2
Särlvik 1977:94	64	41	38	45	
Esping-Anderson 1985:3–5	70[e]				

(*continued*)

Table 5.2 *(Continued)*

	W/X	N/L	X	L	Error
1973 Model	72	32	38	38	−0.6
Särlvik 1977:94	64	38	38	45	
Särlvik 1977:95	73[d]	29[d]			
Petersson and Särlvik 1975:88	69[e]	34			
Esping-Anderson 1985:3–5	69[e]				
1976 Model	71	32	38	38	−0.7
Esping-Anderson 1985:3–5	68[e]				
1979 Model	71	32	38	38	0.2
Esping-Anderson 1985:3–5	70				

[a] Also reported by Converse and Valen (1971).
[b] Using additional information reported by Berglund and Lindstrom (1978:180).
[c] Survey definition narrower than model definition.
[d] Survey definitoin broader than model definition.
[e] No definition.

different groups of workers tend to show that industrial workers vote left and socialist at a higher rate than manual wage earners in other sectors, definitional differences most likely account for some part of this sytematic divergence between the model and the surveys. The Swedish results are quite close in the order of magnitude, particularly the proportions of workers voting for the SAP, but they seem to vary quite independently. Finally, the results for the proportion of French workers voting socialist are simply different for the model and the surveys.

The results concerning the proportion of allies voting left and socialist are quite acceptable in the cases of the Finnish and German left-wing parties as well as in the cases of major socialist parties in Denmark and Finland. The model overpredicts systematically the survey results for the Danish Left. The results for the Left in France are very close in their average numerical values but they vary independently. Finally, in Belgium and Norway the results are very close numerically but too sparse to know whether or not they are correlated.

The German results merit a separate comment. In this case we used the values of parameters that characterized the German Left as a whole before 1933 to generate predictions concerning the post-1949 SPD vote. This procedure turned out to be remarkably successful, confirming both the findings of Converse (1969) con-

Table 5.3 The Statistical Fit between Survey and Model Results

	Workers				Allies			
	N	Intercept	Slope	Correlation	N	Intercept	Slope	Correlation
Total Left								
All Cases	38	53	0.20	0.26	28	32	0.01	0.02
without Norway	33	25	0.57	0.56				
without Sweden					22	24	0.15	0.29
Denmark	9	−16	1.42	0.75	4	14	0.25	0.68
Finland	3	41	0.43	0.71	3	−12	1.15	0.99
France	6	3	0.76	0.61	6	31	−0.13	−0.01
Germany	6	19	0.50	0.78	6	−65	2.80	0.94
Norway	5	24	1.29	0.92	2			
Sweden	8	71	0.04	0.25	6	50	−0.62	−0.21
Socialist Only								
All Cases	31	4	0.82	0.73	20	10	0.86	0.79
Denmark	9	−17	0.98	0.82	4	13	0.59	0.59
Finland	3	7	0.80	0.94	3	−16	1.89	0.92
France	6	39	−0.36	−0.43	6	24	−1.00	−0.26
Norway	5	10	0.94	0.93	2			
Sweden	8	65	0.10	0.15	5	28	0.42	0.23

Note: Fit of linear regression with survey results as the dependent variable. When several survey results were available for the same year we took the average of the definitionally closest cases.

cerning the surprising stability of the German partisan patterns and the importance of the structure of competition.

Given all the potential sources of divergence and error, the overall results rest squarely within the realm of plausibility. The extrapolations derived from the model bear a statistical relation to survey results—correlations between model and survey proportions are significant at the 0.05 level for workers voting Left (0.01 without Norway), at the 0.01 level for workers voting socialist, and at the 0.01 level for allies voting socialist. Only in the case of allies voting for the left-wing parties combined are the predictions of the model and the results of surveys statistically independent. Thus the model which characterizes the process of socialist electoral recruitment since the beginning of the century does reproduce results of surveys conducted since about 1950. Clearly, the fit is closer in some countries than in others and the predictions derived from the model do not reproduce survey results with any exactitude. But the evidence is sufficient to establish the validity of the theoretical principle: the importance of class varies historically, and strategies of political parties and other organizations have cumulative consequences for the way individuals vote in particular elections.

HISTORICAL PATTERNS OF CLASS VOTING

Although the reliability of our estimates is far from perfect, the model can be used to open the black box of class voting throughout the entire period of electoral history, following a long line of methodological devices—recall surveys, cohort analysis, and ecological studies—that are being used to get a glimpse of patterns of voting during the period preceding survey studies. The exact numbers may be all inexact but they nevertheless indicate orders of magnitude and the directions of trends.

Some of the trends are perhaps surprising. The proportion of workers voting socialist and left grew rather slowly. Around 1900 this proportion ranged between a few percent in Norway and Sweden to forty percent in Germany, where socialists had competed in elections already for thirty years. Only in Germany just before World War I did more than one-half of the workers vote left.

This discovery becomes immediately less startling, however, when we note that most workers did not vote socialist because they did not vote at all. Universal male suffrage did not predate World War I by many years in most countries, and workers who won the right to vote a few years earlier voted at low rates. The Swedish data, which distinguish turnout by class, indicate that only about one-half of the workers voted in the first election under extended male suffrage in 1911. Still in 1921 the turnout of workers was about 50 percent; it reached about 64 percent by 1928; 72 percent by 1936; and 80 percent by 1948 (Särlvik 1974:391). ("Social Class III" is somewhat broader than our workers.) Most workers who did vote cast their ballots in support of socialists from the beginning. There is no contradiction between our numbers and the ecological cross-sectional studies which show that the Social Democrats won most of industrial workers' vote in 1911 (Johansson 1967). If 50 percent of workers did not vote at all during this election, and if, of all workers who had the right to vote, 38 percent did vote Social Democratic (our estimate for the first election of 1914), then 76 percent of those workers who voted would have voted socialist. Indeed, if we assume more generally that the turnout of workers during the last election before World War I was in the vicinity of 50 percent, then the figures presented in table 5.4 can be read to indicate that of those workers who did vote, perhaps with the exception of France, an overwhelming proportion voted left.

Nevertheless, it is true that in the era that is supposed to be the golden age of class conflict and class-driven behavior probably about as many workers did not vote at all as turned out at the polls to cast their votes for socialists. Mobilization of working-class support took time; workers had to be organized if they were to participate in politics. Indeed, only by the mid-1930s was the process of electoral mobilization almost completed—the rates of voting participation reached the level at which they have rested ever since. The Swedish data indicate as well that the turnout of workers reached the same level as that of other classes. And by 1936 at least one-half, in some countries more than two-thirds, of workers voted socialist or communist. If we assume that about 80 percent of workers voted, then the working-class electorate divided in a typical country between two-thirds who voted for the left-wing parties, one-fifth who did not vote at all, and the remainder who voted for bourgeois parties. Of those workers who did vote at all, about three-fourths voted left.

Table 5.4 Proportion of Workers Voting Left at Various Moments
According to Model Estimates

	1900	1914	1924	1936	1945	1960	1975
Belgium	24	42	48	50	59	75	47
Denmark	31	35	55	68	63	67	57
Finland		50	53	62	84	76	68
France	12	20	37	50	65	50	67
Germany	44	63	58		51	63	70
Norway[a]	4	41	26	68	57	62	54
Sweden		48	48	81	81	88	92

[a] Labour Party estimates.

The more recent numbers are not very different. A glance at the 1975 model estimates show differences among countries but not a change in the order of magnitude since 1936. Indeed, given the errors they contain, our estimates indicate that no major transformation of voting behavior among workers has occurred in the past fifty years. Given that the turnout did increase somewhat after 1936, the 1975 percentages of all workers who had the right to vote indicate that most likely the socialist and the left proportion of the votes actually cast by workers was lower in 1975 than in 1936. But the differences cannot be large.

Thus the first conclusion from the inspection of historical patterns is that the proportion of workers voting socialist and left increased secularly over time, particularly until the mid-1930s, because increasingly more workers turned out at the polls, not because those workers who had voted previously became socialists. Forced to summarize this entire story in a capsule, we would guess that between two-thirds and three-fourths of workers who turn out vote for left wing parties, and for the rest, it is a question of whether they do vote.

Survey studies support this conclusion, at least so far as they indicate no major overall trends since the late 1950s. If we take the surveys closest to 1960, the proportion of workers voting left will range from 45 percent in France (the 1958 figure representing a sharp drop from the 53 percent in 1956) to 85 percent in Denmark. The most recent survey results range in turn from 49 percent in Germany in 1983, (Klingeman 1983) to 75 percent in Sweden in 1979. These ranges are not very different; they are not very different from the model estimates for the same elections, and they are not different from the model estimates for 1936 or 1945. Once the rates of participation became stable, so did the proportion of workers voting left.

These conclusions should not hide, however, important differences among countries. Precisely because neither the model estimates nor the survey reports indicate any overall secular trends, relative differences among countries again come to the fore. Survey studies confirm the prediction that those countries which experienced a milder trade-off among workers are the countries where more workers vote socialist and left. The proportion of workers voting for social democratic, left-socialist, and communist parties has been persistently higher in Denmark, Norway, and Sweden than in Belgium, France, and Germany. In Sweden 76 percent of workers vote left almost regardless of circumstances—the range of survey results is from 80 percent in 1960 to 73 percent in 1976, and the latter election was seen by the Swedish Left as an exceptional disaster (Stephens 1981). In Norway, 76 percent was a good number until 1973, when the proportion of workers voting left fell by seven points. It remained at 70 percent in 1977. Denmark is the country where social democracy suffered ''decomposition'' according to Esping-Anderson (1985). The left-wing parties combined also experienced a loss of support among workers. From the historic level of 85 percent, the proportion of workers voting left fell to 79 percent by 1968, a few percentage points again in 1971, and all the way down to the French or British level by 1973. By 1976 and again in 1978, two-thirds of the Danish workers voted for left-wing parties, more than in 1973 but still somewhat below the level of Sweden.

The rates of left-wing voting among workers are in the light of survey evidence lower in Belgium, France, and Germany. Note that if our estimates are correct, this difference may be a matter of timing rather than average historical levels. Our estimates show that the highest proportion of workers voting left was about the same in all countries except Sweden, but the peaks came at different moments. Unfortunately, no reliable survey information is available for 1960 in Belgium (Hill 1977:69). In 1968 less than one-half of the workers voted socialist and communist in Belgium. In France this proportion seems highly volatile or surveys are highly unreliable—not only are differences between consecutive elections large, but even the differences among surveys conducted before the same election tend to be suspiciously big. Nevertheless, the overall pattern of survey results traces the electoral fates of the French left well and does so particulary for the socialists. The proportion of workers voting left fell sharply from 1956 to 1958 as the result of 1956 and de Gaulle's popularity among workers. Only when the reorganized Socialist Party entered into an alliance with the PCF in 1973 did workers begin to vote for the left-wing parties again. Indeed, the increase from 42 percent in 1968 (44 in 1967) to 63 percent in 1973 is the largest observed in any country at any time. By 1978, surveys show, 57 percent of French workers voted left in the parliamentary election. According to the SOFRES recall survey of the 1981 presidential election, 68 percent of the French workers voted for left-wing candidates in the first round and 72 percent for François Mitterrand during the second round. Finally, in Germany the proportion of workers voting SPD is again lower than in Scandinavia. From 53 percent in 1953, this proportion climbed gradually to 66 percent in 1972. By 1976 it fell sharply, to 53 percent, and one suspects that the debacle of 1983 brought the proportion of workers voting SPD to less than one-half. (The Pappi, 1977, series ends in 1976; the Klingeman, 1983, series which does not distribute "no responses" among parties, gives 44 percent for 1976, 49 percent for 1980 and 1983.)

None of the countries for which information is available for a sufficiently long period, therefore, show a secular trend. In Denmark and France the proportion of workers voting left fell sharply from its historic level and then began to grow again. In Finland and Germany it increased rapidly and then declined. In Norway it fell slightly at one point and in Sweden it remained almost constant. Altogether, these patterns vindicate a rather prescient observation by Lipset, who warned in 1964 against expecting any secular trends in the voting patterns of workers. Anticipations of the decline of workers' support for socialist parties are a favorite pastime of political scientists and editorialists—perhaps because socialist parties seem to all lose and win elections at the same time. The observed patterns however, appear more like movements around some stable level than like secular trends, and they are consistent with our analysis of the limitations of socialist success.

The second finding resulting from the analysis of the historical patterns of workers' voting is that socialist and other left-wing parties increased their vote between 1900 and the mid-1930s because more workers voted for these parties but not because there were more workers in the electorate. Thus, the success of electoral socialism was due to political mobilization, not to industrialization. Indeed, by the time the socialists entered electoral competition or the time when suffrage was extended to male workers, whichever came later, most European countries were about as industrialized as they would ever become, at least if we measure industrialization in terms of the proportion of manual industrial workers in the labor force (see tables 2.3 and 2.5). After the introduction of universal male suffrage, only in Sweden did the proportion of workers in the population grow by one-fourth. In fact, the proportion of workers in the electorate is a relatively poor predictor of the socialist and left vote (see Appendix: table A.3). The socialist share of the vote rose as the proportion of workers who voted socialist rose—workers who were already in the labor force and who had the right to vote.

Thus although cross-sectional studies often show that left-wing parties are stronger in those districts or regions which are more industrialized, the inference that these parties must have grown as the result of industrialization is not warranted. The economic determinism characteristic of the cross-national aggregate data studies of the 1960s and 1970s finds, in general, little support in historical analysis. Neither did "radicalism" result from industrialization nor "deradicalization" from workers' newly acquired material prosperity.

Support for left-wing parties grew because these parties did specific things to their potential supporters, not only because of the economy, culture, and society. Socialist parties organized workers, they turned for support to other groups, they offered specific programs and when in office pursued particular policies. These actions, and the actions of other political actors, eventually brought workers to the polls and made most of them vote left. And when the original reasons which socialists invoked to persuade workers to vote for them lost validity in terms of the everyday experience of workers—when workers became more prosperous—the parties managed to retain workers' support by changing the objectives and the language in which these were constructed. Economic conditions did not find a mechanical reflection in the behavior of workers because political parties take economic conditions—as well as cultural symbols and reference groups—into consideration when they compete for the support of particular groups.

The gap between workers and other groups persisted in spite of socialist efforts to gain support from first the "old" and eventually the "new" middle classes. If our estimates are valid, only in Denmark did the allies eventually vote for the left-wing parties at the same rate as workers. The Danish left was not particularly concerned about the class composition of its electorate (high *k*) and it enjoyed substantial support among workers. Thus it could afford to dedicate itself to the recruitment of allies and progressed rapidly in the light of our estimates from 5 percent in 1900 to 24 percent in 1914, 52 percent in 1924, 66 percent in 1945, to 70 percent in 1960. Denmark is the only country where the difference between the rates at which workers and allies vote left decreased. In all the remaining countries the proportion of allies voting left rarely exceeded 40 percent. The French Left enjoyed the support of one-half of the allies between 1936 and 1946 but lost most of this support subsequently. In Belgium, Finland, and Sweden never more than one-third of the allies voted left according to our estimates. Most countries exhibit something of a trend—the initial efforts of the socialists to conquer the support of all the "exploited and oppressed" seem to have been moderately successful. Here again, however, the mid-1930s witness levels of support which have remained stable ever since (see tables 5.5 and 5.6).

These estimates provide, therefore, no support for the interpretation of the success of left-wing parties among the middle classes as a phenomenon post-dating World War II and associated with the simultaneous abandonment of marxism and nationalization of industry by the social democratic parties. Whatever support socialists and other left parties were to obtain among the broadly and imprecisely defined middle classes was mobilized as they entered into coalitions, alliances, cartels, and fronts during the unstable decades of the 1920s and 1930s. The push toward office workers, which most parties did undertake in the 1950s, served only to replace support from the vanishing "old" middle classes and did not increase the net level of support among allies.

Table 5.5 Proportion of Allies Voting Left at Various Moments
According to Model Estimates

	1900	1914	1924	1936	1945	1960	1975
Belgium	24	33	25	22	25	24	20
Denmark	5	24	52	69	66	70	59
Finland		14	14	14	22	26	28
France	14	21	39	48	52	27	33
Germany	13	26	27		31	34	36
Norway	0	16	22	35	40	42	39
Sweden		16	13	22	23	20	23

Although survey studies differ substantially in the categories they use and their definitions, they permit us to disaggregate the sources of support for left-wing parties during the last thirty years. Lower white-collar employees show a persistently higher level of support for the Left than do the middle and upper echelons of white-collar workers, the nonagricultural petite bourgeoisie, the executives, employers, and professionals, and the farmers.

Although farmers were the first target of socialist recruitment strategies, only in France do farmowners vote left in any sizable numbers. The reason is perhaps that socialists could never quite make up their mind how serious to be about defending private ownership of land and were never sure how successful they might ever become in winning the support of farmowners. Since workers were a small minority of the electorate in several countries at

Table 5.6 Class Voting as Measured by Alford's Index at Various Moments
According to Model Estimates

	1900	1914	1924	1936	1945	1960	1975
Belgium	0	9	23	28	34	51	27
Denmark	26	11	3	-1	-3	-3	-2
Finland		36	39	48	62	50	40
France	-2	-1	-2	2	13	23	34
Germany	31	37	31		20	29	34
Norway[a]	4	32	19	46	37	37	36
Sweden		32	35	59	58	68	69

Note: Alford's index is the difference between the proportions of workers and of allies voting left.

[a] Labour Party estimates.

the turn of the century, in Denmark and France as well as in Bavaria, socialist parties had to venture into the quest for farmers' support for purely tactical reasons. But as late as 1935, at the meeting of the Nordic Social Democratic Cooperative Committee in Helsinki, "all the Scandinavian participants emphasized that their purpose was not to turn the "real" farmers into socialists. This was neither possible nor desirable" (Söderpalm 1975:273). In Norway the Left traditionally obtained the support of fishermen (classified with farmers by surveys) and in Finland of forest owners. But among "real" farmers the Left could muster support only in the socialist fiefdoms in France.

Perhaps surprising are survey reports concerning the petite bourgeoisie, defined variously as self-employed, small businessmen, or *petits artisants et commerçants.* Such people tend to vote left at rates which are higher than those of farmers and not strikingly low—about one-fourth of them normally vote for left-wing parties. Moreover, these results do not support the widely held reputation for political volatility. The support of the petite bourgeoisie does not seem any more erratic than the support of other groups, including workers.

Small businessmen vote left at about the same rate as do executives, professionals, and employers, i.e., the "bourgeoisie" in the narrower although not quite classical sense. Most surveys group together the upper echelons of salaried employees, professionals, whether they are salaried or free, and owners of large enterprises. Their voting patterns are closer to those of the small businessmen than to the lower and even middle ranks of salaried employees (see table 5.7).

These more detailed comparisons again support the general conclusion implied by the model estimates, namely, the relative stability of the gap between workers and other groups. According to our estimates the difference between the proportions of workers and allies voting socialist—Alford's index of class voting—remained rather large in most countries. If two-thirds of workers typically vote left and one-third of allies, the value of 0.33 would characterize the typical index. Another way to read these numbers is to note that at least two-thirds of workers vote for left-wing parties and at least two-thirds of upper echelons of salaried employees, people who are self-employed, free professionals, employers, and farmers vote for bourgeois parties. Thus most of these people vote in a way consistent with their class position. Moreover, these patterns are stable according to surveys as well. They provide no support for the heralded declines of class, ideology, materialism, and the like. Having reached a plateau, typically immediately before World War II, both the proportion of workers voting left and the proportions of other groups go mildly up and down from one election to another. Perhaps the social and cultural meaning of voting behavior has changed, but the numerical relations between class position and voting behavior remain remarkably stable.

CLINCHING EVIDENCE

Ever since the *Communist Manifesto,* one persistent tendency within the socialist and later communist movement has been to insist that the people who sell their labor power for a wage but perform nonmanual tasks in offices or stores are in fact proletarians, workers like other workers. "Educated proletarians," "workers by brain," "office workers" were the optimistic terms in which these people were repeatedly described. Time after time party theoreticians recognized that these "white-collar proletarians" failed as yet to behave like industrial manual workers but this error of their class consciousness was to vanish imminently, perhaps as the result of exhortations by these theoreticians. Social scientists often fall victim to the same wishful thinking and one book after another is written about the "working-class majority."

Yet even if the conditions of work and life of lower-level salaried employees become more and more like those of workers, even if they begin to be unionized at rates almost equal to manual workers, in elections these lower echelons of white-collar wage earners do not behave like workers. Table 5.8 provides more detailed information about survey reports concerning the proportion of lower-level salaried employees voting for left-wing parties. Their proportions are then compared with the rates at which manual workers vote left according to surveys. These reports confirm again that the gap between the two groups has not been closing, at least certainly not because "white-collar proletarians" began to vote for left-wing parties at a higher rate. In Denmark the distance between lower-level salaried employees and manual workers de-

Table 5.7 Proportions of Different Groups of Nonworkers Voting Left According to Surveys

| | Salaried Employees | | | | Owners | | |
	Lower Only	Both Lower and Upper	Upper and Professional	Professional Employees, Executives, Owners	All Owners and Employers	Self-employed Outside Agriculture, Small Business	Farmers
Belgium							
1968		27		12		17	5
Denmark							
1960	62						
1964	65			33		25	6
1966	58						4
1971	60			32		26	6
	40			33		24	4
	43						
	49						
1973	45		21	26	11	15	3
1975	44			24		12	2
	43			37		19	3
	42						
1977	51						
1979	56						
Finland							
1958	19			15			12
1966	38			12		19	17
1972	32						13

	Col 1	Col 2	Col 3	Col 4	Col 5	Col 6
France						
1956	47		17		25	16
1958	43		21		18	17
1967	32	32	18		27	31
	36		18		20	22
	36				22	22
1968	29		12		22	30
1973	51		34		19	9
	37		21		18	21
1978	40		30		22	22
[a]	47		24		37	26
[b]	51		27		36	25
Germany[c]						
1953		29		19		6
		27		11		4
1961		30		14		8
1965		34		18		
1969		46		17		16
1972		50		23		10
1976		39		23		8
Norway						
1957	53		34		30	33
1965	54		27		25	24
	51		22		38	11
1969	54		28		31	19
1973	46		35		27	13

(continued)

Table 5.7 (*Continued*)

	Salaried Employees			Professional Employees, Employers, Executives, Owners	Owners		
	Lower Only	Both Lower and Upper	Upper and Professional		All Owners and Employers	Self-employed Outside Agriculture, Small Business	Farmers
Sweden							
1956		32			17		14
		51					
1960		37			20		8
		39			17		7
		54					
1964	47	42		8	23		7
		53				27	7
1968		47			28		
		56					6
1970		52					
1973		40		18		23	9
		54					
1976	52	27	20			22	
		46					11
1979		45					

[a] Classified by heads of households.

[b] Classified by respondent's own position.

[c] SPD vote

Table 5.8 Proportion of White-collar Employees Voting Left
According to Country and Their Distance from Manual Workers

Denmark

	1960	1964	1966	1971	1973	1975	1977	1979
Esping-Anderson	62		58	60	45	43		56
Berglund and Lindstrom		65						
Damgaard				40				
Børre				43	44	42	51	
Uusitalo				49				
Distance	−23	−20	−28	−28	−13	−18	−16	−9

Finland

	1958	1966	1972
Various	19	38	32
Distance	−49	−42	−42

France

	1956	1958	1967	1968	1973	1978
Sondages	47	43	32	29	37	
Braud			36	38		
Rabier			34			
Le Matin						40
Jaffré						47
Distance	−9	−2	−10	−8	−26	−13

Germany

	1953	1961	1965	1969	1972	1976
Pappi (1973)	27	30	34	46	50	
Pappi (1977)	29					39
Distance	−25	−26	−20	−12	−16	−14

Norway

	1957	1965	1969	1973
Esping-Anderson	53	56	54	46
Distance	−24	−18	−23	−23

(*continued*)

Table 5.8   (*Continued*)

	Sweden							
	1956	1960	1964	1968	1970	1973	1976	1979
Esping-Anderson	51	54	53	56	52	51	46	45
Särlvik	32	37	42	47				
Petersson and Särlvik			47			40		
Distance	−34	−34	−30	−25	−23	−29	−27	−30

Note: Lower white-collar employees in Denmark and Norway. All white-collar employees or "new middle class" in Finland. *Employés* and *cadre moyens* in France. *Angestellte* and *Beamte* in Germany. Lower and middle white-collar employees in Sweden.

Distance is measured as the difference between average survey reports for lower-level salaried employees and average reports for workers.

clined after 1973 but only because fewer workers voted left. The French patterns are as always volatile but not indicative of any trends (but see Adam 1983:230). In Germany the same pattern occurred as in Denmark, although here the SPD at least made clear progress among the *Beamte und Angestellte* until 1972. In Norway both the proportion of lower-level salaried employees voting left and their distance from manual workers remained the same. In Sweden, where lower and middle echelons of salaried employees are grouped together, the move toward wage earners in the late 1950s produced only a slight increase in support and this support eroded sharply after 1976, restoring the historic gap. Nothing in these patterns indicates that there are better grounds today for expecting salaried employees to vote like manual workers than have existed in the past.

We discuss these historical patterns of voting behavior among salaried employees because these people are often viewed as workers and expected to behave like workers. We have treated such people, however, not as workers but as one of the groups within the middle classes. The theory we developed was based on the hypothesis that workers—manual workers in mining, manufacturing, construction, transport, and agriculture—are less likely to respond to socialist and other left-wing appeals when these parties seek the electoral support of members of other groups. Among these groups we included nonmanual wage earners and even the lower level salaried employees thus drawing the line between manual workers in industry, transport, and agriculture, on the one hand, and even the bottom echelons of clerical, commercial, and technical personnel. We postulated, in other words, that class membership becomes less important to manual workers when parties try to lump them together with "workers by brain" and we expected to find empirically an electoral trade-off between workers defined narrowly and all other groups, including lower-level salaried employees.

Now, the fact that lower level salaried employees vote less often than manual workers for the left-wing parties confirms the validity of our definition but not necessarily the hypothesis concerning the behavior of workers, and the theory concerns the behavior of workers. It might have been true that few salaried employees would vote left, but very much to the regret of manual workers who would have liked to see their office class fellows within the socialist ranks. Neither does our statistical analysis of socialist and left-wing vote shares resolve the issue of the reaction of workers to lower-level salaried employees. This statistical analysis demonstrated that in all cases and countries there has existed a trade-off between the support of allies and the recruitment of workers: the parameter d was always positive as the theory predicted. But the allies are a heterogeneous category that includes middle-level salaried employees, artisans, craftsmen, shopkeepers, and owners of family farms, in addition to the lower echelons of salaried employees. Thus the statistical analysis of the vote demonstrates at best that workers become more difficult to recruit when a party moves for support to a heterogeneous group into which we lumped lower-level salaried employees. But, can it be, perhaps, that there is no trade-off between support specifically by the salaried proletariat and the recruitment of workers? Would the statistical trade-off have been much sharper had we treated lower-level salaried employees as workers and drew the line between them and the rest of the allies?

Surveys permit us to examine these questions at least with reference to the last thirty years or so. We can test the specific hypothesis concerning lower-level salaried employees using the reports of surveys. These reports, to repeat, are not perfectly reliable and observations are scarce, so scarce that we can test the hypothesis only in its simplest form and only by using the crudest statistical techniques. The results are, however, unambiguous: the more lower-level salaried employees vote left or socialist the slower the progress of the party among manual workers is. The change in the proportion of workers voting for socialist and other left-wing parties is invariably related negatively to the proportion of lower-level salaried employees who vote left or socialist. Note that these results concern the lower rungs of salaried employees— the group most likely to be treated as workers. Yet even in this case the salience of class as a motive for voting behavior becomes diluted among manual workers. In the eyes of manual workers, clerical and sales employees are not workers. They may work under similar conditions, they may live under similar conditions, they may be and often are in fact married to each other. But an electoral trade-off occurs right in between them (see table 5.9).

A few numbers derived from Särlvik (1974:397) and Esping-Anderson (1985: chap. 3) may illuminate the reason why this trade-off persists. In an interesting table, Särlvik shows that among manual workers membership in trade unions has a powerful effect on the vote and that this effect is particularly accentuated for first generation workers. Union membership mattered for the voting behavior of Swedish workers; unions had a powerful effect in molding them into left-wing voters. Although such direct data are not available for other countries and other elections, some figures contained in Esping-Anderson's work show a striking difference in the impact of union membership on the voting pattern of workers and salaried employees in Scandinavia. Unionized manual workers vote for left-wing parties at a higher rate than all manual workers, thus at a rate higher than those manual workers who are not members of unions. But salaried employees are less likely to vote for left-wing parties when they are members of unions. In Sweden and Norway this pattern held in every election for which data are available, while in Denmark unionized salaried employees were more likely to vote social democratic and left in the 1975 election. These results seem to indicate that at least in some countries unions do not have the same class-organizing effect on salaried employees as they have on manual workers. Al-

Table 5.9 Statistical Relations between the Proportion of Lower-level Salaried Employees and Allies Voting Left and the Change of the Proportion of Workers Voting Left

	Lower-level Salaried Employees		All Allies Combined	
	Correlation	N	Correlation	N
Total Left				
Pooled	−0.36*	25	−0.36*	19
Denmark	−0.03	7	−0.76	4
Finland		2		2
France	−0.89	5	−0.49	5
Norway	−0.47	4		2
Sweden	−0.23	7	−0.49	6
Socialist				
Pooled	−0.46**	28	−0.27	23
Denmark	−0.39	7	−0.23	4
Finland		2		2
France	−0.88	5	−0.89	5
Germany	−0.34	5	−0.38	5
Norway	−0.65	4		2
Sweden	−0.43	6	−0.43	5

Note: Correlation is the fit of linear regression of the form $\Delta[W(t)/X(t)] = a + b\ N(t)/L(t) + e(t)$, where L and N are defined respectively as lower-level salaried employees and all allies combined. For the listing of lower-level salaried employees see table 5.8. Allies are a weighted sum of groups listed in the text.

*Significant at the 0.05 level.
**Significant at the 0.01 level.

though in these three Scandinavian countries they have become unionized at rates almost equal to those of manual workers, salaried employees do not become members of the working class when they join trade unions (see table 5.10). Note, however, that in Germany salaried employees are more likely to vote SPD when they are union members. Thus, no general conclusions can be drawn.

The trade-off between support by lower-level salaried employees and the recruitment of workers is not the only one parties

Table 5.10   Union Membership and the Vote of Workers
and Lower-level Salaried Employees, According to Surveys

Denmark

	Social Democratic		Total Left	
	1971	1975	1971	1975
All manual workers	60	55[a]	78	67[a]
Trade union members	66	63*	81	80*
All lower-level salaried	41	34	60	43
Trade union members	46	44	54	66

Norway

	1965	1977	1965	1977
All manual workers	69	64	77	70
Trade union members	67	76	75	79
All lower-level salaried	50	38	56	
Trade union members	33	37	38	44

Sweden

	1970	1979	1964[b]	1970	1979
All manual workers	70	70	76	75	75
Trade union members	75	68	81	81	74
All lower-level salaried	48	42		52	45
Trade union members	38	37		41	43

Germany[c]

	Social Democratic Vote						
	1953	1965	1969	1972	1976	1980	1983
Workers:							
Union Members	60	66	64	72	58	61	60
Nonmembers	31	41	45	54	39	44	47

Table 5.10   (*Continued*)

New Middle Classes:							
Union Members	40	42	62	52	51	60	46
Nonmembers	18	27	38	42	28	56	28

Note: Unless otherwise indicated the source is Esping-Anderson (1985: chap. 3).

[a] Børre (1977b).
[b] Särlvik (1974:397).
[c] Klingeman (1983).
* 1977.

encounter. The statistical analysis of the vote shares and of survey reports both demonstrate that there exists a trade-off between the support of allies in general and the mobilization of workers. To defend the thesis of the proletarian unity of workers and lower-level salaried employees one might claim, therefore, that although survey reports indicate that workers do not treat salaried employees as fellow class members, the trade-off with the salaried employees is much weaker than the trade-off with other groups of allies. This may be true, since survey reports are too scarce and too unreliable to provide a firm ground for rejecting this claim. But these reports certainly provide no ground to support the notion that workers react differently to lower-level salaried employees than they do to other groups, except perhaps farmers (see table 5.11).

Indeed, trade-offs between the recruitment of workers and support by lower-level salaried employees, upper-level salaried employees, professionals, and employers, owners of establishments of any size, and the nonagricultural petite bourgeoisie cannot be distinguished. When all the available observations from different countries are pooled, the increase by 1 percent in the support of lower-level salaried employees has the effect of decreasing the change of support among workers by 0.31 percent. The corresponding costs are 0.32 percent when the party gains an additional percentage point from executives, professionals, and employers; 0.61 percent if it wins an additional point among owners who are classified regardless of size in the German and some Swedish surveys; 0.38 percent if it increases its support among owners of small nonagricultural establishments. In turn, the party would re-

Table 5.11 The Trade-off between the Support by Specific Groups of Nonworkers and the Changes of Support by Workers Estimated on the Basis of Survey Reports—Total Left

	Lower-level Salaried Employees	Executives, Professionals, Employers	Owners, Any Size	Small Owners	Farmers
Pooled	−0.31 (0.19; 30)	−0.32 (0.12; 17)	−0.61 (0.21; 9)	−0.38 (0.07; 17)	0.18 (0.04; 26)
Denmark	−0.02 (0.00; 7)	−0.91 (0.28; 5)		−1.13 (0.49; 5)	−2.87 (0.25; 5)
France	−1.48 (0.80; 5)	−1.29 (0.38; 5)		−0.37 (0.01; 5)	1.60 (0.73; 5)
Germany[a]	−0.25 (0.11; 5)		−1.50 (0.42; 5)		0.56 (0.08; 4)
Norway	−0.62 (0.22; 4)	−0.04 (0.00; 4)		−0.36 (0.03; 4)	−0.17 (0.09; 4)
Sweden	−0.14 (0.05; 7)		−0.33 (0.27; 4)	−0.14 (0.04; 3)	0.60 (0.47; 6)

Note: The first line is the slope of the regression coefficient in the model $\Delta[W(t)/X(t)] = a + b[N(t)/L(t)]$, where N and L change according to column titles. The second line gives first the fit, as measured by the squared correlation coefficient, and the number of observations. The pooled analysis includes some cases from Finland but never more than two.

[a] SPD vote.

cruit 0.18 percent more workers when it wins an additional 1 percent of the vote from farmowners. Since the observations on which these numbers are based are few, the definitions often quite inconsistent, and the statistical fit of these relationships is quite mediocre, the most that one can say is that this information does not support the notion that workers react to lower-level salaried employees differently than they do to any other group. Whatever group parties turn to for electoral support, they erode the salience of class and the basis of their support among workers.

Concerned with building a broad base of support, for almost 100 years leaders of left-wing parties have worried whether or not

office employees, sales people, and other nonmanual wage earners can be persuaded that they are proletarians, workers just like
other workers. What they seem not to notice is that they had other
things to worry about. Their problem was not only to convince
white-collar employees that they are workers but also to persuade
workers that white-collar employees are workers. The socialist
party was to be, in Bernstein's words, "an organ of class struggle
which holds the entire class together in spite of its fragmentation
through different employment" (Gay 1970:207). But the party
could no longer hold "the entire class" together when it embraced "the people."

When placed within a historical perspective, survey reports
vindicate both the general posture and the specific hypotheses of
our view of voting behavior. The votes cast by individuals in particular elections can be predicted on the basis of hypotheses concerning the strategies of political parties and other organizations
throughout electoral history. Hence individual acts become intel-
ligible as cumulative consequences of the historical processes in
the course of which multiple political forces compete to impose
particular causes on the behavior of individuals. Whether class
constitutes a cause of the voting behavior of workers at a specific
moment of history depends on the strategies pursued by the left-
wing political parties and the trade-offs they encounter as the consequence of activities of other political parties and forces that
have the effect of organizing, disorganizing, and reorganizing
workers as a class. When left-wing parties turn to salaried employees or the petite bourgeoisie for electoral support, they disor-
ganize workers as a class and they pay electoral costs among
workers. When trade unions are successful in uniting most workers in a centralized and concentrated class organization and when
bourgeois political parties find no particularistic appeals to claim
workers' loyalties, then the pursuit of middle-class votes by the
left-wing parties has little effect on the importance of class and
negligible costs among workers. When the trade unions fail in the
task of organizing workers as a class and other parties appeal to,
and organize, people who are workers as members of other collec-
tivities, class ideology becomes highly fragile and the efforts by
left-wing parties to find electoral support among the middle classes profoundly undermine the salience of class as a cause of individual voting behavior.

Epilogue

Revolutions will not be made by a party, but by the entire nation.

Karl Marx

Models

"Models," Henri Theil observed, "should be used, not believed" (1976:3). They are not simplified descriptions of a complex reality but instruments to be used in analyzing complex situations. Hence we do not pretend that a few simplistic assumptions are sufficient to reconstruct the entire historical experience of electoral socialism. While we would have certainly abandoned the theory if it did not withstand a confrontation with the entire structure of observations, we are undaunted by the lack of descriptive accuracy here and there, now and then. None of the numbers presented above can be taken as exact, but the theory as a whole shows itself capable of generating a compelling tale.

Let us now look at the implications of this analysis with some distance. We think we have demonstrated the following: the process of class organization cannot be reduced to economic conditions, to social structure, or to culture. If the German workers remained narrowly class-oriented throughout the Weimar period, it was not only because of late industrialization, social isolation, or cultural traditions. It was also because the leaders of the SPD, threatened by Bismarck's reforms, Catholic trade unions, national divisions, and eventually communist electoral competition, chose to focus their efforts on organizing workers as a class. We knew for some time that the relation between economic conditions and political behavior is indirect: partly because economic conditions acquire social meaning only in social interactions—as Lockwood pointed out in 1960—and in part because reality is comprehended through symbolic systems which play an autonomous role—the point emphasized by Geertz in 1973. But a part of the reason is autonomously political. Politics cannot be reduced to the economy but neither can it be reduced to society, culture, or discourse; culturalism and sociologism are as pernicious methodologically as is economicism.

The organization of workers as a class is not inevitable. Indeed, people who sell their capacity to work for a wage behave politically as workers only when political parties, trade unions, or someone else organizes them as workers and builds class solidarity into an effective instrument of political struggle. But as long as elections have consequences, any political party, regardless of whether it seeks proximate reforms or ultimate goals, must participate in elections and must compete for votes. And once socialist parties enter the competition for votes, the issue of whether workers can be organized as a class becomes problematic.

The effect of the quest for votes on the organization of workers as a class depends on other participants in the struggles over the political organization of a society. Where the task of forming workers into a class rests primarily on the shoulders of political parties, their dilemma is dramatically sharp. They must choose between keeping the party class pure without any prospects of electoral success or abandoning mobilization in terms of class altogether: the choice to which the SPD before 1933 and the French socialists between 1949 and 1977 gave two extreme answers. In one case workers were organized as a class, but this class was an electoral pressure group constituted to promote the corporate interests of workers. In the other case, class ceases to be a salient principle of political organization. Where, in turn, trade unions are effective in organizing workers as a class, political parties can dedicate some of their efforts to the search for electoral allies. Workers are kept together as a class by the unions; they are mobilized as members of a broader community, "the people," by political parties.

Thus, depending on circumstances, political parties may be

organizing workers as a class, may be organizing the "masses" or "the people," and may be competing for the votes of individuals-citizens regardless of class. Workers may be organized as a class; they may be organized as a class by trade unions and mobilized as members of a broader collectivity by parties; and they may be abandoned altogether as members of a class.

Yet regardless of their strategies, left-wing political parties were unlikely to win an overwhelming majority of votes. Their prospects were limited by the fact that they compete in societies in which there exist real conflicts of interests and values. Whether parties deliberately restrict their appeal to specific groups or attempt to conquer the entire electorate, their opportunities are limited by the heterogeneity of developed capitalist societies. In a heterogeneous society, no party can win the support of everyone without losing the support of someone, because some other party will put in the wedge. Thus no political party can win elections overwhelmingly in a way that could be taken as a clear mandate. Elections are just not a vehicle for radical transformations. They are inherently conservative precisely because they are representative, representative of interests and values in a heterogeneous society.

In retrospect, the error of the early socialists was to have thought that one could precipitate radical social transformations through the electoral process. This belief was based on the assumption that capitalist societies would become almost completely homogeneous in class terms (Birnbaum 1979), dominated by the "immense majority" of workers. Instead, the class structure has become increasingly heterogeneous, and under such conditions elections would not and could not provide a mandate for grand projects for a better future.

Today, 100 years later, left-wing parties face the threat of a secular decline. There is every indication that the proportion of workers in the labor force, in the population, and thus in the electorate, has began to decrease at least after 1960 and is now falling at a precipitous rate, so rapidly that we now speak of "deindustrialization." And we have shown that any decline of the proportion of workers in the electorate reduces the vote-getting capacity of left-wing parties in two ways: not only does their working class base shrink but, with fewer workers among their voters, parties are less willing and able to dedicate their efforts to the conquest of other groups. Thus, as long as parties maintain any privileged ties to workers, deindustrialization reverberates in party halls with an echo: left-wing electoral support diminishes among workers and other supporters simultaneously. The French Communists, the quintessential contemporary instance of a party self-confined within a workers' ghetto, are now struggling literally for electoral survival. But the major social democratic parties are not immune either: as long as they continue to be concerned with the class composition of their electorate, they will bear electoral losses. And they do not have much of a choice: their organizational links, their ideological commitments, their daily habits, and their political projects tie them to their working-class roots. They are thus more likely to turn inward, to their working-class base, and suffer the electoral consequences.

These conclusions do not rehabilitate anarchists and others who 100 years ago opposed electoral participation. Participation was inevitable because elections did and do make a difference for the conditions in which we live, work, and agitate. But the goal with which socialists had entered—to win an electoral mandate for socialism—turned out to be elusive, and the effects on the movement for socialism vindicated the most dire warnings. Organized to represent, electoral parties imposed on the movement for socialism the hierarchy of leaders and followers. Leaders became representatives and the struggle for socialism was delegated to representatives. From the initial claim that the quest for political power was necessary to protect the movement from repression, parties proceeded to reduce the movement for socialism to the quest for political power. They demobilized those potential efforts—cooperatives, councils, and communes—that could not be channeled through elections; they deprived grass roots initiatives of a chance to experiment and grow autonomously; they tamed nascent movements into compliance with electoral tactics. Seducing with the promise of lifting the curtain of socialist society someday, political parties stifled discussion of issues that have no electoral answer and reduced socialist concerns to problems that could be solved by socialist electoral successes. They succeeded in making the very possibility of socialist transformations seem so distant from our daily lives and so unpromising that they themselves no longer know, or care to know, what the curtain may cover. Ashamed of looking too far forward, mortally afraid of appearing irresponsible, left-wing political parties view socialism with embarrassment.

Thus the era of electoral socialism may be over.

Appendix

The Calculations

All of the numbers presented in the text are based on calculating the best fitting values of parameters of the system of equations given by:

$$\Delta W(t) = p[X(t + 1) - (W(t)] - dN(t), \qquad (A.1)$$

$$\Delta N(t) = q[L(t + 1) - N(t)] + c[kW(t) - N(t)], \qquad (A.2)$$

$$Y(t) = W(t) + N(t) + a[1 - X(t) - L(t)]. \qquad (A.3)$$

In this form, however, we could not compare the calculated with the observed values, since neither W nor N are observable from existing historical sources. Electoral statistics inform us only how many people in total voted socialist but not how many workers and allies. Calculating the parameters from the reduced form was also not feasible since some of the parameters occur in nonlinear combinations and they are not identified.

In the practical situation we faced, only X, L, and Y are observable directly. Hence, the descriptive quantities of central interest, W and N, had to be reconstructed somehow during the calculating procedure itself. Our strategy was to fit to the sum, Y, which is observable, by direct use of equations (A.1) through (A.3). As a consequence, the initial conditions for W and N became parameters of the distribution to be fitted, along with the parameters p, d, q, c, k, and a. The subsequent values for $W(t)$ and $N(t)$ were then computed according to the logic of the model. Our criterion of fit has been to minimize the mean square error in prediction of the observed $Y(t)$ series.

Several constraints were imposed on the search. Parameters p, q, and a were restricted to the positive unit interval on descriptive grounds, while c and k were kept nonnegative. The parameter d was not restricted, to allow the test of its sign crucial for the theory. Finally, the initial conditions were constrained by $W(0) + N(0) = Y(0)$ and $W(0) \ge N(0)$.

Subject to these constraints, repeated optimizations were computed for randomly selected starting points. A number of different algorithms have been used, but the workhorse has been the method of steepest descent. Experience revealed that starting values for parameters within the unit hypercube or in an even smaller portion of that cube in the neighborhood of zero avoided pathological computational problems. After several thousand records were examined, we obtained the values of parameters that generated the best fitting time path for $Y(t)$ conditional on the starting values examined for both initial conditions and initial parameter values.

Not all such paths were accepted, however, since some of the series which fitted well were not feasible descriptively. The model must describe a possible world and we accepted only those time series in which all the quantities that constitute proportions behaved as such during the period on which the calculation was based as well as during the "forseeable future" of the forthcoming five elections. In the case of the Belgian Socialist Party we could not obtain a series that would satisfy this criterion.

Thus the final result of these calculations consisted of the values of parameters that generated the best fitting time path of the total vote and under which all quantities that constitute proportions assumed values within the unit interval, given the previously described constraints on parameters.

The essential difference between our procedure and typical regression techniques is that the series we calculate is conditional only upon the initial values $W(0)$ and $N(0)$, while in regression the prediction depends on each preceding value in the sequence. To generate an equivalent series, we recomputed the prediction for $W(t)$, $N(t)$, and the residual vote in such a way that their sum would equal exactly $Y(t)$, adjusting the error in proportion to the magnitude of the contribution from each source. We then calculated a new prediction for $W(t + 1)$, $N(t + 1)$, and the residual vote, this time conditional on the previously corrected, "error-free" path. All values presented in the text are based on this "error-free" series.

One special difficulty resulted from the fact that we were able to measure the $L(t)$ series only in four countries. In Denmark, France, Germany, and Sweden we were able to distinguish different groups of nonworkers and to count allies as a distinct category. In the remaining three countries—Belgium, Finland, and Norway—we treated all nonworkers as allies, thus eliminating the residual group. Strictly speaking, the results were obtained through somewhat different procedures for the two groups of countries. We decided to treat them together after we discovered that defining $L = 1 - X$ has little effect on the values obtained in the four countries in which full information about class structure could be used. Nevertheless, in some cases this procedural difference may have mattered, particularly in artificially elevating the carrying capacities in Norway. Lacking precise numbers we could not calculate exactly the advantages of the unlimited pure supraclass strategy in Belgium, Finland, and Norway.

Table A.1 presents the fit of the model and values of parameters. The "smooth" series is the one which depends only on the initial conditions while the "adjusted" series is based on the correcting procedure described. Note that in most cases the model fits the time path of the vote very well even when the smooth series is used. The fit of the Belgian vote for the total Left and the Finnish Social Democratic vote are distinctly weaker than for the other countries.

The model fits very well but obtaining good fit is of reduced interest since the time path of the vote is very smooth in most countries. Indeed, quite a few different models fit well, even models which are nonsensical from a descriptive or a theoretical point of view. Table A.2 presents the fit of a number of such "naïve" models, obtained in all cases by ordinary least squares. Some of these models fit as well as ours. They are, however, often nonsensical either because the values of parameters are de-

Table A.1 Fit of the Model and Values of Parameters

Country	Fit		Parameter Values					Period	Number of Elections
	Smooth	Adjusted	p	d	q	c	k		
			Total Left						
Belgium	0.16	0.30	0.124	0.137	0.180	0.750	0.139	1894–1971	20
Denmark	0.92	0.94	0.038	0.002	0.050	0.014	1.020	1901–1971	28
Finland	0.15	0.73	0.180	0.095	0.009	0.019	0.369	1908–1972	25
France	0.75	0.84	0.086	0.090	0.109	0.827	0.630	1902–1968	18
Germany	0.87	0.92	0.092	0.130	0.000	0.124	0.629	1874–1933	21
Norway	0.98	0.98	0.033	0.009	0.000	0.282	2.800	1897–1969	21
Sweden	0.87	0.89	0.139	0.073	0.002	0.197	0.239	1911–1964	18
			Socialists Only						
Denmark	0.84	0.86	0.126	0.017	0.000	0.431	0.412	1894–1971	20
Finland	0.17	0.16	0.041	0.058	0.047	0.361	0.250	1901–1971	28
France	0.65	0.40	0.127	1.182	0.000	0.669	0.222	1902–1968	25
Germany	0.70	0.74	0.214	3.571	0.064	1.554	0.000	1874–1933	21
Norway	0.93	0.93	0.055	0.001	0.000	0.198	1.114	1897–1969	21
Sweden	0.85	0.85	0.078	0.060	0.045	0.251	0.288	1911–1964	18

scriptively impossible or because proportions of workers and allies associated with voting left according to these models range far
outside the unit interval. Fit is a very weak criterion in evaluating
a model for a theory.

A question which is important in interpreting the numerical

Table A.2 Fit of the Model and Some of Its Naive Competitors

The naïve models are:

I: $Y(t) = m_0 + m_1 X(t)$
II: $Y(t) = m_0 + m_1 Y(t - 1)$
III: $Y(t) = m_0 + m_1 X(t) + m_2 Y(t - 1)$
IV: $Y(t) = m_0 + m_1 X(t) + m_2 L(t)$
V: $Y(t) = m_0 + m_1 X(t) + m_2 L(t) + m_3 Y(t - 1)$
VI: $Y(t) = m_0 + m_1 X(t) + m_2 L(t) + m_3 Y(t - 1) + m_4 t$
Where: $Y(t)$ is the socialist vote share of the electorate,
        $X(t)$ is the proportion of workers in the electorate,
        $L(t)$ is the proportion of allies in the electorate, and
        $t = 0, 1, 2, \ldots$ represents time.

The fit is as follows:

Country	Our Model	Naïve Models					
		I	II	III	IV	V	VI
Total Left							
Belgium	0.30	0.05	0.11	0.13	n.a.	n.a.	0.08
Denmark	0.94	0.56	0.93	0.93	0.84	0.93	0.95
Finland	0.73	0.04	0.71	0.70	n.a.	n.a.	0.77
France	0.84	0.42	0.77	0.76	0.38	0.74	0.74
Germany	0.92	0.67	0.90	0.93	0.92	0.93	0.93
Norway	0.98	0.00	0.98	0.98	n.a.	n.a.	0.97
Sweden	0.89	0.65	0.87	0.87	0.70	0.86	0.93
Socialists Only							
Denmark	0.86	0.37	0.84	0.83	0.82	0.86	0.88
Finland	0.16	0.00	0.22	0.20	n.a.	n.a.	0.21
France	0.40	0.00	0.16	0.20	0.00	0.14	0.14
Germany	0.74	0.81	0.73	0.83	0.81	0.82	0.82
Norway	0.92	0.02	0.91	0.90	n.a.	n.a.	0.92
Sweden	0.85	0.59	0.83	0.82	0.70	0.82	0.89

Note: Fit is measured as R^2 corrected for degrees of freedom for all the naïve
models.

results analyzed in the text concerns the precision of the calculated values of parameters. One way to examine this question is to ask how much would the fit deteriorate if the value of a particular parameter was slightly different, say by plus or minus 0.01 or 0.05 away from its best value. The results are presented in Table A.3 for the three theoretically important parameters: p, d, and k. The explained variance is quite sensitive to the values of p and d; it is less sensitive to the values of k, which occurs in the model nonlinearly with c. Note in particular the sensitivity with regard to the parameter d in the case of the Danish Left and the two Norwegian cases. In Denmark the best value of d was extremely low, namely, 0.002. With this value, the model accounts for 0.9155 percent of the variance of the left vote. If the parameter d were taken to be lower by 0.01, that is, if we took the value of -0.008, the model would explain 0.8904 percent of the variance, 2.5 percent less. Hence although the calculated value of d is extremely low, we are reassured that it is positive. The same is true of Norway.

These results are less reassuring, however, with regard to the parameter d in the case of major socialist parties, where the fit tends to be quite insensitive to perturbations. We have performed, therefore, the following experiment. We took the parameters from each country and used them to generate the smooth time series with initial conditions of another country. We then measured the fit of this series based on one country's parameters to the observed series of the other country. If there were no differences across countries in their parameter structure, then the fit should have been the same regardless which set of parameters was used: this was the null hypothesis. The results are presented in table A.4. The crucial distinction to be tested was between Sweden and Denmark, on the one hand, and France and Germany, on the other hand, since several interpretations in the text assumed that the estimated differences between these pairs of countries were nonaccidental. The results strongly support this distinction.

THE DATA

Two sets of data were required to conduct the numerical analyses and estimating computations: the distribution of people into classes and their distribution according to votes for parties. These re-

Table A.3   Sensitivity Analysis: Proportion of Variance Explained When
Selected Parameters Are Changed by −0.05, −0.01, +0.01, +0.05
Around the Best Fitting Values—Smooth Series

	−0.05	−0.01	Best	+0.01	+0.05
Total Left					
Parameter p					
Belgium	−2.5927	0.0882	0.1625	0.1067	−0.8675
Denmark	−0.5743	0.8904	0.9155	0.8952	0.6510
Finland	0.7224	0.7254	0.7250	0.7243	0.7197
France	0.7988	0.8409	0.8425	0.8414	0.8133
Germany	0.1639	0.8598	0.8694	0.8440	0.5473
Norway	−11.1150	0.7018	0.9765	0.7603	−2.4264
Sweden	0.5148	0.8653	0.8708	0.8575	0.6911
Parameter d					
Belgium	−0.6459	0.1003	0.1625	0.1772	−0.2160
Denmark	0.2399	0.8865	0.9155	0.8943	0.3341
Finland	0.7139	0.7239	0.7250	0.7254	0.7144
France	0.8325	0.8422	0.8425	0.8419	0.8290
Germany	0.8307	0.8674	0.8694	0.8687	0.8428
Norway	−2.0225	0.9011	0.9765	0.9240	0.1338
Sweden	0.8514	0.8701	0.8708	0.8701	0.8529
Parameter k					
Belgium	0.1525	0.1611	0.1625	0.1635	0.1647
Denmark	0.9155	0.9155	0.9155	0.9155	0.9153
Finland	0.7250	0.7250	0.7250	0.7250	0.7250
France	0.8425	0.8425	0.8425	0.8425	0.8425
Germany	0.8690	0.8693	0.8694	0.8694	0.8692
Norway	0.9760	0.9765	0.9765	0.9764	0.9759
Sweden	0.8664	0.8707	0.8708	0.8706	0.8659
Socialist Only					
Parameter p					
Denmark	0.5214	0.8309	0.8408	0.8372	0.7493
Finland	−5.9082	0.0557	0.1650	0.0472	−1.4080
France	−0.5892	0.6052	0.6475	0.6134	−0.1018
Germany	0.1339	0.6838	0.7044	0.6982	0.5121
Norway	−2.1776	0.8648	0.9334	0.8767	0.0625
Sweden	−1.2460	0.7944	0.8485	0.8059	0.1058

(*continued*)

Table A.3   (*Continued*)

	−0.05	−0.01	Best	+0.01	+0.05
Parameter *d*					
Denmark	0.6794	0.8338	0.8408	0.8374	0.7397
Finland	−3.1025	0.0329	0.1650	0.0746	−2.1861
France	0.6381	0.6471	0.6475	0.6472	0.6394
Germany	0.7037	0.7044	0.7044	0.7044	0.7039
Norway	0.7157	0.9263	0.9334	0.9261	0.7846
Sweden	0.7519	0.8464	0.8485	0.8428	0.7476
Parameter *k*					
Denmark	0.8302	0.8402	0.8408	0.8405	0.8321
Finland	0.1614	0.1648	0.1650	0.1650	0.1623
France	0.4899	0.6421	0.6475	0.6432	0.5550
Germany	−7.6785	0.5926	0.7044	0.6393	−0.0776
Norway	0.9316	0.9333	0.9334	0.9333	0.9318
Sweden	0.8447	0.8483	0.8485	0.8485	0.8461

Note: Fit is calculated by subtracting the ratio of error variance to vote variance from unity.

quirements determined our choice of countries, which was totally opportunistic. We would have very much liked to analyze other cases but only in the seven countries was the time series of the vote sufficiently long and the information concerning class structure manageable to warrant statistical analyses. We could not use Austria, Italy, and Spain, all of which had major socialist and other left-wing parties, because these countries did not have a sufficient number of elections. We did not use the United Kingdom because the census information concerning class reported for England and Wales was separate from that for Scotland and because it was reported in an extremely detailed or excessively aggregated fashion. We found that to reconstruct the British class structure would have taken resources we did not have. Finally, we did not study the Netherlands, which would have been theoretically interesting, and Switzerland because we ran out of time and money. To reconstruct the class structure for one country from the beginning of the century took a team of four persons about six months. Analyses of each case took, at the minimum,

Table A.4 Fit of the Smooth Time Series Generated by Imposing Parameters from One Country on Observations from Another Country: Major Socialist Parties

	Observations from			
	Sweden	Denmark	France	Germany
Parameters from				
Sweden	0.85	0.72	−18.07	−1.66
Denmark	0.33	0.84	−24.10	−2.64
France	−2.93	−2.67	0.65	0.33
Germany	−1.48	−5.78	−0.66	0.70

Note: Fit is calculated by substracting the ratio of error variance to vote variance from unity.

about another four months of work. Thus we were forced to close the analysis mostly for practical reasons.

With regard to class structure the procedure utilized was different for Denmark, France, Germany, and Sweden, where detailed information was available, than for Belgium, Finland, and Norway, where only numbers of workers could be measured. Detailed information concerning the evolution of class structure was gathered for Denmark, 1901–60; France, 1901–68; Germany, 1882–1933 and 1950–61; and Sweden, 1900–1960. Full documentation of the sources and an explanation of procedures utilized to reconstruct the information is available on request. The bibliography of research reports and other writings is attached to this Appendix.

The data are unique in a number of ways. They portray the evolution of the entire adult population, not only those recognized by census takers as economically active or gainfully employed. The adult population is partitioned into a variety of categories narrower than social classes. Each category is further divided by sex and by relation to economic activity. The categories, and to the extent possible their content, are the same in all countries and over time in each country. Finally, in most cases we reconstructed the age categories necessary to determine the class composition of the population eligible to vote in national elections.

Basic data sources consisted of the enumerations of the entire population conducted by the national census bureaus. Although we have not attempted to assess the reliability of the original information, we have supplemented these data with the results of independently conducted censuses of agricultural and industrial establishments whenever these were available. We have adjusted the censuses of occupations to make the sectoral and status distinctions as consistent as it was possible within each country.

Our data are based on industrial or collective classifications, rather than on occupational or individual distinctions. For example, our category of manual workers in industry includes all manual workers in industrial establishments, whether they are assembly-line workers, drivers, or janitors. Altogether we used twenty-two categories, of which fourteen constitute core categories common to the four countries.

01 Manual Workers in Industry
Industrial sectors include mining, manufacturing and handicrafts, construction, and electric, gas and waterworks. Manual workers are those listed in the censuses as *Arbeiter, ouvrier,* and *arbejedere;* unless they were obviously misclassified, as were, for example, the Swedish barbers, listed together with other people who cut hair under "leather industry workers."

02 Manual Workers in Transport
Transport includes those sectors involved in moving people and goods. Communication sectors—post office, telegraph, etc.—are not included here.

03 Manual Workers in Agriculture
Agriculture comprises all agricultural activities such as forestry, gardening, fishing, animal breeding, and dairy production. Only those manual workers who work for a wage are included here, and only if they receive some payment in cash, live in a household separate from their employer, and do not own the land which they farm.

11 Manual Workers in Nonproductive Sectors
Nonproductive sectors comprise all sectors other than those listed above, that is, commerce, communication, services, and public administration. Two nonproductive sectors, however, are counted separately as categories 15 and 16.

12 Nonmanual Employees in Productive Sectors
Salaried employees, typically office and technical personnel, in industry, transport, and agriculture, as defined for categories 01, 02, and 03.

13 Nonmanual Employees in Nonproductive Sectors
Salaried employees, typically office, technical, and sales personnel, in the nonproductive sectors as defined for category 11.

14 Supervisory Personnel in Productive Sectors
Used only in Sweden. Such persons are included in category 12 in other countries.

15 Domestic Servants

16 Public Order Employees
Included here are the professional military, police and fire personnel, forest rangers, customs officials, and the like. Except for the highest ranks, all levels of the military are included here, whether they are identified in the censuses as ''manual'' or ''nonmanual.''

21 Nonagricultural Petite Bourgeoisie
Includes all those in nonagricultural sectors who own workshops, stores, shops, etc. but do not employ anyone outside their family. Independent professionals, such as doctors and lawyers, are included here even if they are employers.

22 Agricultural Petite Bourgeoisie
Includes all those in agriculture who own land but do not permanently employ anyone outside their family. In Sweden this category simply includes all those who owned or rented between 2 and 100 hectares of arable land.

23 Agricultural Bourgeoisie
Includes all those who own and/or control agricultural establishments which employ laborers outside of the family. This category is not used in Sweden.

24 Dependent Agricultural Labor
Includes agricultural laborers who received payment in kind and/or room and board from their employer and/or who were legally tied to land or the employer. During recent years this category includes all those who own some land but cannot live only from cultivating it.

31 Nonagricultural Bourgeoisie
Includes all those who own or manage nonagricultural establishments which employ wage labor as well as the highest echelons of state officials, if the censuses allow their identification. In Sweden this category further includes those who own or rent over 100 hectares of arable land.

41 Students Living in a Separate Household
This is just a fraction of students: those who do not live in their

parents' household. Other students were classified as dependents and distributed according to the category of the head of household. In France this category is not used since all students are listed as dependents.

42 Dependent on Public Assistance: Permanently Institutionalized

This category shows greater inconsistency—within and across countries—than any other. It is usually a residual category used to list those who receive public assistance or who are institutionalized in prisons and asylums and do not have any known occupation.

43 Unemployed

This category is used only in France. Elsewhere the unemployed are listed in the category of their regular or most recent occupation. This category is not a measure of unemployment.

The remaining categories change from country to country. For Denmark and Germany we have:

49 Rentiers and Retired

This category includes rentiers and all those retired, regardless of their occupation before retirement.

For Sweden:

49 Otherwise Unclassifiable

Includes a small number of otherwise unclassifiable individuals, typically widows about whom no information is available.

09 Manual Workers Retired from Productive Sectors

Includes all those whose preretirement occupations would have placed them in categories 01, 02, or 03.

19 Other Retired Wage Earners

Those whose occupations before retirement would have placed them in categories beginning with 1 as the first digit.

29 Retired Petite Bourgeoisie

39 Retired Bourgeoisie and Rentiers

For France between 1901 and 1936 we have:

49 All Dependents

For these years it was not possible to distribute dependents according to the occupation of the head of household.

39 Rentiers and All Retired

For France after 1954 we used:
49 Inactive Heads of Households
09/19 Retired Petite Bourgeoisie
39 Retired Bourgeoisie

All of these categories, unless otherwise indicated, were cross-classified by sex and by status—either gainfully employed or dependent.

To constitute the category of workers we added the categories 01, 02, 03, and 09 or some part of retired people whenever retired workers were not listed separately. Adult dependents were classified by the position of the head of the household. Allies were defined as those listed in the categories 11, 12, 13, and 22 in Denmark and Germany; those listed as 11, 12, 13, 14, 19, and 22 in Sweden; and persons listed as 11, 12, 13, 19, and 22 in France.

In Belgium, Finland, and Norway we were unable to distinguish among different groups of nonworkers. Workers were defined in these countries as those listed in categories 01, 02, and 03, and all the remaining adults were treated as allies for the purposes of calculating the parameters. The data for these three countries are not as reliable as those for the four countries for which full information was available.

In order to calculate proportions of workers and allies in the electorate, we used the information concerning elgibility criteria based on age and sex. We could not take into account other criteria, typically concerning residence.

To interpolate the census information for the dates of elections, we used information derived from the censuses of industrial establishments whenever possible. These censuses typically list workers who are currently employed each year in establishments of some minimal size. They are, therefore, much more sensitive to short-term variations. To extrapolate the trends in class structure beyond the date of the last census we used a straight line. There are good reasons to believe that, as a result, we overestimated the proportion of workers in the electorate during the 1970s. If we are to believe such survey studies, the decrease in the proportion of workers was much more rapid than one would expect from extrapolating earlier trends.

The data concerning election results were derived mainly from Mackie and Rose (1974) and, whenever necessary, supplemented or updated from other sources. Only in France, where party lines are quite fluid, some difficulties appeared. To separate the SFIO from the Radical Socialists in 1924 we used the distribution of the vote between them in 1919. This procedure was validated by the number given by Duverger (1965:82): our result was 16.05 and his 16.21 percent. In 1967 and 1968 we left the MRG votes together with the Socialists.

All of the vote shares used in the analysis constitute proportions of the entire electorate, not of the votes actually cast.

The data concerning class structure were reconstructed by teams which were composed of the following persons:

Denmark: Richard Jankowski, Ernest Underhill
France: Phillip Jackson, Adam Przeworski, Barnett Rubin, Ernest Underhill
Germany: Richard Jankowski, Adam Przeworski, Ernest Underhill
Sweden: Amy Beth Bridges, Robert Melville, Adam Przeworski, Ernest Underhill
Belgium: Barnett Rubin
Finland: Ernest Underhill
Norway: Robert Melville, Ernest Underhill

Most of the work was organized and supervised by Ernest Underhill. Final data tables were cleaned and prepared by Ernest Underhill and Michael Wallerstein.

Bibliography: Documents Available for Distribution

Jankowski, Richard. 1978. The evolution of class structure of Germany, 1882–1933 and 1950–61. Data Report.

Przeworski, Adam, and Ernest Underhill. 1978. The evolution of class structure of Sweden, 1900–1960.

Przeworski, Adam, Ernest Underhill, and Michael Wallerstein. 1978. The evolution of class structure in Denmark, 1901–60; France, 1901–68; Germany, 1882–1933 and 1950–61; and Sweden, 1900–1960: Basic data tables. University of Chicago.

Przeworski, Adam, Barnett R. Rubin, and Ernest Underhill. 1980. The evolution of class structure of France, 1901–60. *Economic Development and Cultural Change* 28, no. 4 (July):725–52.

Rubin, Barnett, R. 1978. The evolution of class structure of France, 1901–68. Data Report.
Underhill, Ernest. 1978. The evolution of class structure of Denmark, 1901–60. Data Report.
———. 1978. The evolution of class structure of Sweden, 1900–1960. Data Report.

Bibliography

Abraham, David. 1981. Corporatist compromise and the re-emergence of the labor/capital conflict in Weimar Germany. *Political Power and Social Theory* 2:59–109.

_____. 1982a. Review essay: The S.P.D. from socialist ghetto to post-Godesberg cul-de-sac. *Journal of Modern History* 51:417–50.

_____. 1982b. 'Economic Democracy' as a labor alternative to the 'Growth Strategy' in the Weimar Republic . . . and why it will return in the post-Godesberg, post-Keynes period. Princeton University. Typescript.

Adam, Gerard. 1983. *Le pouvoir syndical.* Paris: Dunod.

Adam, Gerard et al. 1970. *L'ouvrier français en 1970.* Paris: Armand Colin.

Alford, Robert. 1963. *Party and society.* Chicago: Rand McNally.

_____. 1967. Class voting in the Anglo-American political systems. In *Party systems and voter alignments,* edited by S. M. Lipset and Stein Rokkan. New York: The Free Press.

Allardt, Erik. 1964. Patterns of class conflict and working class consciousness. In *Cleavages, ideologies, and party systems,* edited by Erik Allardt. Helsinki: Westermarck Society.

_____. 1970. Types of protest and alienation. In *Mass politics,* edited by Erik Allardt and Stein Rokkan. Studies in Political Sociology. New York: The Free Press.

Allardt, Erik, and Pertti Pesonen. 1967. Cleavages in Finnish politics. In

Party systems and voter alignments, edited by S. M. Lipset and Stein Rokkan. New York: The Free Press.

Allardt, Erik, and Włodzimierz Wesołowski, eds. 1978. *Social structure and change: Finland and Poland in comparative perspective.* Warsaw: Polish Scientific Publishers.

Althusser, Luis. 1971. Ideology and ideological apparatuses. In *Lenin and philosophy.* New York: Monthly Review Press.

Andrae, Carl-Goran. 1969. The popular movements and the process of mobilization in Sweden. *Social Science Information* 8:65–79.

————. 1975. The Swedish labor movement and the 1917–1918 revolution. In *Sweden's development from poverty to affluence,* edited by Steven Koblik. Minneapolis: University of Minnesota Press.

Bain, G. S., and Robert Price. 1980. *Profiles of union growth: A comparative statistical portrait of eight countries.* Oxford: Basil Blackwell.

Balibar, Etienne. 1970. Fundamental concepts of historical materialism. In *Reading Capital,* edited by Luis Althusser and Etienne Balibar. New York: Pantheon Books.

Bartolini, Stefano. 1979. La sinistra nei sistemi partitici europei (1917–1978): una analisi comparata della sua dimensione e compozisione e dei problemi di sviluppo elettorale. *Rivista Italiana di Scienza Politica* 9.

Beer, Samuel. 1969. *British politics in the collectivist age.* 2d ed. New York: Vintage Press.

Bell, Daniel. 1968. Socialism. *International encyclopedia of the social sciences.* Vol. 15. New York: Macmillan.

Berelson, Bernard R., Paul F. Lazarsfeld, and William N. McPhee. 1954. *Voting: A study of opinion formation in a presidential campaign.* University of Chicago Press.

Bergier, J. F. 1973. The industrial bourgeoisie and the rise of the working class. In *The Fontana economic history of Europe,* edited by C. M. Cippola. London: Penguin.

Berglund, Sten, and Ulf Lindstrom. 1978. *The Scandinavian party system(s).* Lund: Studentlitteratur.

Bergounioux, Alain, and Bernard Manin. 1979. *La social-démocratie ou le compromis.* Paris: Presses Universitaires de France.

Berlinguer, Enrico. 1973. The lessons of Chile. *The Italian Communist* 5–6.

Bernstein, Eduard. 1961. *Evolutionary socialism.* New York: Schocken Books.

Birnbaum, Pierre. 1978. La question des élections dans la pensée socialiste. In *Critique de pratique politique,* edited by Pierre Birnbaum and J. M. Vincent. Paris: Gallileo.

————. 1979. *Les peuples et les gros: L'histoire d'un myth.* Paris: Grasset et Fasquelle.

Bodin, Luis, and Jean Touchard. 1961. *Front populaire, 1936.* Paris: Armand Colin.

Boltanski, Luc. 1982. *Les cadres: La formation d'un group social.* Paris: Les Editions de Minuit.

Booth, D. E. 1978. Collective action, Marx's class theory, and the union movement. *Journal of Economic Issues* 12:263–85.

Børre, Ole. 1974. Denmark's protest election of December 1973. *Scandinavian Political Studies* 9:197–204.

————. 1977a. Recent trends in Danish voting behavior. In *Scandinavia at the polls: Recent political trends in Denmark, Norway, and Sweden,* edited by Karl H. Cerny. Washington, D.C.: American Enterprise Institute for Public Policy Research.

————. 1977b. Personal correspondence.

Børre, Ole, Hans Jorgen Nielsen, Steen Sauerberg, and Torben Worre. 1976. *Vaelgere I 70'Erne.* Copenhagen: Akademisk Forlag.

Børre, Ole, and Jan Stehouwer. 1968. *Partistyrke og Social Struktur, 1960.* Aarhus: Akademisk Boghandel.

————. 1970. *Fire Folketinksvalg, 1960–1968.* Aarhus: Akademisk Boghandel.

Braga, Giorgio. 1956. *Il Communismo fra gli Italiani.* Milan Comunità.

Braud, Philippe. 1973. *Le comportement électoral en France.* Paris: Presses Universitaires de France.

Bull, Edward. 1922. Die Entwicklung der Arbeiterbewegung in den drei skandinavischen Ländern. *Archives fur Geschichte des Sozialismus* 10:329–61.

Bull, Edward, Jr. 1955. Industrial workers and their employers in Norway around 1900. *Scandinavian Economic History Review* 3:64–84.

Cazals, Rémi. 1978. *Avec les ouvriers de Mazamet.* Paris: F. Maspero.

Chodak, Szymon, ed. 1962. *Systemy Partyjne Wspolczesnego Kapitalizmu.* Warsaw: Ksiazka i Wiedza.

Christiansen, Niels Finn. 1978. Reformism within Danish social democracy until the 1930s. *Scandinavian Journal of History* 3:297–322.

Conradt, David, and Dwight Lambert. 1974. Party system, social structure, and competitive politics in West Germany: An ecological analysis of the 1972 federal election. *Comparative Politics* 7:61–87.

Converse, Philip E. 1958. The shifting role of class in political behavior and attitudes. In *Readings in social psychology,* edited by E. Maccoby, T. Newcomb, and E. Matley. 3d ed. New York: Holt, Rinehart & Winston.

————. 1969. Of time and partisan stability. *Comparative Political Studies* 2(July):139–71.

Converse, Philip E., and Henry Valen. 1971. Dimensions of cleavage and perceived party distances in Norwegian voting. *Scandinavian Political Studies* 6:107–52.

Craig, F. W. S., ed. 1969. *British parliamentary election results, 1918–1949*. Glasgow: Political Reference Publications.

Damgaard, Erik. 1974. Stability and change in the Danish party systems over a half century. *Scandinavian Political Studies* 9:103–25.

Daniel, Jean. 1978. Editorial. *Le Nouvel Observateur*. Paris.

Delruelle, Nicole, René Evalenko, and William Fraeys. 1970. *Le comportement politique des électeurs belges*. Brussels: Presses universitaires de Bruxelles.

Derfler, Leslie. 1973. *Socialism since Marx: A century of the European left*. New York: St. Martin's Press.

Desmet, R. E., and René Evalenko. 1956. *Les élections belges: Explication de la repartition géographique de suffrage*. Brussels: Institut de Sociologie Solvay.

Dogan, Mattei. 1960. Le vote ouvrier en Europe occidentale. *Revue Française de Sociologie* 1:25–44.

————. 1965. Le vote ouvrier en France: Analyse écologique des élections de 1962. *Revue Française de Sociologie* 6:435–71.

Downs, Anthony. 1957. *An economic theory of democracy*. New York: Harper and Row.

Droz, Jacques. 1966. *Le socialisme démocratique*. Paris: Armand Colin.

Dupeux, George, with the collaboration of François Goguel, Jean Stoetzel, and Jean Touchard. *1958 French national election survey*. Ann Arbor: Interuniversity Consortium for Political and Social Research (ICPSR) #7278.

Duverger, Maurice. 1965. *Political parties*. New York: John Wiley & Sons.

Edel, Matthew. 1979. A note on collective action, marxism, and the prisoner's dilemma. *Journal of Economic Issues* 13:751–61.

Elvander, Nils. 1979. *Scandinavian social democracy: Its strength and weakness*. Stockholm: Almqvist och Wiksell.

Engels, Frederick. n.d. *A contribution to the critique of the social democratic draft program of 1891*. Moscow: Foreign Languages Publishing House.

————. 1942. *The origin of the family, private property, and the state*. New York: International Publishers.

————. 1958. *The condition of the working class in England in 1844*. New York: Macmillan.

————. 1960. Introduction (1895) to Karl Marx, *The class struggles in France, 1848 to 1850*. Moscow: Progress Publishers.

Engels, Frederick, and Karl Marx. 1935. *Correspondence 1846–1895*. New York: International Publishers.

————. 1975. *Social démocratie*. Edited by Roger Dangeville. Paris: 10/18.

Ensor, R. C. K. 1908. *Modern socialism as set forth by the socialists in their speeches, writings, and programmes.* New York: Charles Scribner's Sons.

Esping-Anderson, Gosta. 1979. Comparative social policy and political conflict in advanced welfare state: Denmark and Sweden. *International Journal of Health Services* 9:269–93.

———. 1985. *Politics against markets: The social democratic road to power.* Princeton: Princeton University Press.

Fiechtier, Jean-Jacques. 1965. *Le socialisme français: De l'affaire Dreyfus à la grande guerre.* Geneva: Librairie Droz.

Furet, François. 1963. Pour une définition des classes inférieures à l'époque moderne. *Annales: Économies, Sociétés, Civilisations* 18.

Fusilier, Raymond. 1954. *Le parti socialiste suédois: Son organisation.* Paris: Les Éditions Ouvrières.

Gay, Peter. 1970. *The dilemma of democratic socialism.* New York: Collier Books.

Geertz, Clifford. 1973. *The interpretation of cultures.* New York: Basic Books.

Geiger, Theodor. 1932. *Die Soziale Schichtung des Deutschen Volkes.* Stuttgart.

Gerstlé, Jacques. 1979. *Le langage des socialistes.* Paris: Stanké.

Goldberg, Samuel. 1958. *Introduction to difference equations.* New York: John Wiley and Sons.

Goldthorpe, J. H. et al. 1969. *The affluent worker in class structure.* Cambridge: Cambridge University Press.

Gornick, Vivian. 1977. *The romance of American communism.* New York: Basic Books.

Gramsci, Antonio. 1971. *Prison notebooks.* New York: International Publishers.

Green, Nathanael. 1971. Introduction. *European socialism since World War I.* Chicago: Quadrangle Books.

Guerin, Daniel. 1970. *Anarchism: From theory to practice.* New York: Monthly Review Press.

Guinchard, Axel Johan Josef. 1913. *Historical and statistical handbook.* 2 vols. Stockholm: P. A. Norstedt & Söder.

Gunsche, Karl-Ludwig, and Klaus Lantermann. 1979. *Historia de la internacional socialista.* Mexico: Nueva Sociedad.

Guttsman, W. L. 1981. *The German Social Democratic Party, 1875–1933: From ghetto to government.* Boston: George Allen & Unwin.

Hamon, Leo, ed. 1962. *Les nouveaux comportements politiques de la classe ouvrière.* Paris: Presses Universitaires de France.

Haupt, George. 1980. *L'Historien et le mouvement social.* Paris: Maspero.

Heady, Bruce. 1970. Trade unions and national wages policies. *The Journal of Politics* 31:407–39.

Heidar, Knut. 1977. The Norwegian Labour Party: Social democracy in a periphery of Europe. In *Social democratic parties in Western Europe*, edited by William E. Paterson and Alastair H. Thomas. Beckenham: Croom Helm.

Helander, Voitto. 1982. A liberal-corporatist sub-system in action: The incomes policy system in Finland. In *Patterns of corporatist policy-making*, edited by Gerhard Lehmbruch and Philippe C. Schmitter. London: SAGE.

Henderson, Arthur. 1918. *The aims of labour.* 2d ed. New York: B. W. Huebsch.

Hentilä, Seppo. 1978. The origins of the *folkhem* ideology in Swedish social democracy. *Scandinavian Journal of History* 3:323–45.

Hill, Keith. 1977. Belgium: Political change in a segmented society. In *Electoral behavior: A comparative handbook*, edited by Richard Rose. New York: The Free Press.

Hirschleifer, Jack. 1976. Comment on Sam Peltzman, Toward a more general theory of regulation. *Journal of Law and Economics.* 19:238–40.

Hobsbawm, Eric. 1962. *The age of revolution.* New York: New American Library.

———. 1964. *Labouring men; studies in the history of labour.* London: Weidenfeld and Nicolson.

———. 1973. *Revolutionaries.* New York: New American Library.

———. 1978. The forward march of labour halted? *Marxism Today* (September) :279–86.

Horkheimer, Max. 1973. The authoritarian state. *Telos* 15:3–24.

Howard, Dick. 1974. Re-reading Luxemburg. *Telos* 18:89–107.

Hunt, Richard N. 1970. *German social democracy 1918–1933.* Chicago: Quadrangle Books.

Jaffré, Jerome. 1980. The French electorate in March 1978. In *The French National Assembly Election of 1978*, edited by H. R. Penniman. Washington, D.C.: American Enterprise Institute for Public Policy Research.

Jaurès, Jean. 1971. *L'esprit du socialisme.* Paris: Denoël.

Johanson, Curt. 1972. *Lantarbetarna i Uppland, 1918–1930. Studia Historica Upsalensia XXXII.* Uppsala: Scandinavian University Books.

Johansson, Ole. 1967. Socialdemokratins valjare 1911 och 1914. *Historisk Tidskrift.*

Joll, James. 1966. *The second international, 1889–1914.* New York: Harper and Row.

Katznelson, Ira. 1982. Class formation and the state: Nineteenth-century England in American perspective. Paper presented at the SSRC Conference on States and Social Structures, Mt. Kisko, New York.

Kautsky, Karl. 1971. *The class struggle.* New York: W. W. Norton.

Kircheimer, Otto. 1966. The transformation of the Western European party systems. In *Political parties and political development,* edited by Joseph LaPalombara and Myron Weiner. Princeton: Princeton University Press.

Klingemann, Hans-Dieter. 1983. Sozialstrukturelle Bestimmungsgründe Langfristiger Veränderungen des Wählerverhaltens. Basistabellen. Manuscript.

Konopnicki, Guy. 1979. *Vive le centenaire du P.C.F.* Paris: Editions Libres.

Krantz, Olle, and Carl-Axel Nilsson. 1975. *Swedish national product, 1861–1970.* Lund.

Ladyka, Teodor. 1972. *Polska Partia Socjalistyczna (Frakcja Rewolucyjna) w Latach 1906–1914.* Warsaw: Ksiazka i Wiedza.

Lafferty, William A. 1971. *Economic development and the response of labor in Scandinavia.* Oslo: Universitetsforlaget.

Landauer, Carl. 1959. *European socialism.* 2 vols. Berkeley: University of California Press.

―――. 1961. The Guesdists and the small farmer: Early erosion of French marxism. *International Review of Social History* 6:212–25.

―――. 1967. The origins of socialist reformism in France. *International Review of Social History* 21:81–107.

Laski, Harold. 1935. *Democracy in crisis.* Chapel Hill: University of North Carolina Press.

Lehmbruch, Gerhard. 1982. Neo-corporatism and the function of representative institutions. Paper presented at the Conference on Representation and the State, Stanford University.

Leser, Norbert. 1976. Austro-Marxism: A reappraisal. *Journal of Contemporary History* 11:133–48.

Levin, Leif, Bo Jansson, and Dag Sorbom. 1972. *The Swedish electorate 1887–1968.* Stockholm: Almqvist och Wiksell.

Lipset, Martin S. 1963. *Political man.* Garden City: Doubleday.

―――. 1964. The changing class structure and contemporary European politics. *Daedalus* 93:271–301.

Lockwood, David. 1960. The 'new working class'. *Archives Europeens de Sociologie* 1:248–60.

Lukács, György. 1971. *History and class-consciousness.* Cambridge, Mass. MIT Press.

Luxemburg, Rosa. 1967. *The Russian revolution and Leninism or Marxism?* Ann Arbor: University of Michigan Press.

―――. 1970. The mass strike, the political party, and the trade unions. In *Rosa Luxemburg Speaks,* edited by M. A. Waters. New York: Pathfinder Press.

Lyman, Richard. 1957. *The first Labour government, 1924.* London: Chapman and Hall.

Mabille, Xavier, and Val R. Lorwin. 1977. The Belgian socialist party. In *Social democratic parties in Western Europe*, edited by William E. Paterson and Alastair H. Thomas. London: Croom Helm.

McDonald, Ian, and Robert Solow. 1981. Wage bargaining and employment. *American Economic Review* 71:896–908.

McKibbin, Ross. 1974. *Evolution of the Labour Party.* London: Oxford University Press.

Mackie, Thomas and Richard Rose. 1974. *The International Almanac of Electoral History.* New York: Free Press.

McLellan, David. 1971. *The thought of Karl Marx.* New York: Harper and Row.

Mandel, Ernest. 1971. *The formation of the economic thought of Karl Marx.* New York: Monthly Review Press.

Marcus, Steven. 1975. *Engels, Manchester and the working class.* New York: Vintage Books.

Markham, James M. 1983. Blue collar Ruhr Valley moves to the right. *International Herald Tribune* 26–27 March.

Martin, Andrew. 1975. Is democratic control of capitalist economies possible? In *Stress and contradiction in modern capitalism*, edited by Leon N. Lindberg et al. Lexington: Lexington Books.

Martin, Penny Gil. 1972. *Party strategies and social change: The Norwegian Labour Party.* Ph.D. diss., Yale University. University microfilm #72–31450.

Marx, Karl. n.d. *The poverty of philosophy.* Moscow: Progress Publishers.

———. 1879. Interview. *The Chicago Tribune.* 5 January.

———. 1952. *The class struggles in France, 1848–1850.* Moscow: Progress Publishers.

———. 1960. *The eighteenth brumaire of Louis Bonaparte.* Moscow: Progress Publishers.

———. 1974. Inaugural address to the International Working Men's Association. In *The First International and after*, edited by David Fernbach. London: Penguin.

Marx, Karl, and Frederick Engels. 1967. *The communist manifesto.* Edited by Harold Laski. New York: Pantheon Books.

———. 1969. *Selected works in three volumes (MESW).* Moscow: Progress Publishers.

Le Matin. 1978. Le dossier des legislatives 1978. Numero Hors Serie.

Menil De, George. 1971. *Bargaining: Monopoly power vs. union power.* Cambridge: Harvard University Press.

Michelat, Guy, and Michel Simon. 1975. Categories socio-professionelles en milieu ouvrier et comportement politique. *Revue Française de Science Politique* 25:291–316.

―――. 1977. *Classe, religion et comportement politique.* Paris: Editions Sociales-Messidor.

Michels, Robert. 1962. *Political parties: A sociological study of the oligarchical tendencies of modern democracy.* New York: Collier Books.

Miliband, Ralph. 1970. *The state in capitalist society.* New York: Basic Books.

―――. 1972. *Parliamentary socialism: A study in the politics of labour.* 2d ed. London: Merlin Press.

―――. 1977. *Marxism and politics.* Oxford: Oxford University Press.

Mitchell, Harvey, and Peter N. Stearns. 1971. *Workers and protest: The European labor movement, the working classes, and the origins of social democracy, 1890–1914.* Itasca, Illinois: F. E. Peacock Publishers.

Le Monde. 1973. Les forces politiques et les élections de mars 1973.

Neimark. M. A. 1976. *Belgiiskaya Socjalisticheskaya Partya: Ideologia i Politika. 1945–1975.* Moscow: Izdatelstvo 'Nauka'.

Newmann, Sigmund, ed. 1956. *Modern political parties; approaches to comparative politics.* Chicago: University of Chicago Press.

Nicolaus, Martin. 1967. Proletariat and the middle class in Marx: Hegelian coreography and the capitalist dialectic. *Studies on the Left* 7:22–49.

Offe, Claus, and Helmuth Wiesenthal. 1980. Two logics of collective action: Theoretical notes on social class and organizational forms. In *Political power and social theory,* edited by Maurice Zetlin. Greenwich: JAI Press.

Okasaki, Ayanori. 1958. *Histoire du Japon: L'Economie et la population.* Paris: Presses Universitaires de France.

Olson, Mancur, Jr. 1971. *The logic of collective action.* Rev. ed. New York: Schocken Books.

Organization for Economic Co-operation and Development. 1979. *Collective bargaining and government policies in ten OECD countries.* Paris: OECD.

Panitch, Leo. 1981. Trade unions and the capitalist state. *New Left Review* 125:21–46.

Pappi, Franz U. 1973. Parteiensystem und sozialstruktur in der BundesRepublik. *Politische Vierteljahresschrift* 14:191–213.

―――. 1977. Sozialstruktur, gessellschaftliche wertorientierungen und wahlabsicht. *Politische Vierteljahresschrift* 18:195–230.

Parti Communiste Français. 1971. *Traité marxiste d'économie politique: Le capitalisme monopoliste d'État.* 2 vols. Paris: Éditions Sociales.

Paterson, William E. 1977. The German Social Democratic Party. In *Social democratic parties in Western Europe,* edited by William E. Paterson and Alastair H. Thomas. London: Croom Helm.

Paterson, William E. and A. H. Thomas, eds. 1977. *Social Democratic Parties in Western Europe.* London: Croom Helm.

Pesonen, Pertti. 1968. *An election in Finland: Party activities and voter reactions.* New Haven: Yale University Press.

————. 1974. Finland: party support in a fragmented system. In *Electoral Behavior: A comparative handbook.* Ed. by Richard Rose. New York: The Free Press.

Petersson, Olaf, and Bo Särlvik. 1975. *The 1973 election.* Vol 3 of *General Elections 1973.* Stockholm: Central Bureau of Statistics.

Pizzorno, Alessandro. 1966. Introduzione allo studio della partecipazione politica. *Quaderni di Sociologia* 15:235–86.

————. 1978. Political exchange and collective identity in industrial conflict. In *The resurgence of class conflict in Western Europe since 1968,* edited by Colin Crouch and Alessandro Pizzorno. London: Macmillan.

Plekhanov, Georgij V. 1965. *Sochynenya.* Vol. 11. Moscow.

Poulantzas, Nicos. 1973. *Political power and social classes.* London: New Left Books.

————. 1974. *Les classes sociales dans le capitalisme aujourd'hui.* Paris: Seuil.

Przemiany w strukturze klasy robotniczej w krajach kapitalistycznych. 1963. Warsaw: Ksiazka i Wiedza.

Przeworski, Adam. 1975. Institutionalization of voting patterns, or is mobilization the source of decay? *American Political Science Review.* 69:49–67.

Przeworski, Adam, Ernest Underhill, and Michael Wallerstein. 1978. The evolution of class structure in Denmark, 1901–60; France, 1901–68; Germany, 1882–1933 and 1950–61; and Sweden, 1900–1960: Basic data tables. University of Chicago. Typescript.

Rabier, Jean-Claude. 1978. On the political behavior of French workers. *Acta Sociologica* 21:355–70.

Rabier, Jean-Claude, and Ronald Ingelhart. 1973. *European Communities Study.* Ann Arbor: Interuniversity Consortium for Political and Social Research (ICPSR) #7330.

Ranger, Jean. 1969. L'évolution du vote communiste en France depuis 1945. In *Le communisme en France,* edited by Frederick Bon et al. Paris: Armand Colin.

Riker, William H. 1962. *The theory of political coalitions.* New Haven: Yale University Press.

Rimbert, Pierre. 1955. *Partis politiques et classes sociales en France.* Paris: Fondation des Sciences Politiques.

Roemer, John E. 1979. Mass action is not individually rational: Reply. *Journal of Economic Issues* 13:763–67.

Rokkan, Stein. 1966. Norway: Numerical democracy and corporate pluralism. In *Political opposition in western democracies,* edited by Robert Dahl. New Haven: Yale University Press.

_____. 1967. Geography, religion, and social class: Crosscutting cleavages in Norwegian politics. In *Party systems and voter alignments,* edited by S. M. Lipset and Stein Rokkan. New York: The Free Press.

Rokkan, Stein, and Henry Valen. 1962. The mobilization of the periphery. In *Approaches to the study of political participation,* edited by Stein Rokkan. Bergen: Michelsen Institute.

Rose, Richard. 1980. *Electoral participation: A comparative analysis.* Beverly Hills: Sage Publications.

Rose, Richard, and Derek Urwin. 1969. Social cohesion, political parties and strains in regimes. *Comparative Political Studies* 2:7–67.

Rosenberg, Arthur. 1965. *Democracy and socialism.* Boston: Beacon Press.

Roth, Guenther. 1963. *The social democrats in imperial Germany: A study in working class isolation and national integration.* Totowa: Bedminster Press.

Sainsbury, Diane. 1980. *Swedish social democratic ideology and electoral politics, 1944–1948.* Stockholm: Almqvist och Wiksell.

Särlvik, Bo. 1960. *Swedish national election survey.* Ann Arbor: Interuniversity Consortium for Political and Social Research (ICPSR) #7366.

_____. 1964. *The social determinants of voting in Sweden.* ICPSR #7339.

_____. 1966. Political stability and change in the Swedish electorate. *Scandinavian Political Studies* 1:188–222.

_____. 1967. Party politics and electoral opinion formation: A study of issues in Swedish politics, 1956–1960. *Scandinavian Political Studies* 2:167–202.

_____. 1969. Socioeconomic determinants of voting behavior in the Swedish electorate. *Comparative Political Studies* 2:99–135.

_____. 1970. Voting behavior in shifting 'election winds': An overview of the Swedish elections, 1964–1968. *Scandinavian Political Studies* 5:241–83.

_____. 1974. Sweden: The social bases of the parties in a developmental perspective. In *Electoral behavior: A comparative handbook,* edited by Richard Rose. New York: Free Press.

_____. 1977. Recent electoral trends in Sweden. In *Scandinavia at the polls,* edited by Karl Cerny. Washington, D.C.: American Enterprise Institute for Public Policy Research.

Sartre, Jean-Paul. 1958. *The communists and the peace*. New York: George Braziller.

————. 1960. *Critique de la raison dialectique*. Paris: Gallimard.

————. 1973. Élections, piège à cons. *Les Temps Modernes* 318:1099–1108.

Scase, Richard. 1977. *Social democracy in capitalist society*. London: Croom Helm.

Schelling, Thomas C. 1978. *Micromotives and macrobehavior*. New York: W. W. Norton.

Schlesinger, John. 1975. The primary goals of political parties: A clarification of positive theory. *American Political Science Review*. 68:840–49.

Schmitter, Philippe C. 1974. Still the century of corporatism? In *The New Corporatism*, edited by Frederick Pike and Thomas Stritch. Notre Dame: University of Notre Dame Press.

Schmitter, Philippe C. 1984. Neo-corporatism and the state. Working Paper no. 106. Florence: European University Institute.

Schorske, Carl E. 1972. *German social democracy 1905–1917: The development of the great schism*. New York: Harper and Row.

Schumpeter, Joseph. 1942. *Capitalism, socialism, and democracy*. New York: Harper and Row.

Schwerin, Don S. 1980. The limits of organization as a response to wage-price problem. In *Challenge to Governance*, edited by Richard Rose. Beverly Hills: Sage.

Sellier, François. 1976. Les problèmes du travail en France 1920–74. Rapport au 4ᵉ congres mondial de l'AIRP. Geneva. Typescript.

Shell, Kurt. 1962. *The transformation of Austrian socialism*. New York: State University of New York Press.

Skirda, Alexandre. 1979. Presentation. In *Le socialisme des intellectuels*, edited by Jan Waclav Makhaiski. Paris: Seuil.

Söderpalm, Sven Anders. 1975. The crisis agreement and the social democratic road to power. In *Sweden's development from poverty to affluence, 1750–1970*, edited by Steven Kublik. Minneapolis: University of Minnesota Press.

SOFRES. 1981.

Soikkanen, Hannu. 1978. Revisionism, reformism and the Finnish labour movement before the first world war. *Scandinavian Journal of History* 3:347–60.

Sombart, Werner. 1909. *Socialism and the social movement*. London: J. M. Dent & Sons.

Sondages Revue Française de l' opinion publique. 1960, 1973. Paris: Editions Le Chancelier.

Stehouwer, Jan. 1967. Long term ecological analysis of electoral statistics in Denmark. *Scandinavian Political Studies* 2:94–117.

Stephens, John D. 1981. The changing Swedish electorate: Class voting, contextual effects, and voter volatility. *Comparative Political Studies* 14:163–204.

Streeck, Wolfgang. 1984. Neo-corporatist industrial relations and the economic crisis in West Germany. In *Order and Conflict in Contemporary Capitalism*, edited by John H. Goldthorpe. Oxford: Clarendon Press.

Sully, Melanie A. 1977. The socialist party of Austria. In *Social democratic parties in Western Europe*, edited by William E. Paterson and Alastair H. Thomas. London: Croom Helm.

Svensson, Paul. 1974. Support for the Danish social democratic party 1924–1939—growth and response. *Scandinavian Political Studies* 9:127–46.

Sylos Labini, Paolo. 1972. Sviluppo economico e classi sociali in Italia. *Quaderni de Sociologia* 21:371–443.

Tarschys, Daniel. 1977. The changing basis of radical socialism in Scandinavia. In *Scandinavia at the polls*, edited by Karl H. Cerny. Washington, D.C.: American Enterprise Institute of Public Policy Research.

Tawney, R. H. 1923. *The British labour movement*. New York: Yale University Press.

Theil, Henry. 1976. *Econometrics*. New York: John Wiley & Sons.

Thomas, Alastair H. 1977. The Danish social democratic party. In *Social democratic parties in western Europe*, edited by William E. Paterson and Alastair H. Thomas. London: Croom Helm.

Thompson, E. P. 1963. *The making of the English working class*. New York: Vintage.

Tingsten, Herbert. 1973. *The Swedish social democrats*. Totowa: Bedminster Press.

Tomasson, Richard. 1969. The extraordinary success of the Swedish social democrats. *Journal of Politics* 31:772–98.

———. 1970. *Sweden: Prototype of modern society*. New York: Random House.

Touchard, Jean. 1977. *La gauche en France depuis 1900*. Paris: Seuil.

Toutain, J-C. 1963. La population de la France de 1700 a 1959. *Cahiers de l'Institut de Science Économique Appliquée*. Serie AF.3:3–247.

Urry, John. 1973. Towards a structural theory of the middle class. *Acta Sociologica* 16:175–87.

Usitalo, Hannu. 1975. *Class structure and party choice: A Scandinavian comparison*. Helsinki: University of Helsinki Research Reports, no. 10.

Valen, Henry, and Willy Martinussen. 1977. Electoral trends and foreign politics in Norway: The 1973 Storting election and the EEC issue. In *Scandinavia at the polls*, edited by Karl H. Cerny. Washington, D.C.: American Enterprise Institute of Public Policy Research.

Visser, Jelle, 1983. Dimensions of union growth in postwar Western
Europe. Working Paper no. 89. Florence: European University
Institute.

Wallerstein, Michael. 1983. Working class solidarity and rational behavior. University of Chicago. Typescript.

Windmuller, John P. 1975. The authority of national trade union confederations: a comparative analysis. In *Union Power and Public Policy*, edited by D. B. Lipsky. Ithaca, NY: Cornell University.

Windmuller, John P. 1981. Concentration trends in union structure: an
international comparison. *Industrial and Labor Relations Review.*
35:43–57.

Wittman, Donald A. 1973. Parties as utility maximizers. *American Political Science Review.* 67:490–98.

————. 1983. Candidate motivation: A synthesis of alternative theories.
American Political Science Review. 77:142–57.

Wright, Erik Olin. 1976. Class boundaries in advanced capitalist societies. *New Left Review* 98:3–42.

Name Index

Subject Index